*Off they go, getting lifts to the nearest shops, from friendly motorists.*

# the harp beat rock gazetteer of great britain
## a geographical guide to rock music past & present
**compiled by pete frame**
**with a foreword by jeff lynne**

**First published in Great Britain in 1989
by Banyan Books Limited, 50 Margaret Street, London W1N 7FD.**

**Exclusive Distributors in U.K. by**
**Biblios Publishers Distribution Services Ltd**
**Star Road,**
**Partridge Green,**
**West Sussex RH13 8LD. U.K.**

Copyright © Pete Frame
ISBN No: 0-9506402-6-3

**Typeset by A.J. Latham Limited, Dunstable, Bedfordshire, U.K.**

**Printed by South Western Printers, Caerphilly, Glamorgan, U.K.**

**Cover and contents designed by P. St. John Nettleton
at Global Antar.**

All photos in this book are © 1989 Banyan Books, unless
otherwise stated beside the photo.

Picture research by Ashley, Annette, Eddie and Eugen

Extra photo search by Brian Hogg at Lizzard Sound Archives,
Melanie Maker at Global Antar Archives, Phil Smee at Waldos/
Bam Caruso Collections and Pete Flanagan at the Zippo Music Vaults.

Further photo thanks go to The Chrysalis Press Office, Matt and
Barbara at WEA (UK), Iain at RunRig, Linda Valentine at Phonogram
and Donato Cinicolo 3rd.

... *Rambles in Essex*
*Rambles in Epping Forest*
*Rambles in Hertfordshire*
*Rambles in East Cornwall*
*Rambles in South Devon*
*Rambles in The Wye Valley*
*Rambles in Somerset*
*Rambles in The Chiltern Country*
*Rambles around The Cambrian
  Coast*
*Rambles in The Cotswolds*

*He who " foots it " need not stick to roads.*

**the harp beat rock gazetteer of great britain**
**a geographical guide to rock music past & present**
**compiled by pete frame**
**with a foreword by jeff lynne**

**The author would like to thank** Jackie Adams, Chloe Alexander, Clive Anderson, Hugh Ashley, Barry Ballard, Ian Barclay, Stephanie Barnes, Graham Battey, Dawn Bebe, Eugen Beer, Don Berrow, Danny Betesh, Will Birch, Johnny Black, Karl Blanch, Eddie Blower, Richard Boon, John Braley, David Brown, Paul Burnell, Alan Cackett, Melissa Cambridge, Tim Carson, Jane Chapman, Paul Charles, Chris Charlesworth, Andy Cheeseman, Pam Cheshire, Andy Childs, Alan Clayson, Pete Clements, Paul Cole, Luke Crampton, Jamie Crick, Nigel Cross, Sophie Culmer, Terance Dale, Brian Dann, Trevor Dann, Mike Darkside, Gareth Davies, Geoff Davies, Jez Davies, Mike Davies, Ed Douglas, Bill Drummond, Chris Duke, Tim Earnshaw, John Ellis, Royston Ellis, Angela Evans, Julian Evans, Roan Fair, Tim Finlay, John Fleet, David Ford, David Freeman, Mariella Frostrup, Trevor Fry, Craig Gerrard, Robert Gillatt, Mark Glyn Jones, Kevin Golding, Simon Goodwin, Robert Gurney, Jon Hammond, Colin Hill, R S Hill, Paul Harris, Richard Hoare, Brian Hogg, Howard Holmes, ZaZa Horne, Guy Hornsby, Mick Houghton, Terry Hounsome, Kevin Howlett, Patrick Humphries, Jerry James, David Johnson, Gary Jones, Mark Jones, Tim Jones, Steve Kingston, Jane Kutlay, Eileen Kyte, Bob Lamb, Bob Langley, Nick Langley, Peter Latham, Alastair Law, Barry Lazell, Spencer Leigh, Martin Lever, Peter Levy, John Lewin, Jeremy Lewis, Polly Lloyd, Brian Long, Richard Lowe, Carl McLean, Ian McLean, Colin Macleod, David Marlow, Pat Marsh, Steve Massam, I Mercer, John Morgan, Andy Murray, Fraser Nash, Chrissie Oakes, Peter O'Brien, Johnny Ogden, Baz Oldfield, John Oley, John Peel, Robin Pike, John Platt, Pauline Poole, Julie Porter, Mark Pendergast, Mark Price, Rocky Prior, Andy Pyle, John Quinn, Patrick Raftery, Mike Read, Dafydd Rees, Bill Reeves, David Revill, Ira Robbins, Louie Robinson, Neil Robinson, Nick Robinson, John Rogan, Robin Ross, Barry Rutter, James Scanlon, Cathy Shea, Paul Simmons, Jim Simpson, Dave Sims, Carol Singleton, Steve Singleton, Clive Skelhon, Ken Slater, Sharon Smale, Keith Smith, Jan Sneum, Anne Spencer, Colleen Staplehurst, Hilda Stark, Martin Stephenson, Mark Stewart, Neil Storey, John Sugar, John Taighton, Derm Tanner, Kevin Thomas, Paul Thompson, Alan Timms, Eric Tingley, John Tobler, Pete Trewavas, Chris Turley, Robin Valk, Matthew Wells, Charles White, Richard Williams, Jim Wiltshire, Paul Wood, Tony Worgan and Susan Young **for their assistance in the compilation of this book.**

If you ever thought it would be nice to know where everybody you ever heard of came from, where they went, and some of the naughty things they got up to, then this is the book for you. I was pleased to see that I come from Birmingham, lucky really, what with me accent, and living so close by. This book is packed with historical goodies and hundreds of things you didn't know.

**Jeff Lynne**

## Page Nº    County

### ENGLAND

| Page Nº | County |
|---|---|
| 10 | Avon |
| 12 | Bedfordshire |
| 14 | Berkshire |
| 17 | Buckinghamshire |
| 20 | Cambridgeshire |
| 22 | Cheshire |
| 23 | Cleveland |
| 24 | Cornwall |
| 25 | Cumbria |
| 26 | Derbyshire |
| 27 | Devon |
| 28 | Dorset |
| 30 | Durham |
| 31 | Essex |
| 36 | Gloucestershire |
| 37 | Hampshire |
| 41 | Hereford and Worcester |
| 42 | Hertfordshire |
| 47 | Humberside |
| 48 | Isle of Man |
| 49 | Isle of Wight |
| 50 | Kent |
| 54 | Lancashire |
| 57 | Leicestershire |
| 58 | Lincolnshire |
| 59 | Liverpool |
| 140 | London (Greater) |
| 66 | Manchester (Greater) |
| 70 | Merseyside (ex Liverpool) |
| 74 | Middlesex |
| 78 | Norfolk |
| 79 | Northamptonshire |
| 80 | Northumberland |
| 81 | Nottinghamshire |
| 82 | Oxfordshire |
| 84 | Shropshire |
| 85 | Somerset |
| 88 | Staffordshire |
| 89 | Suffolk |
| 90 | Surrey |
| 95 | Sussex, East |
| 98 | Sussex, West |
| 99 | Tyne and Wear |
| 102 | Warwickshire |
| 103 | West Midlands |
| 109 | Wiltshire |
| 110 | Yorkshire, North |
| 112 | Yorkshire, South |
| 116 | Yorkshire, West |

## NORTHERN IRELAND

| | |
|---|---|
| 118 | Antrim |
| 118 | Armagh |
| 118 | Down |
| 118 | Londonderry |
| 119 | Tyrone |

| | |
|---|---|
| 120 | **EIRE** |

## SCOTLAND

| | |
|---|---|
| 123 | Borders |
| 124 | Central |
| 124 | Dumfries and Galloway |
| 125 | Fife |
| 126 | Grampian |
| 127 | Highlands |
| 128 | Lothian |
| 127 | Orkneys |
| 127 | Shetlands |
| 130 | Strathclyde |
| 132 | Tayside |

## WALES

| | |
|---|---|
| 134 | Clywed |
| 134 | Dyfed |
| 135 | Glamorgan, Mid |
| 136 | Glamorgan, South |
| 138 | Glamorgan, West |
| 138 | Gwent |
| 138 | Gwynedd |
| 139 | Powys |

© Global Antar Archive

Rockfield Studios in Wales: it was over these green hills that The Teardrop Explodes keyboard player David Balfe was chased by their drummer Gary Dwyer who was armed with a shotgun. The reason given was 'Musical differences'.

Sol Studios in Cookham, Berkshire. Once owned by Gus Dudgeon & where Elton John recorded many a hit, it is now owned by ex-Yardbird guitarist Jimmy Page

48 Margaret St, in the late sixties a different kind of rubbish clustered around the front door of what was once The Speakeasy, London's trendiest muso haunt in W1

The Dial House in Sheffield. Def Leppard are used to playing somewhat larger venues these days. See page 115

East Kilbride National Engineering Lab. This building of staggering beauty and architectural importance was where Midge Ure served as an apprentice. See page 130

**29 Joan Cresc, London SE9: The flamboyant birthplace of one 'Boy' George. Turn to the inside back cover to see what became of his taste in home life.**

**Charterhouse School, Godalming, Surrey where many a member of Genesis, Rivers Job and Jonathan King went. See page 92**

© Global Antar Archive

**Angeluccis in Frith St, London W1 is from where Mark Knopfler steps out of in Dire Straits 'Wild West End' opus.**

# AVON

## BATH

After localised success as Graduate, Curt Smith and Roland Orzabal became Tears For Fears and put Bath on the map with a string of top ten hits. They first met at Beechen Cliff School.

Bath University produced Naked Eyes (hot in the States in the mid 80s but soon forgotten here). Mark Kelly from Marillion was a student at the Academy of Art.

The Mirror (massive locally in the mid 60s) and Interview (new wave) are among the few local acts to have made national ripples.

Local residents include Peter Gabriel and Hugh Cornwell from the Stranglers.

Made world famous by Peter Gabriel, Solsbury Hill is a local landmark.

Before forming the Thompson Twins, Tom Bailey had a music workshop in Bath.

The celebrated Bath Festivals of the early 70s were actually held in Somerset — at Shepton Mallet.

## BRISTOL

Birthplace of Russ Conway 2.9.27; Roger Cook, 19.8.40 (Blue Mink, etc); Roger Greenaway, 23.8.42 (David and Jonathan, etc); drummer/singer Robert Wyatt, 1945 (Soft Machine); drummer Timmie Donald, 1946 (White Trash); journalist Julie Burchill; singer Nik Kershaw, 1.3.58; guitarist Wayne Hussey, 26.5.59 (The Mission); Sarah Dallen, 17.12.62, and Keren Woodward, 2.4.63 (they met at school and later moved to London to form Bananarama).

Adam & the Ants drummer Merrick went to Blackwell Comprehensive; Harriet Wheeler and David Gavurin of The Sundays met at Bristol University; Hugh Cornwell of the Stranglers studied biochemistry at the University; and Bob Geldof's sister was said to have been a teacher at Churchill School.

Home base for a bewildering array of idiosyncratic bands, like The Cougars, Force West, Johnny Carr & the Cadillacs (all 60s), Magic Muscle, Subway Sect, Glaxo Babies, Vice Squad, The Cortinas, Essential Bop, Mystery Guests, The Numbers, Private Dicks (all 70s), The Pop Group, Maximum Joy, Rip Rig And Panic, Pigbag, Electric Guitars, Mark Stewart & The Mafia, Jo Boxers, The Chesterfields, Blue Aeroplanes (all 80s). The latest wave includes The Seers, Brilliant Corners, Rhythm Party ("just like Bros only better looking"), The Driscolls, The Helmets, Rorschach, The Loggerheads, and more!

Local clubs/venues have included Colston Hall (package shows/big deals), Electric Village at the Locarno (progressive), the Granary (70s/80s), the Dugout, the Barclay Centre, Trinity Hall (new wave), and the Anson Rooms.

First local group to make waves were The Kestrels, containing Roger Cook, Roger Greenaway and Tony Burrows. Cook and Greenaway wrote millions of hits (like I'd Like To Teach The World To Sing) and Burrows was in millions of groups — like The Pipkins, Edison Lighthouse, and The Flowerpot Men.

Acker Bilk formed his Paramount Jazz Band in Bristol in early 58, playing local pubs before moving to London.

A few hours before his fatal car crash in April 60, Eddie Cochran played his last gig at Bristol Hippodrome. The same venue saw the start of the Wings tour in May 73; the first scheduled tour by an ex-Beatle since their last foray in 1966.

In Sept 60 The Shadows played their first gig without Cliff — at Colston Hall.

In the early 60s, American star Big Dee Erwin got lost on his way to Colston Hall. He stopped outside the bowling alley in Kingswood to ask directions and gave a helpful schoolboy half a crown and his autograph!

In January 64, the Stones (on tour with the Ronettes) were refused admission to the Royal Hotel on College Green for sartorial irregularities. The Animals subsequently suffered the same fate.

Ronnie Lane of The Small Faces wrote the lyrics to Itchycoo Park in a Bristol hotel room after perusing a local tourism brochure which spoke of dreaming spires and a bridge of sighs.

For a BBC television show in 1970, Simon & Garfunkel played an unannounced concert at the Arnolfini Theatre on Narrow Quay.

Away from the glare of dubious publicity, Erasure played their first ever gig at the tiny Western Star Domino Club, off Broadmoor, in November 85.

It was while Paul McCartney was in Bristol visiting his girlfriend Jane Asher (appearing at the Old Vic in early 66) that he was drawn to an old clothes shop called Daisy Hawkins. The name inspired a new song, but by the time it was recorded a few weeks later, it had metamorphosed into Eleanor Rigby.

Bristol has been mentioned (if not immortalised) in several songs — in-

avon

© Apple · Dezo Hoffman

**Weston-Super-Mare – Dezo Hoffman's unique early photo of the fab tour**

© Zippo Records ltd/Anter Archives

**Magic Muscle: reunited in Bath**

**Is this the way to Keynsham?**

## WESTON-SUPER-MARE

Birthplace of Deep Purple guitarist Richie Blackmore, 14.4.45.

Dezo Hoffmann's famous photos of the Beatles cavorting on the beach in Victorian bathing costumes were taken here in July 63.

One of the few groups to make it out of town was rock'n'roll band Fumble.

In 1986, Vivian Stanshall entered Broadway Lodge to curb his reliance on pills and booze.

cluding The Bristol Steam Convention Blues by The Byrds, and Bristol And Miami by Selecter.

## KEYNSHAM

Through his incessant advertising on Radio Luxembourg, Horace Batchelor – inventor of "the Infradraw Method for the Football Pools" – gave this town legendary status. The Bonzo Dog Band later revived the name as the title of their fourth album.

## PENSFORD

Birthplace of Mr Acker Bilk, 28.1.29. He broke out of the jazz clubs with the 1960 hit Summer Set – dedicated to his beloved county . . . of which Pensford is no longer part! He could play clarinet better than he could spell.

## YATTON

Home base for idiosyncratic early 70s group Stackridge, who immortalised the town in Spaceships Over Yatton. Members James Warren and Andy Davis later formed the Korgis, internationally successful with Everybody's Got To Learn Sometime.

# BEDFORDSHIRE

## BEDFORD

Tony Poole and Ross McGeeney, the instigators of 70s band Starry Eyed And Laughing, met at Bedford Modern School.

The Kursaal Flyers played their final gig at the Nite Spot in 1977. Roadie Glen Churchman was moved to disrobe on stage ... resulting in local paper headline "Punk Rock Group Simulates Homosexual Acts On Stage"!

## DUNSTABLE

Birthplace of singer Duke D'Mond, 25.2.45 (Barron Knights).

The California Ballroom at the foot of Dunstable Downs was the county's hottest venue during the 60s, when everyone from the Stones to The Who, Roy Orbison to Tina Turner played there. The bar overlooked the back of the stage, allowing dumb-ass punters to pour beer on Pink Floyd (Feb 67), whose innovations were beyond their understanding. It survived until punk (when Rat Scabies was refused service at the nearby Windsock pub) but was then bulldozed to make way for a housing estate.

The town's other venue was the much posher Civic Hall. Almost every big group has visited, including Wishbone Ash who made their world debut there in November 69.

## LEIGHTON BUZZARD

Home of The Barron Knights, pop funsters for nigh on 30 years, and Kajagoogoo, whose five minute career peaked on their debut hit, Too Shy. The latter evolved from Art Nouveau, who also made a couple of indie records.

Both The Clash and The Damned played very early provincial gigs at the Tiddenfoot Leisure Centre, just a kiss away from the scene of the Great Train Robbery starring Pistols collaborator Ronnie Biggs.

## LUTON

A grim place ... but during the 60s, it was jumping! The Majestic Ballroom in Mill Street (later a bingo hall) presented everyone from The Beatles down — and The Supremes, who were playing a package show at the Ritz, dropped down to the Dolphin coffee bar in Waller Street (now crushed under the Arndale Centre) to see where the action was!

When not a disco/local group venue, the Dolphin was a folk club presenting the likes of Donovan, Julie Felix and Tom Paxton.

In January 65, PJ Proby's troubles started when he split his trousers on-stage at the Ritz in Gordon Street.

Luton was teeming with groups like The Avengers, The Scimitars, McGregors Engine, Jaxon's Dogfood ... but the first to make a record were Bryan & The Brunelles.

After playing at the local Beachcomber Club (part of the Caesars Palace complex), two Blackpool bods moved down to join two Lutonians as Jethro Tull. To support himself, singer Ian Anderson (who lived in Studley Road) worked as a cleaner at the ABC cinema in George Street and earned a local rep as the nutter who walked around town with a lampshade on his head.

Tull guitarist Mick Abrahams (born 7.4.43) later started Blodwyn Pig with various mates including bassist Andy Pyle (who'd worked as a mechanic at Shaw & Kilburn's in Dunstable Road). Pyle was later in the Kinks with another Luton lad, John Gosling — graduate of the Grammar School, now the Sixth Form College.

Punk group UK Decay created a bit of excitement, but the town's most celebrated export is Paul Young (born Grove Road Maternity Hospital on 17.1.56), who used to live up Wigmore Lane and worked for a while at Vauxhall Motors ... as did Luton's very first pop act The Mudlarks, who reached the 1958 top three with Lollipop! Their first gigs were at the Wesleyan Church in Chapel Street and they used to live round the corner from the Three Horseshoes in Leagrave.

In January 70, Yes elbowed guitarist Pete Banks after a dubious gig at the College of Technology in Park Square — and the same venue saw the conclusion of Mott The Hoople's variety tour, where they shared the bill with Max Wall and a knife thrower who used the group for target practice against the dressing room door! Ian Dury was an art teacher there.

Elton John's straw boaters are made at Olney's hat factory and stars like U2, Eurythmics and Phil Collins have their natty leather trousers made at Peter Kay's place in Dudley Street.

Shirley Bassey made her first public appearance in Luton — in a touring revue, Memories Of Al Jolson — and

# bedfordshire

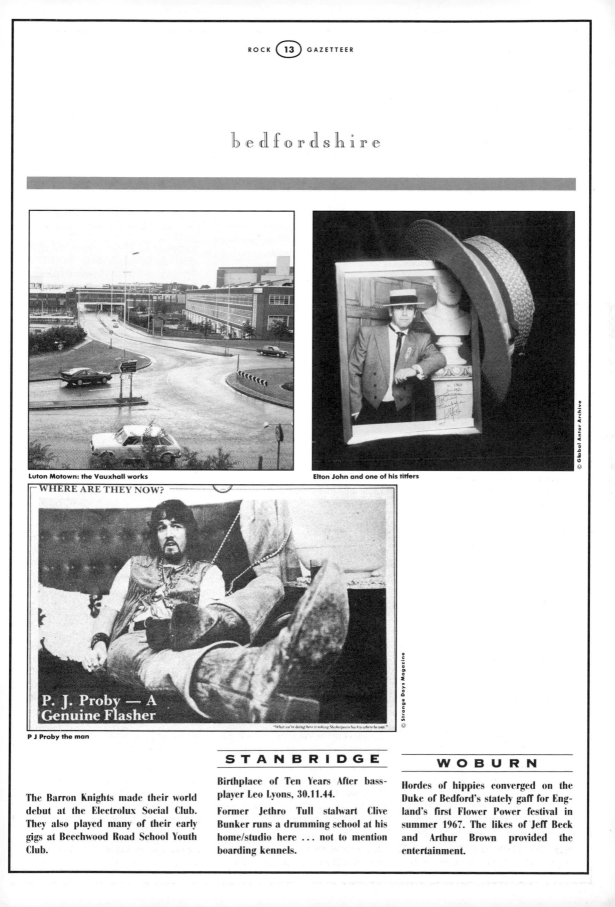

Luton Motown: the Vauxhall works

© Global Antar Archive

Elton John and one of his titfers

**WHERE ARE THEY NOW?**

P. J. Proby — A Genuine Flasher

"What we're doing here is taking Shakespeare back to where he was."

© Strange Days Magazine

P J Proby the man

The Barron Knights made their world debut at the Electrolux Social Club. They also played many of their early gigs at Beechwood Road School Youth Club.

## STANBRIDGE

Birthplace of Ten Years After bass-player Leo Lyons, 30.11.44.

Former Jethro Tull stalwart Clive Bunker runs a drumming school at his home/studio here ... not to mention boarding kennels.

## WOBURN

Hordes of hippies converged on the Duke of Bedford's stately gaff for England's first Flower Power festival in summer 1967. The likes of Jeff Beck and Arthur Brown provided the entertainment.

# BERKSHIRE

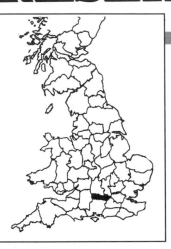

## ALDERMASTON

Among the Campaign for Nuclear Disarmament marchers of the early 60s were Rod Stewart, Chris Dreja (Yardbirds) and Paul Jones (Manfred Mann).

## ASCOT

In May 69, John Lennon laid out £145,000 for Tittenhurst Park, a Georgian mansion set in 72 acres, at Sunningdale. When he moved to America in September 73, Ringo bought it.

David Bowie was an extra in The Virgin Soldiers, filmed on location at Ascot in summer 68.

In 1970, Leapy Lee and his mate Alan Lake (husband of Diana Dors) became involved in a pub fracas at the Red Lion in Sunningdale. The relief manager was knifed and Leapy was sent to prison for three years (to see a super-abundance of Little Arrows), Lake for eighteen months. At the time, Lee was living at Cedar Wood in Larch Avenue; Lake and Dors at Orchard Manor, Shrubs Hill.

## BURNHAM

Birthplace of Tracey Ullman, 30.12.59 (three top ten hits in 1983).

## BRACKNELL

Them Howlin' Horrors were tipped for stardom in 1984 ... but nothing happened!

Two of Yardbird Keith Relf's sons (April, his widow, lives here) have a band; they made their debut at South Hill Park Community Centre.

## BRAY

Home of Howard Jones.

Rod's gaff – pic courtesy of F R Kemmet

# berkshire

The Fox and Hounds in Caversham, where the Nurk Twins played a secret show to Paul McCartneys cousin

The first local musician to find national acclaim was blues singer/guitarist Mike Cooper in the late 60s and R&B combo Jive Alive have been going for almost 20 years.

In June 71, after ten years in different locations, the National Jazz Blues & Rock Festival moved to Reading where it has since remained. In its first year, there were 112 drug arrests in what the News Of The World called "a jamboree of pop and pot".

Hatched in a semi-derelict Cemetery Junction squat, next door to the Sikh Temple, Clayson & The Argonauts were Melody Maker's pick-to-click in 1976, but global fame proved elusive. So disturbing was an early performance at the Target pub in Hosier Street, that the landlord produced a revolver and hustled the group from the premises.

In 1978, before The Buggles hit, Trevor Horn was making ends meet by playing bass in the resident band at the Top Rank.

Twelfth Night were heavy metal hopefuls in the early 80s, while The Lemon Kittens were imaginative arty types.

Robyn Hitchcock mentions Reading in his song I Often Dream Of Trains.

Van Morrison recorded some demos at Audiogenic Studios in Crown Street. Locals say that while he was ensconced there, the place was as impregnable as Fort Knox!

## CAVERSHAM

In April 60, John Lennon and Paul McCartney spent a week's holiday here, staying at the Fox And Hounds on the junction of Westfield and Gosbrook Roads. (The landlady was Paul's cousin). It was here that they played an Everly-style acoustic set under the name of the Nurk Twins.

## LAMBOURN

Charisma boss Tony Stratton Smith lived here in the early 80s, when his interest in horse racing eclipsed his enthusiasm for the record biz.

## NEWBURY

In October 67, Mick Jagger purchased a country estate, Stargroves. Producer Jimmy Miller also lives in Newbury.

## PANGBOURNE

Jimmy Page lived here in the mid seventies.

## PURLEY

Deep Purple's Ian Gillan lived here during the early 80s and played for the local police football team.

## READING

Birthplace of Vincent Crane, 21.5.43 (Atomic Rooster); Mike Oldfield, 15.5.53.

Students passing through the University included Arthur Brown (The Crazy World Of) and Andy Mackay (Roxy Music). The neo-mod group Secret Affair made their debut at the Uni in January 79, supporting the Jam.

Marianne Faithfull was educated at St Joseph's Convent.

## SLOUGH

Birthplace of Cliff Bennett, 4.6.40 (Got To Get You Into My Life); drummer Dave Ballinger, 17.1.41 (Barron Knights); singer Rod Evans, 19.1.47 (Deep Purple); drummer Mark Brzezicki, 21.6.57 (Big Country).

The Beatles/Roy Orbison tour opened at Slough Adelphi in May 63.

# berkshire

The Maze were late 60s locals; Ian Paice left them to drum in Deep Purple Sledgehammer were 80s heavy metal grinders.

Police shot their video of Roxanne at the Fulcrum Centre; Kate Bush filmed Army Dreamers in Black Park – also the location for the video promoting Bob Marley's Buffalo Soldier.

## STOKE POGES

The video for the Human League hit Don't You Want Me was shot in the grounds of the Stoke Palace Hotel in Stoke Green.

## STREATLEY

Martin Rushent's Genetic Studio is located at Wood Cottage on Streatley Hill.

## WINDSOR

The Ricky Tick was a prime mid 60s Rhythm & blues club, featuring the likes of Zoot Money, John Mayall, Graham Bond, etc. For the famous Yardbirds scene in the movie Blow Up, the club was meticulously reconstructed at Elstree Studios.

In August 63, The Rolling Stones played the Star & Garter pub – without illness-prone Brian Jones, but it was at the Ricky Tick Club that Jones met Linda Lawrence, later to be mother of his child. For a while they lived with her parents in Windsor.

Windsor residents include Elton John and Jimmy Page, who bought Michael Caine's old house in May 80. It was there, nine months later, that John Bonham died after an intense vodka binge.

Genetic Studios

The Slough Adelphi

Rod Stewart also lived here, with Deirdre Harrington during the early 70s, at Cranbourne Court – a mansion he purchased from Lord Bethell for around £89,000. You'd pay that much for a chicken coop in Windsor these days.

For its 6th and 7th years (July 66 and August 67), the National Jazz Blues & Rock Festival was held at Balloon Meadow on Windsor Racecourse. In 66, Cream unveiled themselves and The Who smashed up their equipment; 67 was dominated by flower power and marked the debuts of Fleetwood Mac and Chicken Shack.

## WOKINGHAM

Wooderay Studios at Manor Farm in Finch Hampstead Road started small but now attracts the likes of Then Jerico and All About Eve.

Sixties popsters Marmalade, still big on the cabaret circuit, are now based here.

# BUCKINGHAMSHIRE

## AMERSHAM

Birthplace of Butch Baker, 16.7.41 (Barron Knights); Tim Rice, 10.11.44.

## ASTON CLINTON

Tamla Motown's first UK outlet was the Oriole label, based in premises opposite the Rising Sun pub (now a derelict plastics factory).

## AYLESBURY

Friars club started in 1969, at the British Legion Hall in Walton Street. Mott the Hoople and Genesis were audience faves.

The Borough Assembly Hall in th Market Square was known as the Grosvenor in the 60s, when everyone from Johnny Kidd to Jimi Hendrix played there, and Friars in the 70s, when the club outgrew its first venue. When Genesis played there in June 71, Peter Gabriel leapt off the stage during an overenthusiastic interpretation of The Knife and broke his ankle. David Bowie previewed his Ziggy Stardust show there in January 72.

In 1961, Bill Wyman was on holiday in Aylesbury and was taken to see Dickie Demon & The Barron Knights (as they were then known) at the Grosvenor. What he actually saw was his future, determining there and then to join a group.

When the Assemby Hall was closed for redevelopment, Friars moved to the Reg Maxwell Hall in the Civic Centre and the jollity continued until promoter David Stopps discovered Howard Jones (who first played there in May 82) and quit the club to manage him.

In the late 70s, the town's biggest star was John Otway; born at 17 Whitehall Street and educated at Queens Park Junior School. He worked for the council as a dustman until fame tapped him on the shoulder.

Otway and his sidekick Wild Willy Barrett caused mayhem on the national new wave circuit until a gig coincided with a World Cup match. Barrett made the wrong choice and the duo split.

Other local residents include jazz-rock saxophonist Lol Coxhill, Pete Trewavas from Marillion, Bill Drummond from the Timelords and Ian Gillan from Deep Purple, who lives in the hinterlands.

Other local groups included The Vice Creems (punks, led by Zigzag magazine editor Kris Needs), The Stowaways (guitarist Mick Lister was later in The Truth), Orthi, The Haircuts, The Disco Students, The Blood Oranges, Danny Picasso & The Last Good Kiss, The Robins, The Feckin Ejits, and Big Big Sun (late 80s Atlantic signing).

In January 77, Keith Richards found himself in Crown Court on drug charges (see Newport Pagnell). After a three day trial he was found half guilty and fined £1000.

The Coventry Automatics, supporting The Clash at Friars, changed their name to The Specials on the day of the gig (June 78).

The Grange Secondary School was responsible for the education of John Otway, Wild Willy Barrett, Robin Boult (Big Big Sun), Pete Trewavas (Marillion), Kris Needs (Zigzag), David Rohoman (Kilburn & The High Roads).

In the 80s, the town's hottest band was Marillion, who really got going after Fish moved here in January 81. They lived communally at 64 Weston Road, Aston Clinton. Following their first flush of success, they bought houses in the town: Fish lived at 18 Albert Street, Mark Kelly at 42 Willow Road, and Pete Trewavas at 15 Mount Pleasant. All have since moved to more palatial residences.

Their local boozer was Seatons (now closed) on the Market Square — setting for their first hit, Market Square Heroes ... inspired by the town's very first punk, known locally as Brick.

## BEACONSFIELD

Birthplace of New Seeker Paul Layton, 4.8.47.

## BLETCHLEY

Wilton Hall was a major 60s venue. Jeff Beck, The Animals and all the R&B/blues crowd played there — as did Pink Floyd on one of their first provincial forays, November 66.

## BRILL

Birthplace of drummer Mick Pointer, 22.7.56 (Marillion).

# buckinghamshire

## CAR-CRASH STONE ON DRUG CHARGES

**By EDWARD LAXTON**

ROLLING STONES' lead guitarist Keith Richard was charged yesterday with possessing cannabis and cocaine.

He was also charged with three driving offences, and bailed to appear in court next month at Newport Pagnell, Bucks.

The charges follow a crash on the M1 nearly three months ago when Richard was returning from a Stones concert.

His car careered off the motorway and crashed through a fence into a field. No other vehicle was involved.

After the crash his Bentley was searched at the local police station.

When he was arrested he asked police for ten weeks' bail so that he could complete the Stones' tour of Europe and go on to America.

But both trips turned sour.

In France, his four-year-old son Tara died from a 'flu virus.

In America, the big bicentenary concert was cancelled.

Meanwhile the US drugs enforcement agency had learned of the impending charges, and asked Thames Valley police to keep them informed.

Yesterday Richard arrived at Newport Pagnell police station with his solicitor in a Ford Granada limousine—chauffeur driven.

*Keef crashes somewhere off Newport Pagnell*

## BUCKINGHAM

Former Whitesnake guitarist Bernie Marsden went to Buckingham School and still lives in town.

Locally based Liquid Gold had two top tenners in 1980.

## CHESHAM

Art Garfunkel made his UK solo debut at the Trap Door folk club, just off the High Street, in 1965.

## CUDDINGTON

Until he moved to Wales in 1988, Labi Siffre lived in the thatched house next to the Crown public house. Heavy Metal group Lone Star also lived in the village during the mid 80s.

## HIGH WYCOMBE

Birthplace of Martha, 16.6.66 (Paul McCartney's sheepdog).

Students passing through the Royal Grammar School include Tom Springfield (The Springfields), Ian Dury and Ted Speight (who were in a skiffle group there and re-united in Kilburn & The High Roads), Howard Jones.

The first floor room above the Nag's Head on the London Road has always presented excellent up and coming groups — from Fleetwood Mac to Elvis Costello and beyond. The ebullient promoter, Ron Watts, intermittently led R&B/cajun band Brewers Droop — which for a while contained Mark Knopfler playing his first professional role.

Unannounced and uninvited, the Sex Pistols played at the College of Art's Valentine Dance in February 76 — supporting Screaming Lord Sutch.

The Town Hall was the first gig on the seminal Bunch Of Stiffs tour of October 77. It marked the debut of Ian Dury & The Blockheads; other stars included Elvis Costello and Nick Lowe.

While waiting for fame to tap him on the shoulder, Howard Jones was employed in the stock control department at the Perfawrap cling film factory.

Late 70s R&B group Long Tall Shorty looked promising for a while; in the 60s, The Peasants looked like making it.

Among the stars living in the hinterlands beyond the town are Ian Anderson (Jethro Tull) and Stewart Copeland (Police).

## MILTON KEYNES

Milton Keynes Bowl has presented numerous rock concerts, starting with Police in July 80. (Bowl? More like a mud-filled flanease!) Status Quo played their farewell gigs there (they came back, of course) and Michael Jackson blocked roads in all directions in 1988.

Local resident Eddie Stanton got together with Wild Willy Barrett to record Milton Keynes We Love You. The Style Council's tribute was rather more equivocal.

The video for Cliff Richard's Wired For Sound was shot in the shopping centre, adjacent to the excellent bookshop Fagins.

Home of Acid House executant Jolly Roger.

Once the guitarist with Jethro Tull and Blodwyn Pig, Mick Abrahams moved here to become a financial consultant with Allied Dunbar.

# buckinghamshire

Tingewick Village pond, – the contractors used the wrong sort of clay!

Jimmy Saville fund raising

With Thanks to Janet Rowe

## NEWPORT PAGNELL

In May 76, following a Stones concert at Stafford, Keith Richards' car swerved off the M1, burst through a hedge and came to rest in a ploughed field. He was arrested for drug possession.

## PRINCES RISBOROUGH

Birthplace of Nigel Harrison, bassplayer in Blondie. His first group was Farm, whose drummer Paul Hammond replaced Carl Palmer in Atomic Rooster.

During 1975, John Otway lived in a tent in the hills near Whiteleaf Cross — chronicled in his song Louisa On A Horse. He later moved to his girlfriend's house in Place Farm Way — the title of another song.

## STOKE MANDEVILLE

Robert Wyatt recuperated at Stoke Mandeville Hospital after fracturing his spine. Jimmy Saville raises millions for new buildings and equipment, and puts in many hours on the wards.

## STOWE

Passing through this exclusive public school were George Melly (more interested in Bessie Smith), Richard Branson, and Roger Hodgson of Supertramp.

The Beatles played here in April 63. It was the first time they'd even seen a public school and were astonished and delighted that the audience remained seated and silent throughout the entire performance.

## TINGEWICK

Duran Duran's Andy Taylor played in the village hall gig to raise funds for landscaping the village pond (December 88).

## WENDOVER

The Well Head pub was a cool venue in the late 80s, when groups like The Housemartins and The Mighty Lemon Drops were regulars.

Marillion men Mark Kelly and Steve Rothery bought homes here when they made a bit of cash.

## WINGRAVE

Ian Dury's band Kilburn & The High Roads lived in the vicarage during their 70s heyday. Local kids would sit on the railings by the village pond and listen to their rehearsals. Peter Cook lived here too as a matter of interest.

# CAMBRIDGESHIRE

## CAMBRIDGE

Birthplace of Syd Barrett, 6.1.46, subsequently a pupil at Cambridge High School For Boys, where he met Roger Waters. After moving to London, they formed Pink Floyd, who later paid homage to their roots on Grantchester Meadows.

Barrett later returned to the city to pursue a sporadic solo career and lead ill-fated group Stars.

Premier late 60s local group was Jokers Wild, comprising Dave Gilmour (later in Floyd), Rick Wills (later in Foreigner) and Willie Wilson (later in Quiver). Also Wages of Sin and Little Women (both featuring Jerry Shirley, later of Humble Pie).

In the 70s, came multifarious eccentric pop rockers including Duke Duke & The Dukes and The Soft Boys, the latter containing Kimberley Rew and led by Robyn Hitchcock, who could often be found busking in Lion Yard.

The Cambridge Folk Festival, held annually at Cherry Hinton has always presented top-line international acts — including Paul Simon, Paul Butterfield, Bo Diddley, Jimmy Page and Roy Harper, Tom Rush, etc etc.

Also born in Cambridge were Olivia Newton John, 26.9.48; guitarist Tim Renwick, 7.8.49 (Quiver/Mike & The Mechanics . . . he also went to the High School For Boys).

University alumni include Nick Drake, Jonathan King, Tim Curry, Kimberley Rew, Fred Frith and Chris Cutler (Henry Cow), Pete Atkin and Clive James, Simon Boswell (Advertising), Julie Covington, late 80s singer/song writers Andy White and John Wesley Harding.

It was at a party in Cambridge that Andrew Oldham first met his protegee Marianne Faithfull.

Venues come and go, including the Dorothy Ballroom (which once throbbed to The Beatles but is now a steak house), the Corn Exchange (recently refurbished), the Great Northern Hotel in Station Road (which stopped presenting live gigs after noise complaints and later became the short-lived City Limits), the Burleigh Arms in Maid's Causeway (put on Darling Buds, Wedding Present, etc until ubiquitous complaining neighbour caused recent closure), the Alma Brewery (sporadic local group showcase), and various University halls.

**Julian Cope goes Spaceward**

In January 81, Jerry Dammers and Terry Hall of The Specials were each fined £400 plus costs for using threatening words and behaviour likely to cause a breach of the peace at a concert on Midsummer Common.

Eighties groups include The Dolly Mixtures, The Frigidaires, Cri de Coeur, Exploding Hamsters, The Great Divide, Perfect Vision, Andy Goes Shopping and The Roaring Boys, who extricated a massive advance from CBS and promptly went phut!

Current faves include The Fruit Bats, The Bible, and Jack The Bear.

Spaceward Studio started in a basement at 20 Victoria Street, where early clients included The Soft Boys, Tubeway Army and Stiff Little Fingers.

## FOXTON

UK residence of Rick Wills, bass player with Foreigner.

## GREAT PAXTON

Birthplace of Terry Reid, 13.11.49.

## PETERBOROUGH

Birthplace of actor Paul Nicholas, 3.12.45 (he scored hits in the mid-70s, but in 1964 was playing piano in Screaming Lord Sutch's Savages!); singer Andy Bell, 25.4.64 (Erasure).

New wave groups included The APF Brigade, The Destructors and The Name.

In 1978, punk group The Dole dedicated their single New Wave Love to a local vicar's daughter, who was later accused by their manager of being a disruptive influence and breaking up the band!

# cambridgeshire

## SOMERSHAM

Home of Stranglers bassist Jean Jacques Burnel.

## STAPLEFORD

Birthplace of Stan Cullimore, 6.4.62 (Housemartins).

## STRETHAM

Second and last home of Spaceward Studio was the Old School House, where Julian Cope, The Bible, and many more recorded. Closed in 1988.

## THRIPLOW

Operational base for The Fruit Bats and Jack The Bear.

Syd Barrett outside his old Cambridge home

The late Nick Drake

# CHESHIRE

## ALSAGER

Before he started the Thompson Twins, Tom Bailey studied music at Alsager College.

## CHESTER

Top 60s groups were Four Hits and A Miss, and The Black Abbots — led by Russ Abbot (born here on 16.9.47).

Before becoming guitar star of Fairport Convention, Richard Thompson was a stained glass designer. An example of his work can be seen in St Columbus Church.

Bomb Disneyland are current indie faves.

## MACCLESFIELD

Birthplace of blues pioneer John Mayall, 29.11.33.

With Joy Division poised for international recognition, charismatic singer Ian Curtis took his life at his parents home in May 80.

New Order drummer Stephen Morris was expelled from King's School.

## RUNCORN

The Elite coffee bar was a popular 60s hang-out.

## SANDBACH

Clive Gregson was a teacher here until he went back to Manchester to start Any Trouble.

Home of aptly named new wavers The Pits.

St. Columbus, Chester —
and example of Richard Thompsons' early craft

## WARRINGTON

Birthplace of Rick Astley, 6.2.66.

After he made it, George Harrison bought a house for his parents at nearby Appleton.

Home of 60s psychedelic band Fairytale; recorded for Decca but got lost along the way.

Deep Purple made their UK debut at the Red Lion Hotel in July 68.

## WIDNES

The Queens Hall was the town's first rock venue; The Beatles, Gerry & The Pacemakers, and all the Liverpool groups played there. The Regal Club and Columbia Hall were popular later.

It was whilst waiting for the milk train on Widnes station, after a local folk club gig in 1964, that Paul Simon — yearning to be back in London in the arms of his beloved Kathy — began writing Homeward Bound.

Home base for 60s also-rans, The Addicts.

## WILMSLOW

Pogue Jem Finer was educated at Wilmslow Grammar School.

# CLEVELAND

A hot mid 60s R&B group was The Roadrunners, who moved to London in 1967. Their line-up included Paul Rodgers, Mick Moody (later in Whitesnake) and Bruce Thomas (later in The Attractions).

Martin Fry made his public debut with Vice Versa at new wave club the Rock Garden.

Several of Chris Rea's songs contain local references: Steel River is the Tees, and Stainsby Girls School is in the suburb of Acklam.

## HARTLEPOOL

Birthplace of bass player Mod Rogan, 3.2.44 (The Roulettes); guitarist Jeremy Spencer, 4.7.48 (Fleetwood Mac).

## KIRKLEAVINGTON

During the 60s, the Country Club presented every group ever invented. Now called Martha's Vineyard.

## MIDDLESBROUGH

Birthplace of drummer Pete York, 15.8.42 (Spencer Davis Group); singer Paul Rodgers, 17.12.49 (Free/Bad Company); singer Chris Rea, 1951; singer Claire Hammil, 1955; bassist Pete Trewavas, 15.1.59 (Marillion) ... not to mention East Enders star Wendy Richard, who allowed Mike Sarne to seduce her on his 1962 chart topper Come Outside.

Rocker Terry Dene made his variety debut at the Empire in June 57.

In July 63, The Rolling Stones played their first gig outside London — at the town's Alcove Club.

**Middlesborough lad Rea**

© WEA Records (U.K.)

## REDCAR

The Coatham Bowl was and is a popular venue.

## SALTBURN-BY-THE-SEA

Birthplace of heavy metal titan David Coverdale, 21.9.51 (Deep Purple, Whitesnake). His first group was called Denver Mule.

## STOCKTON-ON-TEES

A skyline of tall chimneys belching shit into the overcast sky. Undoubtedly the inspiration for Stars Fell On Stockton, the b-side of The Shadows' 1962 chart topper Wonderful Land.

Stockton Hippodrome has presented star-studded pantomimes since the year dot. Marty Wilde was in Babes In The Wood, Cliff Richard remembers how lonely the beach was (well it was January!),

Birthplace of singer/songwriter Lesley Duncan.

# CORNWALL

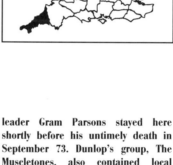

## ALTARNUN

Local residents include Tony Butler of Big Country and Robert Smith of The Cure.

## BOSCASTLE

Graham Bond's description of nearby Bossiney Waterfall and Rocky Valley inspired Pete Brown to write Tickets To Waterfalls for the first Jack Bruce album. When Bond died, his friend Pete Bailey scattered his ashes here.

## BUDE

The Headland Pavilion has promoted weekly Saturday night dances since the early 60s. The Ebony Combo played summer-long residencies and in 1970 achieved a degree of national notoriety under the name Hard Meat.

## DAVIDSTOW

Chilli Willi & The Red Hot Peppers cut their album Bongos Over Balham at the Lucky Abattoir Studios and Elvis Costello & The Attractions had their first rehearsals in the village hall.

## GOLANT

Home of The Mechanics (nothing to do with Mike), who are resident session players at Sawmills Studio — approachable only by boat! New Model Army recently stated that they'd never record anywhere else!

## HELSTON

Home of Ian Dunlop, member of seminal US folk-rock group The International Submarine Band, whose leader Gram Parsons stayed here shortly before his untimely death in September 73. Dunlop's group, The Museletones, also contained local resident Terry Clements — former sax player with Janis Joplin's Kosmic Blues Band.

## LAUNCESTON

The White Horse Inn was a regular Friday night gig through the early 80s ... favourites were local group Brainiac 5.

## LISKEARD

Home of Charlie & The Wide Boys (who made waves on the London pub rock circuit) and 70s chanteuse Lesley Duncan.

## LOOE

Home of legendary (within a five mile radius of here) late 60s psychedelic outfit Constable Zippo's Electric Commode Band and current bizarros Dan Gleebits & The Bull Bags Boogie Band.

## PARR

Paul Whaley, drummer with San Franciscan power trio Blue Cheer, was working in a bakery here during the early 80s!

## PENZANCE

Elvis Costello & The Attractions made their world debut at the Garden in July 77.

Home of Danny's Passions (first Cornish band to record), COB (Clive's Original Band ... whose albums now fetch upwards of 100 quid) and idiosyncratic pub rockers Brainiac 5 (whose guitarist, Charles Taylor, now runs the Reckless Records empire).

## REDRUTH

The Quasar Coffee Bar was the cool meeting place and The Room At The Top was a folk club presenting the likes of Ralph McTell and Stefan Grossman.

## ST AUSTELL

The Cornwall Colisseum at Carlyon Bay is the largest venue in the south west ... used for big national tours.

## ST GERMANS

Siouxsie & The Banshees and The Cure are among headliners at the Elephant Fayre — annual three day mixed media gatherings held on Lord Eliot's estate in the early 80s.

# CUMBRIA

*Cornwall continued...............*

## ST IVES

Birthplace of drummer Mick Fleetwood, 24.6.44 (Fleetwood Mac).

Donovan, John Renbourn and Ralph Metell were among the early beatnik/folkie community spending summers here in the early 60s.

## TRURO

From whence came guitarist Keith Lucas, leader of London punk group 999.

Home of The Famous Jug Band.

## WADEBRIDGE

Home of psychedelic group Onyx, who recorded for Pye, CBS and Parlophone but made only local impact.

Also from Cornwall are guitarist Jon Mark (Mark Almond and John Mayall's Bluesbreakers) and Debbie from My Bloody Valentine ... not to mention Roxy Music sax player Andy Mackay, who was born here on 23.7.46.

## BARROW-IN-FURNESS

Birthplace of bassplayer Glenn Cornick, 24.4.47 (Jethro Tull).

## CARLISLE

Birthplace of singer Mike Harrison, 30.9.42, and bassplayer Greg Ridley, 23.10.43 (Spooky Tooth). Originally called the VIPs, they moved to London as the first band signed to the Island label. They subsequently changed their name to Art, then Spooky Tooth. When they broke up, Harrison adopted another Carlisle bunch, Junkyard Angel, as his backing group.

## EGREMONT

Home of It Bites, who were all schoolfriends. They moved down to London in 1986 to hit the top ten with Calling All The Heroes.

Incidentally, William Wordsworth lived around here too.

## ULLSWATER

Location for Spandau Ballet's Musclebound video.

## WIGTON

Author and broadcaster Melvyn Bragg played tea-chest bass in Wigton Grammar's skiffle group.

**Charles Taylor, Brainiac 5**

Mike Harrison

**The underrated Mike Harrison solo LP**

**Rockin' Melv**

# DERBYSHIRE

## BAKEWELL

Birthplace of Long John Baldry, 12.1.41.

## BUXTON

Scene of the Buxton Rock Festival of July 74. The Faces, Mott The Hoople and Captain Beefheart headlined.

Echo & The Bunnymen filmed their Crocodiles video at the Pavilion.

The Fusion Club was the cool late 70s hangout; the Queens Park Hotel in Park Road is a late 80s venue.

## DERBY

Birthplace of Kevin Coyne, 27.1.44; bassplayer John Wetton, 1950 (Asia).

Harry Webb and his group, The Drifters, played their first provincial gig at a Derby ballroom — using the name Cliff Richard for the first time (June 58).

## CHESTERFIELD

Birthplace of Tom Bailey, 18.1.56. He left Chesterfield Grammar to attend music college but returned to start the Thompson Twins in late 77. Also the birthplace of Mark Shaw, 10.6.61 (singer with Then Jerico).

The Victoria Hall was the town's hottest venue in the 60s, when Cream, The Nice, King Crimson, etc played there.

Original Buxton programme, The New York Dolls The Faces & Mott The Hoople on the same bill!

Bunnymen Buxton live recording

© Global Antar Archive

© WEA Records (U.K.)

# DEVON

## ASHBURTON

Once the singer in Reading group Kerry Rapid & his Blue Stars, Alan Hope was later the landlord of the Golden Lion pub in Ashburton. Standing as Monster Raving Loony candidate for the local council, he found himself elected ... the party's greatest (possibly only) political triumph!

## BARNSTAPLE

Local residents include Dave Brock (Hawkwind), Gilli Smyth (Gong) and Harvey Bainbridge (Sonic Assassins).

Most famous band was Spirit Of John Morgan — three turn of the 70s blues/rock/humour albums.

## BIDEFORD

Birthplace of Marcus Lillington, 28.2.67 (Breathe).

## DARTMOOR

The sleeve of the Yes album Tormato was shot at Yes Tor.

## EXETER

Birthplace of singer Tony Burrows, 14.4.42 (Edison Lighthouse). Home of Hawkwind dancer Stacia.

Principal Edwards Magic Theatre (signed to John Peel's Dandelion label) formed at the University.

Steve Upton and Martin Turner first met in Dirty Dot's Cafe. There they put together The Empty Vessels, soon to evolve into Wishbone Ash.

## EXMOUTH

Birthplace of Pearl Carr, who with husband Teddy Johnson, carried our 1959 Eurovision hopes with Sing Little Birdie!

## HOLSWORTHY

The Memorial Hall was a notable 60s gig — presenting the likes of Them and Jeff Beck's Tridents.

The Old Vicarage in nearby Pyworthy is the home of Hidden Drive Recording Studios, run by former Van Der Graaf Generator drummer Guy Evans.

## KINGSBRIDGE

Slade guitarist Dave Hill was born at Fleet Castle, 4.4.46. He moved to the Midlands as a child.

## OKEHAMPTON

T V Smith and Gaye Advert moved to London to ride the 1977 boom with their punk band The Adverts.

Home of the idiosyncratic Avant Gardener (recorded for Appaloosa and Virgin).

## PAIGNTON

In 1978, former 50s rocker Rory Blackwell was entertainments manager at the Devon Coast Country Club.

## PLYMOUTH

Birthplace of jazz and avant garde composer Mike Westbrook.

The Van Dike Club was an important 70s progressive venue, presenting everyone from T Rex to Derek & the Dominoes. In 1971, Fairport were on-stage when the place was raided ... Dave Swarbrick was busted for possession! Vinegar Joe (with Robert Palmer and Elkie Brooks) made their debut here in November 71.

Also operated by Peter Vandike, Woods was a primo punk venue. The Pistols played one of their Spots (Sex Pistols On Tour Secretly) gigs here.

Emerson Lake & Palmer made their world debut at the Guildhall in August 70.

## TAVISTOCK

Birthplace of Kinks bass player Pete Quaife, 27.12.43.

The church at Brentor was pictured on the sleeve of the first McGuinness Flint album.

Local new wavers Amebix made mild national ripples.

## TIVERTON

Just outside the town, The Fisherman's Cot at Bickleigh is where Paul Simon started writing Bridge Over Troubled Water.

# DORSET

continued..............

## TORQUAY

Birthplace of comedian Peter Cook, 17.11.37 (compere of bizarre TV rock show Revolver); bassplayer Martin Turner, 1.10.47 (Wishbone Ash).

Current home of 50s thrush Ruby Murray, who held the record for most UK top tenners . . . until Madonna came along 25 years later.

Local groups include The Rustiks (managed by Brian Epstein) and Peter & The Wolves (four late 60s MGM singles).

Most successful recent indie band is The Morrisons.

## TOTNES

Birthplace of Jimmy Cauty, once in Zodiac Mindwarp's Love Reaction and Brilliant; now half of The Timelords and The Justified Ancients of Mu Mu.

© Global Antar Archive

**Zoot Money**

## BOURNEMOUTH

Many illustrious stars have appeared here in pantomime: in 1962 Adam Faith played Aladdin (whilst his Roulettes played Chinese policemen), for example.

Forgotten (by most people) local groups include Albatross, Dave Anthony's Moods, The Capitta All Stars, The Freebooters, The Future Classics, The G Men, King Harry, Gringo, The Track Marks, Once Bitten, Raw Deal, Tetrad and Jack-Knife. The Dowlands had a minor hit with the Beatles song 'All My Loving', but none of The Nite People's eight singles made any impact. Two thirds of the calmest jazz trio The Peddlers were from Bournemouth; they scored a top twenty hit with Birth in 1969.

The first local musician to make a national impression was John Rostill, who moved to London to join The Shadows in October 63.

The same month, Zoot Money moved up to join Alexis Korner's Blues Inc. A well known window cleaner/prankster/R&B fanatic, Zoot had played in numerous local outfits, including the Jan Ralfini Band, the Sands Combo, the Don Robb Band and his own jazz/blues groups. In London he formed The Big Roll Band

– one of the era's more spectacular R&B outfits – which through drug metamorphosis became Dantalian's Chariot. Now a musician/actor, he can be spied in several commercials.

Zoot's principal crony in Bournemouth (and London) was Andy Somers, later to become famous as Andy Summers, guitarist in The Police.

Chirpy pirate disc jockey Tony Blackburn – later the first DJ to play a record on Radio One – was a local laddie, best remembered for his early 60s group Tony Blackburn & The Rovers. Lead guitarist in that ensemble was Al Stewart, soon to make it big on the London folk circuit.

Stewart was one of many locals who visited Strike Music Shop to take guitar lessons from the area's most gifted musician, Robert Fripp. He played in The Ravens (with Gordon Haskell, later vocalist in King Crimson), The League Of Gentlemen (a name he resurrected briefly in the 70s), and then joined Pete and Mike Giles in Giles Giles and Fripp.

The Giles brothers had served their apprenticeship with the aforementioned Dowlands and Trend Setters Ltd. Their alliance with Fripp began with a month of rehearsal at the Beacon Hotel.

All three moved to London, and in 1969 became King Crimson – with the addition of another pal from Bournemouth, Greg Lake. He'd been in local groups like Shame and Shylimbs. After less than two years in King Crimson, he formed one of the 70s most successful supergroups, Emerson Lake & Palmer.

Other Bournemouth luminaries include drummer Lee Kerslake (a stalwart of Uriah heep), John Hawken (Nashville Teens pianist), Richard Palmer James

dorset

(Supertramp vocalist for a while), bass player John Wetton (graduate of Family, Roxy Music, Asia and various other bands), Anita Harris (educated at the Convent Of The Cross).

Promoter Mel Bush works from an office in Wolverton Road.

In June 65, David Bowie tried out his new group Davy Jones & The Lower Third at the Pavilion.

The Fall's song Bournemouth Runner was written after they'd stayed in a hotel near the Winter Gardens. A guy in the next room died while they were there.

Local band Seven seem poised for stardom.

## LULWORTH COVE

The video for Ten Pole Tudor's last minor hit, Throwing My Baby Out With The Bathwater, was filmed here.

## POOLE

In August 65, John Lennon purchased a bungalow in Panorama Road, Sandbanks for his Aunt Mimi.

New wave band The Tours were signed to Virgin, but dissolved almost immediately. Leader Richard Mazda then formed The Cosmetics, who played Portugal, Japan and various other places with Tom Robinson. Mazda became hot-shot producer of not only Tom but Wall Of Voodoo, Alternative TV, The Fall, and more.

## SHAFTESBURY

Mark Price from All About Eve was the short-trousered kid pushing his bike up the cobbled hill (just behind the High Street) in the old Hovis television ad.

Mark Price dreams about flowers and harbours whilst earning a crust.

© Tele Pictorials

## SWANAGE

Big Country shot the video for In A Big Country on Swanage Beach.

## WIMBOURNE

Birthplace of Robert Fripp, gentleman and guitarist. Famed for adding intricate decoration to many an album, notably those of King Crimson, a group he has led (on and off) for twenty years.

Still resides in the area, in a noble Edwin Lutyens house which he shares with his wife, Toyah Wilcox.

The Martian Schoolgirls were a punk group from here.

John's Aunt Mimi, at home in Poole.

# DURHAM

## BISHOP AUCKLAND

Home of the splendidly named Flatcap & Whippet label.

Local resident Chris Oddy was bass player in The Humblebums — fronted by Billy Connolly and Gerry Rafferty.

## CHESTER LE STREET

Shadows guitarist Bruce Welch lived at 15 Broadwood View and attended Red Rose School.

## CONSETT

A bunch of enterprising locals have formed the Consett Music Project, getting grants to build a studio and rehearsal rooms. They teach schoolchildren recording and engineering techniques and other skills appropriate to the post- steelworks era, and they promote local bands and worthies — like miner/poet/pit-song specialist Jock Purdon.

Hottest local band is Aiming At America.

The Works and the Stanley Fordham Arms are good venues ... but usually only promote on giro day.

## COXHOE

Home of respected jazz-rock guitarist Martin Holder.

## DARLINGTON

Penetration singer Pauline Murray went to Darlington Art College.

Tom Jones used to cavort at the La Bamba Club — now extinct.

## DURHAM

Birthplace of Peanut Langford, 10.4.43 (Barron Knights); Chad Stuart, 10.12.43 (half of Chad & Jeremy); drummer Alan White, 14.6.49 (Yes); keyboard player Alan Clark, 5.3.52 (Dire Straits); singer Pauline Murray, 8.3.58 (Penetration ... who used to rehearse in St Margarets Church Hall).

Birthplace also of drummer Martyn Atkins, who lived on the Newton Hall housing estate and went to Wearside School. Played in local 70s progressive group Mynd until he auditioned for Johnny Rotten and got the job in PIL. Also had his own band, Brian Brain.

Prefab Sprout used to play to an average audience of 8 at the Brewers Arms (now a nightclub called Brodies) in Gilesgate ... "it was as if a spacecraft came through the roof, took them away, and beamed them into stardom" says a local.

Barking Billy & The Rhythm Dogs are R&B executants; the Ray Stubbs All Stars (ditto); Swimmer Leon are tipped as next big local band; Gerbils In Red Wine have the best name!

Venues include The Angel (who boast "the loudest juke box in the North East"), the Queens Head, and Fowlers Yard Community Centre.

## FATFIELD

Birthplace of Animals organist Alan Price 19.4.42.

## FERRYHILL

Pauline Murray was raised in this wee village, just south of Spennymoor. It was here in 1977 that she formed the early punk group Penetration, whose record Silent Community aroused local ire.

## LANGLEY PARK

Former Railway Street resident Paul Ellis moved to London to play keyboards for Hot Chocolate, Billy Ocean and Pepsi & Shirlie.

Despite their album title, Prefab Sprout don't come from here ... but Paddy McAloon used to get his hair cut at the barber's shop in Front Street!

A fast-rising band that do come from here are called Somebody Famous.

## PITY ME

There has to be a bizarre story behind the name of this village, where Terry Gavagan runs the 24 track Guardian Studio ... as used by John Miles, among others. The booth is said to be haunted by a little girl, who many claim to have heard!

## SEAHAM

Three schoolfriends formed The Reptile House, The Kings of Cotton, and finally The Kane Gang, who made the charts in 1984.

# ESSEX

### (including boroughs in Greater London area)

continued...............

## WITTON GILBERT

This is where Prefab Sprout actually hail from. They used to run the local garage and filling station while planning their international breakout. Petrol purchasers were invited inside to buy second hand albums.

(above) Kamem of Epping

(below) Feelgoods in The Admiral Jellicoe

© WEA Records (U.K.)

© United Artists Records

## BARKING

Birthplace of Brian Poole, 2.11.41; guitarist Ricky West, 7.5.43 (Tremeloes); Billy Bragg, 20.12.57; guitarist Dave Evans, better known as The Edge, 8.8.61 (U2 . . . born at Barking Maternity Hospital).

Brian Poole & The Tremeloes were the town's hottest act in the 60s — replacing The King Brothers who ruled in the 50s.

## BASILDON

Birthplace of Vince Clarke, 3.7.60, Andy Fletcher, 8.7.60, and Martin Gore, 23.7.61 — all three of whom (together with Chigwell born Dave Gahan) formed synth-pop group Depeche Mode. They played their first gig at St Nicholas School.

Clarke soon split to start Yazoo with Alison Moyet, another Basildon native (formerly fronting Southend band The Screaming Abdabs).

## BILLERICAY

Born here in 1942, Ian Dury drew on local knowledge to pillory typical sub-urban swag-artist Billericay Dickie — self-satisfied all mouth-and-trousers

brickie. Among his conquests were Janet from the Isle of Thanet and a nice bit of posh from Burnham on Crouch . . . but hopefully not Alison Moyet, born here on 18.6.61.

## BRENTWOOD

Paul Simon makes his UK debut at the Railway Inn folk club in April 64. There he meets Kathy, soon to become his girlfriend and the inspiration behind songs like Homeward Bound and America.

Honey Bane completed her formal education at the St Charles Youth Treatment Centre.

## CANVEY

The rock'n'roll era opened with a 21 year old greengrocers assistant winning the national Best Dressed Teddy Boy contest (Aug 54).

The Fix, Pigboy Charlie, Southside Jug Band, The Flowerpots and The Roamers distilled into Dr Feelgood in 72, and they put Canvey firmly on the rock'n'roll map. The Admiral Jellicoe was their local (probably still is!) Manic guitarist Wilko Johnson split to form his own group, but singer Lee Brilleaux still carries the Feelgood flag.

In the 60s, Wilko (then with The Heap) was the first man on the island with shoulder length hair; ten years later, he was the first with short back and sides!

The Goldmine was a popular new wave/new romantics haunt.

## CHELMSFORD

The Corn Exchange was the hottest 60s venue/mod hang-out.

# essex

Home of Tracie Young, and James Vane, who worked as a hairdresser at Silhouette du Barry.

## CHIGWELL

Birthplace of singer Dave Gahan, 9.5.62 (Depeche Mode).

## CLACTON

Cliff Richard & The Drifters played a four week residency at Butlin's Holiday Camp in August 58. Whilst there, his first single, Move It, began to climb the national chart.

Some 20 years later, Kevin Rowland had a summer job there . . . washing up!

Operational base for 60s beat groups Peter Jay & The Jaywalkers (featuring vocalist Terry Reid) and Dave Curtiss & The Tremors.

Most famous 80s resident was Sade, who grew up there — having been born in Nigeria. Also home for Blockhead sax man Davey Payne.

## COLCHESTER

Home of Twink — drummer with The Pretty Things, Tomorrow and various others. His first group, the Colchester based Fairies were hot on the mid 60s London R&B scene.

The sleeve photo on Fairport Convention's What We Did On Our Holidays was taken in their dressing room during a gig at Essex University.

Home of 80s hopefuls Modern English.

## DAGENHAM

Birthplace of bass player Alan Howard, 17.10.41, and drummer Dave Munden,

Twink trashes a drumkit on T.V.

© Global Antar Visionquest

2.12.43 (both of The Tremeloes); Keith West, 6.12.43 (Teenage Opera); Sandie Shaw, 26.2.47; Mike Nolan, 17.12.54 (Bucks Fizz).

Tony Rivers & The Castaways were a hot local group in the 60s.

Some Bizarre svengali Stevo attended Eastbury Comprehensive.

Vera Lynn could hardly be described as a rock act, but she did make her public singing debut at a Dagenham working man's club.

The Roundhouse in Lodge Avenue was a good venue at the turn of the 70s, when the likes of Bowie and Mott The Hoople would play.

## EAST MERSEA

Yes made their debut well away from the public glare at East Mersea Youth Club in 1968.

## EPPING

Birthplace of singer David Byron, 29.1.47 (Uriah Heep); actor/singer Nick Kamen, 15.4.62.

Following the modification of UK tax laws, Rod Stewart ended his Los Angelean exile and bought an Elizabethan mansion in Epping Forest (1986).

## FRINTON

Birthplace of singer/actor John Leyton 17.2.39. One of producer Joe Meek's hottest acts, he topped 1961 charts with Johnny Remember Me.

Between March 64, when Radio Caroline came on the air, and August 67, when the Government shut them down, most of Britain's pirate radio fleet floated in the calm waters off Frinton — just beyond the three mile

## essex

territorial limit. After Caroline came Atlanta, London, England and 355.

In January 65, gales snapped Caroline's anchor chain and she drifted onto Frinton beach — with the Dutch captain hanging over the bow, shouting "Mayday" at bemused spectators!

### HARLOW

The Naturals were one-hit wonders in 64; they should have known better.

Mark Knopfler was a journalism student at Harlow Tech during 67; guitarist Jim Cregan (Cockney Rebel/ Rod Stewart) went to Harlow Art School.

At an outdoor gig in summer 75 Harlow was the setting for the first large-scale outbreak of Bay City Rollermania.

Home of new wavers The Newtown Neurotics and mid 80s popsters Roman Holiday.

### HOCKLEY

Birthplace of Lesley Wood, 25.1.58 (Au Pairs).

### HORNCHURCH

Home of mod group The Little Roosters.

### ILFORD

Birthplace of trumpeter Kenny Ball, 22.5.31; chanteuse Kathy Kirby, 20.10.40.

Brian Poole & The Tremeloes decided to turn professional after winning a talent competition at Ilford Palais in 1960.

### LEIGH ON SEA

Birthplace of bassplayer Paul Gray.

Fairport Convention's 'What We Did On Our Holidays' sleeve designed on a blackboard at Essex University

© Island Records

### LOUGHTON

Before Dire Straits got going, Mark Knopfler was a lecturer at Loughton Teachers Training College.

### RAYLEIGH

Culture Club made their UK debut (October 81) at Crocs, a club made famous by Depeche Mode. It's now called the Pink Toothbrush.

### ROCHFORD

Home of Eddie & The Hot Rods, one of the 1975 bridges between pub-rock and punk.

### ROMFORD

Birthplace of R&B star Graham Bond; songwriter Chris Andrews, 15.10.42 (also scored a hit of his own, Yesterday Man); bassplayer Cliff Williams, 14.12.49 (AC/DC); singer Pauline Black (Selecter).

The Red Lion was a hot gig in the late 60s.

It was at the Electric Stadium in Chadwell Heath that Marillion (then largely unknown) first saw keyboard player Mark Kelly — and lured him away from the headline band, local hot-shots Chemical Alice. Fish can be a very persuasive guy.

Most successful local group is 5 Star, from Rush Green.

The Purple Hearts were a neo mod group.

### SAFFRON WALDEN

In June 66, following the attempted takeover of his pirate station Radio City, owner Reg Calvert visited the home of rival Oliver Smedley — who reacted to his threatening behaviour by taking down his shotgun and blowing him away. Judge and jury subsequently agreed that he acted in self defence and acquitted him.

Tom Robinson was a pupil at the (Quaker) Friends School ... until his expulsion.

## essex

### SOUTHEND-ON-SEA

Birthplace of Roy Hay, 12.8.61 (Culture Club); Danielle Dax, (Lemon Kittens).

The local rock scene has heaved with vitality since the 50s, when groups like The Barracudas, The Rockerfellers, The Whirlwinds, Force Five, The Avengers and The Monotones ruled the roost.

In the 60s, The Paramounts and The Orioles reigned. The former became Procol Harum while Orioles leader Micky Jupp amassed a cult following in the 70s.

Venues included the Jacobean and the Capri (coffee bars), the Studio, the Nightlife, Shades (a mod club on the seafront), the Cricketers pub and the London Hotel.

Members of groups like The Tradewinds, Saints And Sinners, The Fugitives, Surly Bird, Glory, Cow Pie, Thomahawk, and The Bread And Cheese Hillbillies coalesced into The Kursaal Flyers in 73. They were resident at the Blue Boar until breaking nationally.

Half of Talk Talk came from Southend, as did Arthur Comics (late 70s), Tonight (78), the Steve Hooker Band (R&B) and Leepers (mods).

Bonzos leader Vivian Stanshall went to Southend Grammar and then the Art School.

The pirate station Radio Essex broadcast from Knock John Tower in the Thames estuary, 18 miles off Southend. A successful Post Office prosecution removed it from the air in January 67.

In April 87, Stiff recording star Lew Lewis was jailed for seven years after robbing a post office in Westcliff. He tried to make his getaway on a bicycle!

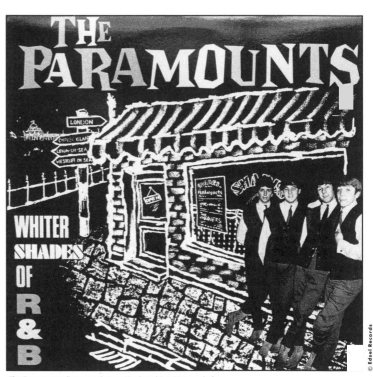

© Edsel Records

The Paramounts fine compilation 'Shades of R & B' named after the Southend club 'Shades' a frequent meeting place for Brooker & Co.

### STANFORD LE HOPE

Guitarist Roy Hay trained and worked as a hairdresser here until Culture Club took off. He lived with his parents in nearby Corringham.

### TILBURY

It was here, in September 47, that six year old Cliff Richard (born in Lucknow, 14.10.40) set foot on English soil for the first time. He and his family had sailed from India, on a troopship, in the wake of Gandhi's successful campaign for home rule.

### UPMINSTER

On his 1981 album, Ian Dury adopted the persona of Lord Upminster.

### WOODFORD

Birthplace of bandleader John Dankworth, 20.9.27.

Deep Purple made a stealthy visit to an Episode Six gig here in July 69 and managed to lure away Ian Gillan and Roger Glover.

## essex

Below: the very envelope in which the lyrics to 'A Whiter Shade of Pale' were sent to Gary Brooker by Keith Reid, the Procul Harum lyricist. Bottom L–R Lew Lewis, Episode Six and Procul Harum products of Essex-ish.

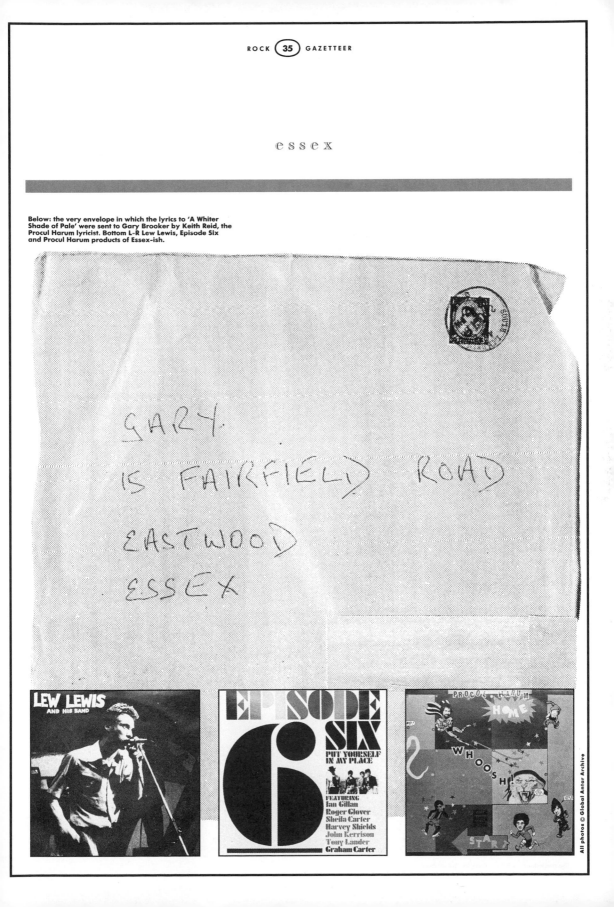

# GLOUCESTERSHIRE

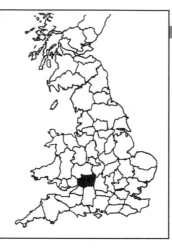

## CHELTENHAM

Birthplace of Rolling Stones founder Brian Jones, 28.2.42. He grew up in Hatherley Road, attending Dean Close Public School in Shelburne Road and Cheltenham Grammar on the Bath Road. An avid R&B fan playing reluctant sax in local rock'n'roll band the Ramrods, he encountered Alexis Korner at the town's jazz club (held in the clubroom at the back of the Alstone Baths) and was encouraged to move to London. Fans still make pilgrimages to his grave in Cheltenham Cemetery.

Also the birthplace of coffee bar rocker and Beatles confederate Tony Sheridan, 21.5.40, and Robert Fisher, 5.11.59 (Climie Fisher).

During his years in the slow lane, Steve Winwood lived in the locality and played a few outdoor benefits near Andoversford.

New wave group Index were based here; Troy Tate later joined the Teardrop Explodes.

Erstwhile Shadow Jet Harris, bankrupt and down on his luck, was fined £150 and banned for a year for driving under the influence (Feb 89).

## CINDERFORD

Birthplace of disc jockey Jimmy Young, who topped the charts twice in 1955.

## CIRENCESTER

Drummer Cozy Powell learned his trade with local 60s beat group The Sorcerers.

## CLEARWELL

In Autumn 73, Deep Purple took over Clearwell Castle to write and rehearse their album Burn. In May 78, Led Zeppelin moved in to work out the set for their imminent tour.

## GLOUCESTER

In February 58, Gloucester magistrates fined fifties rocker Terry Dene £155 after he pleaded guilty to wilful damage/drunk and disorderly charges.

Local resident Jet Harris can often be seen riding around town on his bike.

In 1987, Ashley Hutchings and his Albion Band released the album By Gloucester Docks I Sat Down And Wept.

## NEWENT

Birthplace of pioneer producer Joe Meek, 5.4.29. A local group, The Saxons, were one of his less successful acts.

**The tombstone of Brian Jones in Cheltenham**

# HAMPSHIRE

## ALDERSHOT

Birthplace of producer Mickie Most, 1938.

The Beatles ventured south for the first time in December 60, when they drew less than twenty punters to the Queens Road Palais on the corner of Perowne Street.

Sixties groups included Kevin Manning & The E Types, Kerry Rapid & his Blue Stars, and The Bandits.

## ANDOVER

Birthplace of Manfred Mann co-founder Mike Hugg (11.3.40).

The Troggs put Andover on the rock'n'roll map with their immortal rendition of Wild Thing. Three of their number were born and raised in the town ... bass player Pete Staples (3.5.44), drummer Ronnie Bond (4.5.42) and vocalist Reg Presley (16.6.44).

The only other group laying claim to "the Andover Sound" seems to have been The Loot.

## BASINGSTOKE

A schoolgirl one week, a star the next! Tanita Tikaram (born in Munster, West Germany, on 12.8.69) left Queen Mary's Sixth Form College with three A levels. She played two gigs here in town — a Labour Party benefit at Moose Hall and a support spot at Ruestall Hall — and one at the Mean Fiddler ... where she was discovered and turned into an overnight success!

Local groups include Mega City Four, Go Go Amigo and Papa Brittle (who backed Tanita on her first demos).

## BEAULIEU

Lord Montague's estate was the pastoral setting for annual jazz festivals at the turn of the 60s ... until drunken, lewd, unruly fan behaviour put the lid on them.

## BOTLEY

His Cessna low on fuel, Gary Numan made an emergency landing on the A 3051 Botley to Winchester Road (summer 81). Miraculously, there were no injuries.

**Tanita: bard of Basingstoke**

© WEA Records (U.K.)

## COSHAM

Family home of guitarist Mick Jones (born 27.12.44), who began in Nero & The Gladiators and ended up in Foreigner.

## EASTLEIGH

Home of Heinz — blue-eyed, blond haired protege of producer Joe Meek. Bass player in The Tornados during their Telstar heyday, he soon went solo to reach top five with his Eddie Cochran tribute Just Like Eddie.

## FARNBOROUGH

Local groups included Ace & The Cascades, The Emeralds, The Modern Art of Living, and The Sound Of Time (whose drummer, Dinky Diamond, was later in Sparks).

## FORDINGBRIDGE

Balls, a Brummie supergroup containing Denny Laine and Steve Gibbons, rehearsed here during 1969 before falling flat on their face.

## GOSPORT

Mark Andrews & The Gents were often described as Gosport's answer to Elvis Costello & The Attractions when they made their national bid in the early 80s ... but even they fared better than other local groups like The Classics and The Meddyevils.

The area's most notable export was probably Hookfoot, who backed Elton John at the turn of the 70s and cut five albums for the DJM label. Guitarist Caleb Quaye and drummer Roger Pope became hot session men.

# hampshire

The Highlights of Hayling Island, our hero is seen standing second right

© Fly By Night Management

Simon Dupree & His Big Sound

© Derek Schulman

## HAYLING ISLAND

Birthplace of singer songwriter Julia Fordham.

In 1964, fifteen year old Rick Parfitt played a summer season at the Sunshine Holiday Camp — just him and his guitar. There he met "a couple of birds" and the three of them formed The Highlights, with whom he toured until joining Status Quo in August 67.

## HEADLEY

During summer 70, Led Zeppelin wrote and recorded their third album at Headley Grange — said, by the previous occupants, to have been haunted. The group purchased the property three years later.

## PORTSMOUTH

Birthplace of singer Paul Jones, 24.2.42 (Manfred Mann); singer Roger Hodgson, 21.3.50 (Supertramp).

Local groups include Aubrey Small, Autumn, Blackout, Cherry Smash, The Eyes, The Frames, Gold Dust, Jumbo Root, Last Orders, The Lesser Known Tunisians, Shy, Smiling Hard and The Warm Jets ... but the city has produced bigger names too.

First group to make it on a large scale was Manfred Mann — originally a modern jazz cum R&B octet called the Mann Hugg Blues Brothers. Their commercial peak came in 1964, when Do Wah Diddy Diddy topped both the UK and US charts. Paul Jones was local (but was studying at Oxford) while the others had been drawn to Pompey from

such distant places as Johannesburg and Andover.

Next up were Simon Dupree & The Big Sound, who reached the 1967 top ten with Kites. By 1970, they'd mutated into progressive rock band Gentle Giant (see Southsea).

The most famous Portsmouth resident of recent years has been Joe Jackson, who fronted Arms And Legs before going for the big one.

The Foster Brothers looked set to break out ... but broke up.

The Portsmouth Sinfonia enjoyed the patronage of Brian Eno, who produced two eyebrow raising testaments. Their ever changing composition included some of Deaf School, Alan Clayson (leader of The Argonauts) and Gavin Bryars — who continued working with Eno.

# hampshire

The most newsworthy group of 1989 are E-Coli (medical term for bugs up the bum), who are based in Cowplain and attract attention for their peculiarities rather than their music.

## ROMSEY

After marrying a local girl, Stu James re-located his Liverpool group The Mojos, who saw out the 60s doing cabaret work. Bassist Duncan Campbell later endeared himself to Southampton football club supporters when he wrote and recorded The Saints Song.

## SOUTHAMPTON

In February 57, after days of seasickness, a much relieved Bill Haley, hailed as the King of Rock'n'Roll, stepped off the Queen Elizabeth to start his first UK tour. 5000 fans lined Southampton dock to greet his 17 strong party, which included wives, kids and someone's 77 year old mother!

Birthplace of Benny Hill, 21.1.25 (1971 chart topper with Ernie); Mike Vickers, 18.4.42 (Manfred Mann); singer Jona Lewie, 14.3.47; singer Howard Jones, 23.9.55 (in Hythe).

The most famous local manager and impressario was Reg Calvert, who started out as proprietor of the Band Box, a cellar record shop.

Over the years Southampton has spawned literally hundreds of bands, but few have made waves beyond the immediate vicinity. In the 60s local faves included Brother Bung, Brownhill Stamp Duty, Chances R, The Daisies, Footprints, Globeshow, Barrie James & The Strangers, Midnights, and Tex Roberg, while the 70s saw Agnes Strange, Alco, Big Brother, Bitter Lemmings, The Blazers, Brandy Pope & Sundown, Combustion, Ebony, Ebony

![The Men They Couldn't Hang](© Silvertone Records)

The Men They Couldn't Hang

Fleur De Lys: super rare pic!

© Bam Caruso Archives

Rockers, Games To Avoid, Happy Tobacco, Honky, Iguana, King Rock, Lip Moves, Refugee, Rusty Nail, Rye Whisky, Smacky Davis, Strate Jacket, Sweet Poison, Timepiece, Trader and many more trying their luck.

Among those who gained at least a modicum of national recognition were the Brook Brothers (Everly types who hit the top five with Warpaint in 1961), Fleur De Lys, Fresh (managed by Simon Napier Bell), Heaven, The Quik, The Soul Agents (most famous for their five minute stint as Rod Stewart's backing group), Danny Storm & the Strollers, Jakki Whitren and Wishful Thinking.

For many years, fifties rocker Rory Blackwell held the world record for non-stop drumming — a record he had set in Southampton.

Two of Sigue Sigue Sputnik went to Redbridge Community School — Ray Mayhew and Chris Kavanagh ... they caused a near riot when they appeared at Southampton Gaumont during their brief flicker of fame.

Group most likely to succeed are The Men They Couldn't Hang, who not only come from Southampton but sing about it ... as in Dancing On The Pier and Island In The Rain (which is about the Isle of Wight). Singer Paul Simmons went to Weston Park Boys School with England footballer Graham Roberts.

# hampshire

## SOUTHSEA

Birthplace of Sarah Jane Owen 1957 (Bodysnatchers, Belle Stars), who worked briefly as a lifeguard in Portsmouth.

The three Shulman brothers — Ray, Phil and Derek — lived in Eastney Road. (Ray was born in Portsmouth; the other two moved down from the Gorbals as kids). Their first group was The Howling Wolves; their most famous, Gentle Giant.

The Mann Hugg Blues Brothers, later Manfred Mann, made their debut at Butlins in 1962.

In April 74, Southsea was the location for some of the movie Tommy, directed by Ken Russell. At one stage, the pier mysteriously caught fire, adding immeasurably to the excitement of the film.

## WINCHESTER

Birthplace of Mike Batt, who attended Peter Simmons College and played in various local groups before finding acclaim as Wombles musicmaster.

Fifties rocker Terry Dene was called up for national service and sent to Winchester Barracks, where he proceeded to have a nervous breakdown (January 59). After three months of psychiatric scrutiny he was ejected as unfit for service.

Brian Eno studied at Winchester Art School, where he formed heavy rock group The Maxwell Demon!

The city's magnificent cathedral inspired at least two vinyl excursions. In 1966, the New Vaudeville Band sold a million copies of their quaint Winchester Cathedral and ten years later Graham Nash wrote Cathedral for CSN — after exploring the edifice on an LSD trip, and stumbling across the grave of a soldier who had died on his (Nash's) birthday.

Fairport Convention wrote and rehearsed their classic album Liege And Lief in a Queen Anne mansion at Farley Chamberlayne.

The only local groups to have made any impact are The Life (signed by EMI but immediately dropped!) and Thieves Like Us.

Robyn Hitchcock mentions the city in his song Element Of Light, and Whistle Tester/Q mag editor Mark Ellen went to school here.

## YATELEY

The three popsters who comprise 1988 chart stars Breathe all dwelt here.

Eno on T.V.

© Global Antar Archive

# HEREFORD & WORCESTERSHIRE

## BROMSGROVE

Dire Straits bass player John Illsley was educated at Bromsgrove School.

## EVESHAM

Birthplace of drummer Jim Capaldi, 24.8.44 (Traffic); guitar player Luther Grosvenor, 23.12.49 (Spooky Tooth).

In September 63, Jet Harris and his girlfriend Billie Davis were injured when his chauffeur driven car crashed into a bus. He never reached the charts again.

Local groups include early 80s new wavers The Photos, led by Wendy Wu (they recorded a tribute to Barbarella's in Birmingham), and The Dancing Did (ecologically inclined folk-rockers best known for the song Squashed Things On The Road).

## GREAT MALVERN

Local groups include The Tights (new wave).

Birthplace of the Cherry Red label.

## HEREFORD

Birthplace of guitarist Mick Ralphs, 31.3.48, and organist Verden Allen, 26.5.44. Together with friends, they form Silence who, in 1969, move to London, add vocalist Ian Hunter and find fame as Mott The Hoople.

Ten years later, three more locally born musicians — James Honeyman Scott, 4.11.57; Martin Chambers, 1952; and Pete Farndon, 1953 — moved to London, added vocalist Chrissie Hynde, and found success as The Pretenders.

It was at the town's Municipal Ballroom in March 65 that P J Proby was ordered offstage for an act described by the wife of a tory alderman as "disgusting and obscene".

## HERGEST

Mike Oldfield called his second album Hergest Ridge — after the hill facing his rural retreat.

## KEMPSEY

During his Led Zep days, Robert Plant's only extra-curricular work was producing (and singing backing vocals on) a single by Brummie group Dansette Damage at the Old Smithy Studio in Post Office Lane.

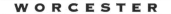
Dansette Damage & Percy in the studio

## KIDDERMINSTER

Birthplace of organist Roger LaVern, 11.11.38 (The Tornados).

Led by Stan Webb and Christine (McVie) Perfect, Chicken Shack were one of the most successful blues-boom bands of the late 60s.

John Bonham's funeral took place near his home at Rushock in October 80.

## REDDITCH

Birthplace of drummer John Bonham, 31.5.48 (Led Zeppelin).

The Cravats were the local punk group.

## ROSS ON WYE

Birthplace of drummer Dale Griffin, 24.10.50 (Mott The Hoople). He and Overend Watts started out in school group The Anchors, who used to play at the town's Hope And Anchor pub.

## STOURPORT

Birthplace of singer Ray Thomas, 29.12.42 (Moody Blues).

Singer/songwriter Clifford T Ward was a local lad. His group Cliff Ward & The Cruisers were mid 60s Midlands favourites.

Home of Rouen, highly touted pop-rockers who mysteriously and sadly nose-dived after massive radio play for their indie single.

## WORCESTER

Birthplace of Dave Mason, 10.5.46. His first group was the locally renowned Hellions, but he made his name in Traffic.

Singer Jess Roden led The Shakedown Sound before moving to London to join the Alan Bown Set.

# HERTFORDSHIRE

## ALDBURY

Owned by ex-Playboy emperor Victor Lownes, the Stocks Country Club was the setting for videos by Madness (It Must Be Love), Fun Boy Three (Summertime), and Kajagoogoo (Hang On Now).

## BARNET

Birthplace of Zombies bass player/songwriter Chris White 7.3.45; singer Andrea Simpson, 12.9.45 (The Caravelles); guitarist Pete Banks, 7.7.47 (Yes); Elaine Paige, 5.3.51.

Lois Lane of The Caravelles was educated at St Martha's Convent.

Ian Dury recorded the demos for New Boots And Panties at Livingston Studios, 32a East Barnet Road, New Barnet.

An early Toyah release was the strangely titled Sheep Farming In Barnet.

## BERKHAMSTED

Home of former Kinks keyboard player John Gosling — currently manager of Graham Webb Music, just off the High Street.

## BISHOPS STORTFORD

Birthplace of Bill Sharpe, 19.11.52, instigator of locally based Shakatak. That group developed out of Tracks, whose bass player was Trevor Horn.

## BOREHAMWOOD

Pink Floyd keyboard player Rick Wright went to Haberdashers' Aske's, a public school in Butterfly Lane. So did Yes bass player Chris Squire.

## BROOKMANS PARK

Birthplace of Tracey Thorn, 26.9.62 (Everything But The Girl) in Peplins Way. Many of her songs are about home life.

Home to 60's crooner Clinton Ford in Mymns Drive.

## BROXBOURNE

Birthplace of drummer Bob Henrit 2.5.46 (Roulettes/Argent/Kinks).

## BUSHEY

Birthplace of Simon LeBon, 27.10.58 (Duran Duran).

The acoustic soft-rock trio America met here at a school for children of US airforce personnel.

Wham! cohorts George Michael and Andrew Ridgeley met at Bushey Meads Comprehensive. Their backing singer Shirlie Holliman — later of Pepsi and Shirlie — was also a pupil there. The lads inveigled their way into the business by chatting up record company exec Mark Dean in the Three Crowns pub.

## CHESHUNT

Birthplace of songwriter/guitarist Russ Ballard 31.1.45 (Roulettes, Argent, solo).

Russ Ballard was educated at Cheshunt Secondary Modern, as was Cliff Richard, who came to live in a Cheshunt council house in 1950. He formed his first group (The Quintones) at the school and after becoming famous returned regularly to perform charity shows. This despite the fact that his prefect's badge was confiscated when he played truant to see his hero Bill Haley. As an aspiring rock'n'roller he would take the Green Line bus to London to play the 2 Is coffee bar, but the travel sickness he suffered provoked a lifelong aversion to buses. His guitarist Ian Samwell wrote Move It while riding on that same bus!

Sixties pop group The Roulettes, originally formed to back Adam Faith, were Cheshunt based — as were their descendants Unit 4 Plus Two. The latter group's winsome frontman Tommy Moeller resurfaced briefly as Whistling Jack Smith.

Other local groups included Dave Sampson & the Hunters (who once backed Cliff at the London Palladium when the Shads were indisposed) and Buster Meikle & the Daybreakers. The Mark Four (containing Cliff Richard's original guitarist Norman Mitham) evolved into psychedelic pop-art group Creation.

The Who played the Wolseley Hall in December 65. Such a lot going on in such a small place!

## CUFFLEY

Birthplace of Zombies guitarist Paul Atkinson 19.3.46.

# hertfordshire

## ELSTREE

Many popsters made a tentative transition from vinyl to celluloid at Elstree Studios — including Cliff Richard (his first film was Serious Charge, with Andrew Ray and Wilfred Pickles). Adam Faith worked in the studio's cutting rooms until the television show Drumbeat made him a star.

## HADLEY WOOD

Home of Shadow Bruce Welch.

## HARPENDEN

Home of Keith Marshall, who reached the 1981 top twenty with Only Crying.

Home to 60's popstar Frank Ifield.

Bananarama's Siobham Fahey lived in Aldwickbury Crescent for many years. She later married Eurythmic Dave Stewart and embarked on a solo career.

## HATFIELD

Birthplace of vocalist Colin Blunstone, 24.6.45 (Zombies); guitarist Mick Taylor, 17.1.48 (Rolling Stones ... he lived at 27 Lockley Crescent); singer Sal Solo, 5.9.54 (Classix Nouveaux).

Among those spending their teenage years in this hum-drum new town were Zombies drummer Hugh Grundy and folk troubadour Donovan, whose appearances on Ready Steady Go catapulted him to overnight stardom in 1965. He lived in Bishops Rise and went to Onslow Secondary Modern — as did Mick Taylor.

Local 60s groups included The Favourite Sons and The Gods, who lost their momentum when guitarist Mick Taylor went off to join John Mayall. The latter also included Ken Hensley (later of Uriah Heep) and John Glascock (later

The Breaks Youth Club in Hatfield, frequently visited by Hawkwind

Hatfield's Onslow School substantially rebuilt after a fire that was started by a pupil, (probably not Donovan)

of Jethro Tull). Glascock (or Brittle Dick, as the Tull guys called him) began his pop career in The Juniors — famed only for their appearance on television's 5 O'Clock Club.

Adam & The Ants made their Stand And Deliver video at Hatfield House.

Progressive group Babe Ruth originally formed in Hatfield, and Free guitarist Paul Kossoff used to live here ... his father still does.

Another local resident is Barbara Gaskin, who teamed up with Dave Stewart to cut the number one hit It's My Party in 1981.

Balls was the absurd name of a much touted 1969 Brum supergroup led by Denny Laine. They made their debut here, at Breaks Youth Club.

## HEMEL HEMPSTEAD

Home of 60s folkie Mick Softley and underrated soulsters the Q Tips. Andy Powell from Wishbone Ash also lived here.

Damned vocalist Dave Vanian is said to have worked in a local shoe shop while formulating his plan of attack.

# hertfordshire

© David F Setford, Knebworth House

**Knebworth chaos**

## HERTFORD

Operational base for mid-60s poppets The Mirage. Six singles failed, but bass player Dee Murray later joined Elton John's first band.

## HITCHIN

Home of hardcore punks Chron Gen.

## KNEBWORTH

During the 70s, the extensive grounds of Knebworth House were frequently transformed into a concert site. The Allman Brothers played there in July 74, Pink Floyd in July 75, the Stones in August 76, and Led Zeppelin played their final UK shows there in August 79.

Support group to the Stones was 10cc, whose set was preceded by a guy who casually strolled to the front of the stage, removed his clothes, masturbated and climaxed to the cheers of the crowd before being roughly bundled off by stewards, who finally realised he wasn't part of the show!

Tears For Fears shot their Mad World video at Knebworth House.

## LETCHWORTH

The Sting Rays got together at St Christophers School. Other pupils included bassplayer Neil Murray (Whitesnake and Vow Wow), guitarist Peter Blegvad (Slapp Happy), synth player Hoagy Davies (son of television Maigret, Rupert Davies; later in Leeds University group She's French with future Buggle Geoff Downes) and saxman Dave Winthrop (Supertramp, Secret Affair).

## LITTLE HADHAM

In 1970, Fairport Convention moved into an old Ind Coope pub on the A 120. Their idyllic life here ended abruptly when a lorry ploughed through Dave Swarbrick's bedroom one Sunday morning. A Dutch driver, anxious not to miss the Harwich ferry, had fallen asleep at the top of the hill approaching the village. Still, they did write Full House there.

## MARKYATE

The Zombies used to rehearse in a room over the local grocery store —

owned by the father of bassplayer Chris White.

## POTTERS BAR

A popular 70s progressive rock venue was Farx.

Home for clarinetist Acker Bilk whose bowler hat hangs in the local barber!

## RADLETT

Home of guitarist Hank Marvin (Shadows, in case you didn't know), guitarist Stuart Taylor (Tornados, Lord Sutch), George Michael, and — until he electrocuted himself in the early 70s — bassist John Rostill (Shadows), who lived in The Avenue.

## RICKMANSWORTH

Jackson Recording Studio has turned out several hits, the biggest being 2-4-6-8 Motorway by Tom Robinson. UFO cut their first album there over six evenings in 1970; it was a fave haunt of all the pub rock generation; Eddie & The Hot Rods and Dr Feelgood recorded there too.

Punk band Anorexia seems to be all this town could muster.

# hertfordshire

## ROYSTON

New wave groups included Terra Cotta and The Dogma Cats.

## ST ALBANS

Birthplace of singer/song writer/keyboard man Rod Argent 14.6.45 (Zombies/Argent), bass player Jim Rodford 7.7.45 (Mike Cotton Sound/Argent/Kinks).

Most celebrated local group was The Zombies, four of whom were mates at the Abbey School while singer Colin Blunstone was a sports fanatic from the Grammar School. Between them they racked up 50 GCEs before She's Not There announced their seductive charm. Despite their academic record, they mis-spelt the title of their finest album Odessey And Oracle!

Other local stars were Maddy Prior (later of Steeleye Span) and Rod Argent's post-Zombies band Argent.

Donovan and Mick Softley were among the crowd of folkies and beatniks who hung around the Cock in St Peters Street during the mid 60s.

Local musicians included bass player Paul Dean, who joined X-Ray Spex, and guitarist Steve Forrest, who joined Silverhead. Local lecturer, poet and writer Jeff Cloves led early 70s group Stardust, who recorded for Sonet.

A great 60s venue (Who, Graham Bond, Small Faces, etc), the Market Hall is no more … and nor are the Co-op Hall, the Faulkner Hall, or the Civil Defence Hall. But they still have the odd gig at the City Hall.

The Pistols played one of their earliest gigs at the art school, and the White Riot tour played the City Hall — after which Joe Strummer was arrested for nicking hotel towels.

The Pioneer Youth Club, next to the fire station, presented all manner of groups — from Arthur Brown to Mott The Hoople to the Average White Band.

The Horn Of Plenty pub on the corner of Victoria Street put on up and coming talent … like Street Band (with Paul Young) who played there a couple of times a month before their hit. Still a rocking venue for the likes of The Groundhogs and Steve Marriott.

A dozen or so local new wavers found a vinyl outlet on Waldo's, a label based at 4 Liverpool Road. Owners Phil Smee and Cally later launched the Bam Caruso label and did sleeve designs for many companies.

Bam Caruso/Waldos are now at 9 Ridgmont Road which is also the office for the new 'Strange Things' record collectors magazine.

Other groups to make their mark were The Bodies, Clive Pig & The Hopeful Chinamen, John Grimaldis Cheap Flights, The Innocent Vicars and The Manic Jabs.

4 Liverpool Road; once home to Waldos, Bam Caruso records & Julian Cope's fan club, now the headquarters of Antar records and publishing.

St Albans Art School before The Sex Pistols arrived...

The Horn of Plenty, St Albans

# hertfordshire

## SOUTH MIMMS

Deep Purple first got together and rehearsed at Deeves Hall, a local farmhouse.

## STEVENAGE

Overspill new town which provided an ideal location for adolescent sex romp Here We Go Round The Mulberry Bush. Another film, Quadrophenia, was dedicated to the kids of Stevenage.

Uriah Heep stalwart Ken Hensley went to Alleynes Grammar School where he fronted Ken & His Cousins. His firs. professional stab was The Jimmy Brown Sound — an R&B outfit named for James Brown. Residents recall that he spent much of the late sixties living in a van.

During the punk era, the hot local band was Restricted Hours. Though they look as though they lived in Oklahoma a century ago, gothic outlaws The Fields Of Nephilim have their roots in Stevenage.

Lesley Woods of the Au Pairs and Sal Solo of Classix Nouveaux also lived in Stevenage.

## TRING

Home of bassplayer Andy Pyle (Blodwyn Pig/Juicy Lucy/Kinks/etc) and former Spooky Tooth frontman Mike Harrison.

Champney's is a local health farm specialising in the rehabilitation of rich fatties. Horrified by his enormity, EMI dispatched Marillion's Fish to Champney's — hoping he would lose half his bodily bulk before meeting various American VIPs. Through strategies he refuses to divulge, he ultimately emerged weighing more than he did when he went in!

Deeves Hall, responsible for unleashing Deep Purple

© Global Antar Archive

## WARE

Kim Wilde went to school here; Chas & Dave lived here in the early 80s.

## WATFORD

Birthplace of Shirlie, 18.4.62 (Pepsi And . . .).

Home of minor league 60s R&B group Cops And Robbers.

Knox, who led punk group the Vibrators, was a student at Watford Art College. There he fronted Knox & The Nightriders.

Recent success is local lad Steve Waddington — half of The Beloved.

Also at the Art School were Colin Newman and Bruce Gill of Wire who rehearsed there alongside The Tea Set who recorded for St Albans label Waldos.

The two bands played early gigs at Carey Place (now demolished) and The Tea Set became world famous due to graffitti on the nearby M1.

Nigel Simpkins released influential electro pop single in 1978 other local notables included Sad Lovers & Giants, Soft Drinks, The Magits, Rudimentary Peni all who released records in the late 70's on local labels.

The Club Foot was held at The Verulam Arms for several packed nights, the pub is owned by Big Joe notable security guard for Bob Dylan & The Stranglers, The Tea Set rehearsed in bomb shelters below the pub, their backing singers were three lasses who left to become Bananarama!

## WELWYN GARDEN CITY

Birthplace of jazz trombonist/Marquee Club owner/pioneer R&B promoter Chris Barber 17.4.30. His Petite Fleur was a worldwide hit in 1959; Lonnie Donegan recorded Rock Island Line whilst a sideman in his trad jazz band. Also born here was Alan Williams, 22.12.50, leader of The Rubettes.

Jazz and rock pub The Cherry Tree hit a glamorous peak in April 69 when Led Zeppelin played there.

A satellite village is the home of the rocking Wilde family ... Marty, Joyce, Ricky and Kim. Popsters all!

The punk explosion saw The Astronauts and Johnny Curious & The Strangers releasing singles.

# HUMBERSIDE

## BEVERLEY

The only venues for local bands appear to be Nellie's pub (the White Horse) and the Regal night club at the old cinema.

## BRIDLINGTON

Birthplace of Bob Wallis, 3.6.34 (leader of popular trad-era band The Storyville Jazz Men).

Radio 270, last to join the pirate fleet in June 66, was broadcast from a converted Dutch lugger moored three miles off the coast. It shut down in August 67, after it had relocated to a mooring off Scarborough.

## HORNSEA

Home of new wavers Indians in Moscow.

## HULL (KINGSTON-UPON-HULL)

Birthplace of 50s swooners Ronnie Hilton, 26.1.26, and David Whitfield, 2.2.26; Shan of the Kaye Sisters, 15.8.38; singer songwriter Philip Goodhand Tait, 3.1.45; Henry Priestman, 21.6.55 (The Christians); Ted Key, 1.7.60, and Hugh Whittaker, 18.5.61 (Housemartins).

Also the birthplace of guitarist Mick Ronson, who formed The Rats with two other local lads, Trevor Bolder and Woody Woodmansey. Two singles failed, but the trio later became famous as David Bowie's Spiders From Mars. Woody, who took his surname from a local village, was last seen drumming with Art Garfunkel.

Buddy Holly & The Crickets played at the Regal cinema in March 58 and stayed at the White Horse Hotel in Jameson Street.

The Silkie got together at Hull University in summer 63 and won the patronage of the Beatles, who wrote and played on their only hit, You've Got To Hide Your Love Away. Other University alumni include Everything But The Girl (Tracey Thorn and Ben Watt, who met there), poet and Scaffolder Roger McGough.

Stiff recording star Wreckless Eric was educated at Hull College of Art, where he also led Addis & the Flip Tops. For part of this period, his residence was a length of sewage pipe which he furnished from local rubbish tips. Brad from The Specials was a fellow student.

Singer/songwriter Michael Chapman was a local schoolteacher and Lene Lovich grew up here (having been born in Detroit).

Punk band Dead Fingers Talk made national waves in the late 70s.

Def Leppard made their first recordings at Fairview Studios in Great Gutter Lane, Willerby.

Self-styled fourth best band in Hull, The Housemartins made their debut at the Hull University bar in October 84. Hugh Whittaker and Ted Key met at Sir Henry Cooper Senior High in Orchard Park; Stan Cullimore (at the Uni) lived at 70 Grafton Street; all drank at the

Grafton pub. Stan and Paul busked in the Whitefriargate pedestrian precinct while refining their act.

Current Housemartins splinter groups include The Penny Candles and Beautiful Self. Also on the scene are the Mighty Strike, Pink Noise, The Brontes and Planet Wilson (who evolved from Red Guitars).

Best local venue is the Adelphi Club at 89 De Grey Street.

Richest ex-resident is Rod Temperton – Hull born and bred. His group Heatwave struck big with Boogie Nights in 1977 and he was soon writing songs for Quincy Jones, Aretha Franklin and other soul stars. Several of his efforts appear on the biggest selling album of all time – Thriller by Michael Jackson.

Although born in Birmingham, Roland Gift grew up in Hull and sang in local groups Blue Kitchen and Acrylic Victims before going back to Brum to make it big with Fine Young Cannibals.

Locals maintain that Hull residents don't want to see bands, they just want to get plastered. At weekends, there are queues to get into pubs, which are controlled by bouncers! Night clubs fall as violent crime rises.

## SCUNTHORPE

Birthplace of Ian Matthews, June 46, who sang in local groups The Classics and Rebels before moving to London to join Fairport Convention.

Also the birthplace of Stella Barker, 1955 (the Belle Stars).

Local folk rockers Amazing Blondel were nationally popular at the turn of the 70s. It is said that Eurythmic Dave Stewart was one of their roadies.

# ISLE OF MAN

## DOUGLAS

Birthplace of Barry Gibb, 1.9.47 (Bee Gees).

Also from the island ... singer Christine Collister.

In August 64, the island's only police dog, on duty to help control 7000 shrieking Rolling Stones fans, reacts to the noise and starts snarling at the crowd. She recovers after several days of cossetting with Winalot and Chum.

## RAMSEY

Radio Caroline North took up position off Ramsey in July 64, transmitting from an old Dutch passenger ferry.

Residents who have benefited from the island's lower rate of personal taxation include John Coghlan (Status Quo), Go West, the Sutherland Brothers, and Rick Wakeman.

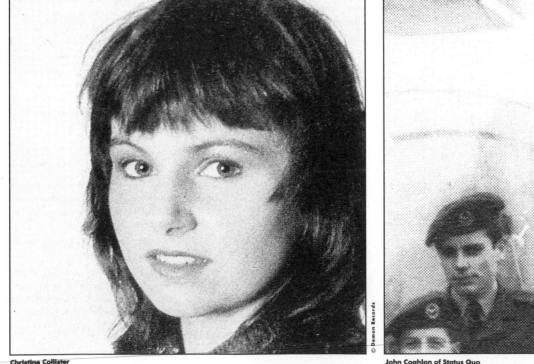

Christine Collister

© Demon Records

John Coghlan of Status Quo

© Global Antar Archive

# ISLE OF WIGHT

## NEWPORT

Birthplace of erstwhile milkman Craig Douglas, 12.8.41, a number one with Only Sixteen.

Three of Level 42 — drummer Phil Gould, guitarist Boon Gould and bassist Mark King — grew up together on the island. Strangely, Mark King was a milkman too.

Three rock festivals were held on the Island. The first, in 68, starred Jefferson Airplane; the second, held at Freshwater Farm, Afton Down in August 69, was memorable for the appearance of Bob Dylan — his first public performance for eons; the third, in August 70, featured Joan Baez and the last major appearance of Jimi Hendrix. The Who played at the last two.

Local groups have included Stormtrooper and Skip Bifferty — when they were hiding from their manager!

Plans to start a group were discussed by Dave Wakeling and Andy Cox while on holiday here. They co-opted local lad David Steele and returned to Birmingham to form the Beat. Steele (later in the Fine Young Cannibals with Cox) was born here on 8.9.60.

Isle of Wight Festival memories, including the remains of the stage.

# KENT

## ASHFORD

Birthplace of Ray Dorset, 21.3.46 (Mungo Jerry).

## BECKENHAM

Birthplace of Peter Frampton, 22.4.50; David Sylvian, 23.2.58 (Japan); Nick Heyward, 20.5.61.

Bill Wyman's formal education was completed at Beckenham Grammar School.

Sedgehill Comprehensive pupils Francis Rossi and Alan Lancaster formed The Scorpions in 1962. It took five years of hard graft before they scored their first hit as Status Quo.

In 1969, David Bowie was a co-founder of the Beckenham Arts Lab, held at the Three Tuns pub in the High Street. During this period, he lived in Foxgrove Road, but by the end of the year, he and Angie had moved into flat 7 of Haddon Hall, a Victorian town house at 42 Southend Road. Other residents included producer Tony Visconti and Bowie's latest backing musicians, The Spiders From Mars.

In summer 69, Bowie also organised Beckenham Free Festival — held at Croydon Road recreation ground, next to the hospital.

Nick Heyward, Les Nemes and Graham Jones all went to Kelsey Park School, where they laid plans for Haircut 100.

## BELTRING

Among the London families who spent their summers picking hops for Whitbreads was that of Chas Hodges — now half of Chas & Dave.

## BEXLEY

Boy George was born in Bexley Hospital on 14.6.61. In July 69, Marianne Faithfull entered the same establishment to cure her heroin addiction.

The Black Prince has been a jazz and rock venue forever. Its heyday was during the 60s R&B boom.

## BEXLEY HEATH

Kate Bush was born at Bexley Heath Maternity Hospital on 30.7.58.

## BROADSTAIRS

Birthplace of Bob Calvert, poet and vocalist with Hawkwind.

## BROMLEY

Birthplace of drummer Alan Blakely, 7.4.42 (The Tremeloes); drummer Topper Headon (The Clash); bassist Norman Cook, 31.7.63 (The Housemartins).

Between 1957 and 1969, David Bowie's home was his parents' house at 4 Plaistow Grove, Sundridge Park. He attended Burnt Ash Junior Mixed, in Rangefield Road, before moving on (September 58) to Bromley Technical High School, in Oakley Road, Keston (now Ravenswood School for Boys). Other pupils at the latter were Peter Frampton, whose father was Bowie's art master, and Billy Idol.

Beatles manager Brian Epstein and disc jockey Brian Matthew planned to build a recording studio/theatre complex in the town during the mid 60s but were thwarted by the local council.

The town's hottest 60s R&B/rock club was the Bromel at Bromley Court Hotel on Bromley Hill.

David and Angela Bowie were married at the Registry Office in Beckenham Lane on 20.3.70.

Among the earliest followers of punk rock were The Bromley Contingent, whose garb attracted much press coverage. Two of their number, Siouxsie and Steve, formed the Banshees, while William Broad soon became famous as Billy Idol. Their initial inspiration was a Sex Pistols gig at Bromley Tech in January 76.

Home of new wave group The Acid Drops.

## CANTERBURY

Former Canterbury Cathedral choirboys include 50s rocker Dickie Pride, Terry Cox (drummer in Pentangle), and teen balladeer Mark Wynter.

During the 60s, the city spawned a plethora of groups: The Earl Gutheridge Explosion, The Four Methods, The Corvettes, The Insect, The Rojeens, and The Wilde Flowers ... out of whom sprang the Soft Machine, Caravan, Kevin Ayers & The Whole World, Matching Mole, Gong, Hatfield & The North, and several more!

# kent

Robert Wyatt, Mike Ratledge, Hugh Hopper, David Sinclair and various other instigators of the group scene first met at Simon Langton School.

Guitarist Steve Hillage went to the University of Kent; Robert Wyatt went to Canterbury College of Art . . . where one of the tutors was Ian Dury. Two of his pupils later joined him in Kilburn & The High Roads — Humphrey Ocean and Keith Lucas (then in Canterbury group Frosty Jodpur; later the leader of punk group 999)

During the early 80s, The Pop Rivits were the hot local group.

Bromley Tech. High School playground

## CHATHAM

When Ringo replaced Pete Best in The Beatles in August 62, one of the first gigs they did was at the Invicta Ballroom.

The Milkshakes made waves and cut records; so did The Prisoners. The former even recorded a song called Chatham Drive.

Other local groups include Thee Mighty Caesars, The Del-Monas, and The Len Bright Combo — led by former Stiff star Wreckless Eric (who lives here and was last seen working as roadie for George Hamilton IV!)

## CHISLEHURST

Birthplace of Susan Dallion, 27.5.57 (better known as Siouxsie).

Chislehurst Caves opened up as a rock venue in the 60s.

## CRAYFORD

Birthplace of bassplayer John Stax, 6.4.44 (Pretty Things).

The Town Hall was a popular venue during the 60s — music, fights and sexual intrigue.

## DARTFORD

Birthplace of Rolling Stones Mick Jagger (26.7.43) and Keith Richards (18.12.43), who attended Maypole County Primary and Westhill Infants respectively, before meeting up at Wentworth County Primary. At 11, Mick went to Dartford Grammar while Keith displayed dwindling enthusiasm for Dartford Tech. Rapport was only estab-lished in 1961, when they chanced to meet on a London to Dartford train . . . an armful of obscure R&B albums brought them together.

Jagger used to live in The Close, Wilmington.

Another graduate of Dartford Grammar was Dick Taylor, original bassplayer in the Stones and later instigator of the Pretty Things. Taylor, 28.1.43, and singer Phil May, 9.11.44, were also born in Dartford — as were bassist Rick Huxley, 5.8.42 (Dave Clark Five);

Joe Leeway from the Thompson Twins grew up here.

After his deification in London, Rusty Egan became the groovy disc jockey at Flicks: "From the Blitz to the sticks — Mondays at Flicks".

# kent

## DEAL

Birthplace of singer Glen Dale 2.4.43 (Fortunes).

## DOVER

Birthplace of Jane Summers, 4.4.61 (The Bodysnatchers).

Home of Vashti, 60s hopeful managed by Andrew Oldham.

For some reason a favourite of American doo-wop groups, The White Cliffs Of Dover was also recorded by The Byrds.

## DOWNHAM

Sixties balladeer/ubiquitous television presenter Mark Wynter was raised and educated here.

## ERITH

Birthplace of 60s singer Bern Elliott, 17.11.42 (originally led The Fenmen, who he dumped for The Clan).

## FOLKESTONE

Birthplace of bassplayer Noel Redding (Jimi Hendrix Experience).

Tofts was a popular 60s hang-out. A showcase for local talent, it was also a regular venue for Ron Wood's Birds and The Freddy Mack Big Band.

## GILLINGHAM

Wang Chung broke through internationally in 1983, but Acker & the Nice Boys found only local acclaim.

## GRAVESEND

During the early 60s, the Royal Daffodil would sail for Calais under the banner Rock Across The Channel! Various groups, from Acker Bilk to The Shadows, would provide music for the revellers.

## HERNE BAY

Erstwhile home of Kevin Ayers, born here on 16.8.45.

## HYTHE

Supertramp formed, lived and rehearsed at Botolphs Bridge House on Burmarsh Road, West Hythe in summer 69.

## KESTON

Bill Wyman moved here in June 66.

## MAIDSTONE

Home of 70s popsters Chicory Tip — chart toppers with Son Of My Father. Before, and after, they were famous they used to play at the London Tavern in Week Street.

The Granada was a 50s/60s package show venue where everyone from Sam Cooke to Screaming Lord Sutch played.

The Royal Star Hotel in the High Street (replaced by a shopping arcade) was a trad jazz/ rock'n'roll stronghold; the Rat Trap was a coffee bar where the likes of Albert Lee would play.

Peter Bellamy, singer in seminal folk group The Young Tradition, attended Maidstone School of Art.

Aspiring new wavers included Stark and the Performing Ferret Band; Alkatrazz were heavy metal also rans.

In November 87, former Clash drummer Topper Headon was jailed for 15 months at Maidstone Crown Court, for supplying heroin to a man who later died.

## MARGATE

As immortalised by Chas & Dave on their 1982 hit.

In July 63, The Beatles played a whole week at the Winter Gardens.

Home of 80s cult singer/writer Paul Roland.

## ORPINGTON

Birthplace of folksinger Ralph McTell, 3.12.44 (in the locality of Farnborough).

## RAMSGATE

Local new wave group The Record Players attracted modest national attention.

## ROCHESTER

Home of late 60s pop group Vanity Fare.

## ST MARY CRAY

One of the earliest instances of rock'n'roll style mayhem happened in April 54, when two gangs of teddy boys met in violent confrontation. 55 were arrested.

A hot 60s gig was the Iron Curtain Club, which presented the likes of The Move.

# kent

## SEVENOAKS

Birthplace of drummer Bill Bruford, 17.5.50 (Yes, King Crimson).

The promotional film clip for Strawberry Fields Forever saw the Beatles cavorting around a dead tree in Knowle Park. They arrived in four matching Austin Minis with blacked-out windows. John Lennon, snooping around local antique shops during a break in filming, bought the old circus poster which inspired Being For The Benefit Of Mr Kite.

Local resident Peter Skellern wrote his instrumental Cold Feet after his tootsies turned into blocks of ice during intense bell ringing practice at the parish church.

## SIDCUP

Birthplace of bassist/producer John Paul Jones, 3.1.46 (Led Zeppelin).

Keith Richards attended Sidcup Art School after being expelled from Dartford Tech for truancy. Other pupils included Dick Taylor and Phil May, who started hot R&B group The Pretty Things there.

## SWANLEY

Birthplace of 60s popster Crispian St Peters, 5.4.44.

## TENTERDEN

Local papers praised the public spirited Paul McCartney who, driving home to Rye, stopped to offer assistance at the scene of an accident on the Appledore Road.

At 16, Tom Robinson was sent to Finchden Manor, a readjustment centre for wayward youths. It was there that he formed his first group, Davanq, in 1971.

## TUNBRIDGE WELLS

Birthplace of Tony Colton, 11.2.42 (leader of 60s R&B group the Crawdaddies).

Home base for 60s pop groups Jason Crest, High Broom and Kippington Lodge, who became Brinsley Schwarz in 1969 after five singles missed the charts. The controversial Anti Nowhere League scored three minor hits in the early 80s.

Sid Vicious attended Sandrock Road Secondary Modern.

Marillion shot the video for Garden Party at Groombridge House.

## WELLING

Kate Bush grew up in a 350 year old farmhouse, not far from Woolwich cemetery.

## WEST MALLING

Scenes for The Beatles' Magical Mystery Tour were shot here in September 67.

## WHITSTABLE

Birthplace of Bette Bright (singer in Deaf School; later married Suggs from Madness).

Derelict gun towers on Shivering Sands, nine miles off the Whitstable coast, became the base for pirate broadcasters Radio Sutch in May 64. Gunboats failed to dislodge him, prompting the news headline "Sutch Turns Back The Navy!" Sutch later sold out to his manager Reg Calvert and the station became Radio City.

In June 64 Radio Invicta began operating from an adjacent fort. Six months later its owner, Tom Pepper, was mysteriously drowned leaving the station. As Radio 390 it continued broadcasting until the passing of the Marine Offences Act.

Seminal Kent group The Wilde Flowers made their world debut at the Bear And Key Hotel in 1963.

Paul Roland

© Bam Caruso Collection

# LANCASHIRE

## ACCRINGTON

Birthplace of Jon Anderson, 25.10.44. He went to St Johns Catholic School before forming The Warriors, whose drummer, Ian Wallace, was later in Bob Dylan's band. Anderson moved to London in 1967 and ultimately formed Yes.

## BLACKBURN

Birthplace of Lionel Morton, 14.8.42 (Four Pennies); Tony Ashton, 1.3.46 (Ashton Gardner & Dyke); Karen Kay, 18.7.47.

Tony Ashton went to St Georges Secondary Modern.

Operational base of The Four Pennies — 1964 chart toppers with Juliet.

In September 56, the town's Watch Committee banned local screenings of the Bill Haley film Rock Around The Clock — in case it provoked teenage riots and crime.

In January 67, a council survey revealed some 4000 holes in the town's roads — a fact noted by John Lennon in the Beatles song A Day In The Life.

The Boomtown Rats made their UK debut at the Lode Star pub in 1977, getting 70 quid for their efforts.

## BLACKPOOL

Birthplace of Cynthia Lennon, 10.9.39; Graham Nash, 2.2.42 (Hollies/CSN); Andy Summers, 31.12.42 (Police); Coleen Nolan, 12.3.65 (Nolans); Chris Lowe, 10.10.59 (Pet Shop Boys).

1957 chart star Russ Hamilton was a redcoat at Butlins Holiday Camp.

It was at the Pavilion Theatre that Lonnie Donegan recorded his 1961 hit, Michael Row The Boat.

Sixties R&B groups included Johnny Breeze & The Atlantics, and The Executives (featuring future NME writer Roy Carr) ... but The Blades, who made their debut at the Holy Family Youth Club in 1963, were to become the most successful. By 1966, they had evolved into The John Evan Band, specialising in blues and soul. They split when singer Ian Anderson and bassist Glenn Cornick (both local lads) moved to Luton in late 67. There they formed Jethro Tull ... soon to include Blackpool pals John Evan, Jeffrey Hammond-Hammond and Barriemore Barlow. Anderson mentions his old home town on the Tull song Going Up The Pool.

Also calling Blackpool home were Roy Harper, The Rockin' Vickers (a wild 60s group through which passed pre-Hawkwind Lemmy), The Wheels (transplanted Belfast R&B merchants), Anti Social and Skrewdriver (belligerent late 70s punks), The Membranes (late 80s indie hopefuls).

Rockin' Vickers leader Harry Feeney now runs a Datsun showroom in Devonshire Road.

During an early 60s tour, Tommy Roe's van broke down enroute to a Blackpool gig. As he stood there looking anxious, a coach bringing Blackpool's football

team home pulled up and transported him to the venue.

In July 64, the Winter Gardens was the setting for Britain's biggest rock riot to date. At a Stones concert, an hysterical element in the audience demolished fixtures and fittings and went generally nutty. Fifty fans needed hospital treatment.

In the early 80s, the town's biggest star was Dave Ball ... half of Soft Cell. He went to Arnold School, and then Blackpool Tech.

## BRIERFIELD

Birthplace of Alan Buck, 7.4.43 (Four Pennies).

## BURNLEY

Birthplace of Bernie Calvert, 16.9.42, and Bobby Elliott, 8.12.42 (both Hollies); Tex Comer, 23.2.49 (Ace ... in fact their hit, How Long, was written about him: he was considering a defection to another group).

The Dolphins were an early 60s beat group; two of their number, Tony Hicks and Bobby Elliott, later joined The Hollies.

Punk groups included The Not Sensibles and The Stiffs.

## CHORLEY

Birthplace of John Foxx, who moved to London in 1974 and formed Ultravox. Under their original name of Tiger Lily, they played their first try-out gig in Chorley.

## DARWIN

Birthplace of Bryn Haworth.

# lancashire

## EARBY

Residents still recall the day in 1964 when The Four Pennies honoured a contract to play the village youth club — even though their record had shot to number one. Utter pandemonium!

## LANCASTER

China Street attracted some national attention in the late 70s.

# 4,000 holes put us on 'pop' map

A TRACK from a new Beatles LP has been banned from some radio stations in Los Angeles and it sings about Blackburn.

The stations which have got hold of advance copies of the LP, "Sergeant Pepper's Lonely Hearts Club Band," have taken exception to the track: "A Day in the Life" because, they say, it refers to drug addiction.

The lyric goes: "Four thousand holes in Blackburn, they had to count them all, now they know how many holes it takes to fill the Albert Hall."

But the Americans think the lyric is: "40,000 holes IN MY ARM!"

## REMOTE

A Lancashire Evening Telegraph story recently pointed out the number of holes in Blackburn roads — 4,000 in all.

Disc and Music Echo's Hollywood reporter, Derek Taylor, said in yesterday's issue: "Any idea that this may encourage people to take drugs is, to say the least, remote."

A spokesman for Nems Enterprises, the Beatle's managers, told the Telegraph today: "Well, it should be good for business in Blackburn when the record is released later this month."

# Digging into the Beatles' past. . .

AMID all the nostalgia this week surrounding the 20th anniversary of the release of the Beatles' epochal LP Sgt. Pepper's Lonely Hearts Club Band, remains the mystery of why one of the tracks, "A Day in the Life" has a line that goes: "I read the news today, oh boy. Four thousand holes in Blackburn, Lancashire." And though the holes were rather small, they had to count them all."

However, today I can point to the man responsible for bringing the state of Blackburn's potholed streets in 1967 to the attention of the Fab Four who immortalised the town in song.

It was veteran East Lancashire freelance journalist Ron Kennedy who spotted a story in these pages of an Evening Telegraph survey on town centre pavements, followed it up with the council to get the now-historic figure of 4,000 holes and sold the story to the national press where it must have been read and remembered by Beatle lyricist John Lennon.

Blackburn's holey state must have made a strong impression on the group, for, the following year the town got another mention from them — in their cartoon film, Yellow Submarine, which includes a clip of the characters amid a land full of holes, of which one of them remarks: "This place reminds me of Blackburn, Lancashire."

However, 20 years on, writer Ron, although he remembers gathering and selling the story on the town's 4,000 holes, hasn't got a more tangible reminder of his starting Blackburn's claim to Beatle fame. "I cleared out all my newspaper cuttings from 1967 years ago," he tells me.

**Newspaper reports from (L) 1967 & (R) 1987: They had to count them all...**

# lancashire

## LYTHAM ST ANNE'S

The Buggs were local hopefuls . . . their drummer joined Alien Sex Fiend.

## MORECAMBE

Birthplace of broadcaster and writer Charlie Gillett, 20.2.42.

## NELSON

Birthplace of Tony Hicks, 16.12.45 (Hollies).

The Imperial Ballroom hosted every major 60s group.

## ORMSKIRK

Birthplace of Les Pattinson, 18.4.58 (Echo & The Bunnymen).

## PRESTON

Birthplace of Keef Hartley, 8.3.44, who played drums for Rory Storm and Freddie Starr before moving to London to join John Mayall and ultimately form his own band. He played at Woodstock but missed inclusion in the movie!

It must be a drummers town . . . also spawning Paul Varley of The Arrows and Fred Kelly of Rare Bird.

One of the most famous natives is that man with the golden trumpet Eddie Calvert, born 15.3.22.

Local groups include David John & The Mood (60s R&B), The Puppets (produced by Joe Meek), and Little Free Rock (70s progressive).

Starting in September 69, the Amethyst Club in Old Cock Yard presented the likes of Genesis, Supertramp and Renaissance (all of whom played for less than 75 quid), while the 70s scene was centred around the Dog & Partridge in Friargate and the Pear Tree Hotel in Bamber Bridge.

Formerly a dress-regulated disco, The Warehouse became the focus of punk activity — but no local bands made it out.

Singer/songwriter Kevin Coyne worked at Whittington Mental Hospital — its influence surfacing in many of his songs.

Preston also gets a mention in Cheap Day Return, from Jethro Tull's Aqualung album.

After leaving school, Les Pattinson — soon to become bass player in Echo & The Bunnymen — was an apprentice boatmaker at Douglas Yard.

Charlie 'Oval' Gillett

© Charlie Gillett

(below) Les Pattinson of Preston

© WEA Records (U.K.)

# LEICESTERSHIRE

## CASTLE DONINGTON

Setting for annual Monsters Of Rock heavy metal festivals.

## LEICESTER

Birthplace of keyboard player Jon Lord, 9.6.41 (Deep Purple); singer Roger Chapman, 8.4.42 (Family); drummer Brian Davison, 25.5.42 (The Nice); bassist Rod Allen, 31.3.44 (Fortunes); drummer Barry Jenkins, 22.12.44 (Animals); keyboard player Tony Kaye, 11.1.46 (Yes); drummer Rob Townsend, 7.7.47 (Family); bass player John Illsley, 24.6.49 (Dire Straits); bass player John Deacon, 19.8.51 (Queen); singer Phil Oakey, 2.10.55 (Human League).

Roger Chapman and Rob Townsend went to Ellis Avenue Boys School; Charlie Whitney went to the Art College, where The Farinas made their debut in 1962.

The Farinas and The Roaring Twenties coalesced into the city's most famous export, Family.

Other local groups include Black Widow (early 70s gothic/sorcery); Le Gay, who moved to London in the progressive 70s and made some headway as Gypsy; Amber Squad, Atrocious Ghastly and The Sinatras (all new wave).

Making waves in 1989 were hot EMI signing Diesel Park West — once known locally as The Filberts. Lead singer John Butler was previously in mid-70s group Widowmaker. Also currently hot are Crazyhead and Gaye Bykers On Acid.

## LOUGHBOROUGH

Birthplace of maverick drummer Viv Prince, 9.8.44 (The Pretty Things); Paul Brindley (The Sundays).

Suzi Quatro made her UK debut at Loughborough University in 72.

## MARKET HARBOROUGH

Birthplace of Simon Park, whose Eye Level reached number one in 73.

Leicester's finest: The Family

& Crazyhead

# LINCOLNSHIRE

## AUTHORPE

Home of Corinne Drewery, vocalist in Swing Out Sister. Her mother runs a hedgehog hospital in the village.

## BOSTON

Richard Green and Ken Popple moved to London to form hot indie band Biff Bang Pow.

## BOURNE

The Corn Exchange presented the likes of Suzie Quatro, but local groups like The Maniacs, The Residents and The Delties all failed ignominiously.

## GRANTHAM

Birthplace of 50s rocker Vince Eager — a Larry Parnes second leaguer.

## LINCOLN

Birthplace of Perry Ford, 30.12.40 (Ivy League).

Home of The Allisons, our 1961 Eurovision song contestants with Are You Sure.

In 1963, the Trust House Hotel refused entry to The Rolling Stones. The place subsequently burned down.

Roxy Music played their first official gig at the Lincoln Festival in May 72. They were bottom of the bill — below such worthies as The Faces, The Beach Boys, and Genesis, whose Peter Gabriel appeared for the first time with a cleavage shaved into his hair. He became increasingly theatrical thereafter. The festival also saw the solo debut of Sandy Denny.

Local groups include The Pseudo Existors (new wave),

## LOUTH

Swing Out Sister's Corinne Drewery attended Monk's Dyke High School and enjoyed the odd tipple in the Golden Fleece.

## SKEGNESS

Birthplace of Graham Bonnet, 1947 (Marbles, Rainbow).

Liverpool group Rory Storme & The Hurricanes were resident at Butlins Holiday Camp in summer 60, 61 and 62. Their last stint was interrupted at the beginning of August when drummer Ringo Starr was called home to join The Beatles.

## SLEAFORD

Birthplace of Lois Lane, 3.4.44 (The Caravelles); lyricist Bernie Taupin, 22.5.50.

## SWARBY

Birthplace of chirpy cockney Joe Brown, 13.5.41. That can't be right ... oh yes, he moved to the East End of London when he was two! (I thought people were supposed to move OUT of London during the war!)

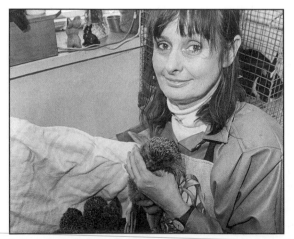

**Authorpes Mrs Drewery**

# LIVERPOOL

## LIVERPOOL

Due to the wealth of talent and plethora of venues, this section is necessarily compressed. Your attention is drawn to Let's Go Down The Cavern by Spencer Leigh, The Scouse Phenomenon by Klaus Schwartze, and In The Footsteps Of The Beatles by Mike Evans and Ron Jones.

Birthplace of (just a few) Ken Dodd, 8.11.29 (fifteen 60s hits!); Brian Epstein, 19.9.34; Michael Cox, 19.3.40 (Joe Meek protege); Billy Fury, 17.4.40; John McNally, 30.8.41 (Searchers founder); Gerry Marsden, 24.9.42 (Gerry & The Pacemakers); Cilla Black, 27.5.43; Jim McCarty, 25.7.43 (Yardbirds); Aynsley Dunbar, 10.1.46 (Journey, Whitesnake); Carol Decker, 10.9.57 (T'Pau); Ian McCulloch, 5.5.59 (Echo & The Bunnymen); Holly Johnson, 9.2.60 (Frankie Goes To Hollywood); Colin Vearncombe, 25.6.62 (Black).

First local chart stars were Frankie Vaughan, Lita Roza, Michael Holliday, and teenage balladeer Russ Hamilton, who lived at 158 Beacon Lane, Everton.

Then came pre-Beatle boom rockers like Lance Fortune, The Vernons Girls, Johnny Gentle, Michael Cox, and Billy Fury, who was discovered in Marty Wilde's dressing room (see Birkenhead).

The most influential gigs were Buddy Holly's appearance at the Philharmonic Hall on Hope Street in March 58, and the Gene Vincent/Eddie Cochran package at the Empire in March 60.

Also, Roy Rogers rode Trigger from the Adelphi Hotel down Lime Street to the Empire Theatre ... and it was only weeks later that poor old Trigger died!

Beatles landmarks: Ringo Starr was born in the Dingle at 9 Madryn Street (off High Park Street) in Liverpool 8, on 7.7.40. While still a toddler, he moved around the corner to 10 Admiral Grove, where he stayed until moving to London in 1964. A sickly child, he spent many months in the Royal Children's Hospital in Myrtle Street. He was educated at St Silas Primary in Pengwern Street and Dingle Vale Secondary Modern. His local pub was the Empress in High Park Street — as pictured on his album Sentimental Journey.

John Lennon was born at Oxford Street Maternity Hospital (just across the road from the Roman Catholic Cathedral) on 9.10.40. His early boyhood was spent at 9 Newcastle Road, Liverpool 15 (just around the corner from Penny Lane) and he later moved — with Aunt Mimi and Uncle George — to Mendips, 251 Menlove Avenue, Woolton, Liverpool 25 (just around the corner from Strawberry Fields).

He went to Dovedale Primary in Dovedale Road, Liverpool 18, and Quarry Bank Grammar in Harthill Road. He started at the Art College in Hope Street in 1957, meeting Bill Harry (Merseybeat publisher), Stuart Sutcliffe (Silver Beatle) and Cynthia Powell — soon to become his wife.

After their Register Office wedding at 64 Mount Pleasant, he and Cynthia honeymooned/lived in Brian Epstein's flat at 36 Falkner Street.

© Global Antar Archive

John's Aunt Mimis house
'Mendips', 251 Menlove Avenue

# liverpool

Their son Julian was born at Sefton General in Smithdown Road on 8.4.63.

Paul McCartney was born at Walton Hospital in Rice Lane, Liverpool 9, on 18.6.42. As a baby, he lived at 10 Sunbury Road, Anfield but later lived at 20 Forthlin Road, Allerton ... his home until moving to London. He went to Joseph Williams Primary in Naylorsfield Road, Belle Vale, Liverpool 25 and then Liverpool Institute in Mount Street, where he met George.

George Harrison was born at 12 Arnold Grove, Wavertree, Liverpool 15. For a while he lived at 174 Mackets Lane, Hunts Cross, Liverpool 25. (see also Speke).

Stuart Sutcliffe had a studio/flat in the basement of 7 Percy Street. He also shared a flat with Lennon at 3 Gambier Terrace.

Pete Best (born in Madras, India) attended Collegiate Grammar School in Shaw Street, Liverpool 6. His mother operated the Casbah Club in the cellar of their house at 8 Hayman's Green, West Derby.

Brian Epstein's NEMS Record Shop was at 12 Whitechapel; he administered the Beatles from an upstairs office. The Epstein family home was at 197 Queens Drive in Liverpool 15. He is buried at the Kirkdale Jewish Cemetery, Longmoor Lane, Liverpool 9.

The Quarrymen made their debut at a Roseberry Street open air carnival in May 57, and later played at St Barnabus Church Hall in Penny Lane, and the Broadway Conservative Club in Broad Lane, Norris Green, Liverpool 11.

John and Paul first met at a Quarrymen gig at St Peter's Church Hall in Church Road, Woolton in July 57.

Complete with barber shop and bank, Penny Lane is in Liverpool 18 — though souvenir hunters have convinced the council not to erect any more signs.

Strawberry Fields is a Salvation Army Children's Home in Beaconsfield Road, Liverpool 25.

A statue of Eleanor Rigby can be seen in Stanley Street. The sculptor was former rock'n'roller Tommy Steele, who charged half a sixpence for his work (but never got it!).

The ferry across the Mersey, as advertised by Gerry & The Pacemakers, leaves from the Landing Stage — as did the Royal Iris, often used for rock cruises.

Beatles contemporaries included The Searchers, Kingsize Taylor & The Dominoes, Rory Storm & The Hurricanes, The Big Three, Gerry & The Pacemakers, The Swinging Blue Jeans, Cilla Black, The Remo Four, Faron's Flamingos, The Dennisons, The Merseybeats, Billy J Kramer & The Coasters, Lee Curtis & The All Stars, The Fourmost, Freddie Starr & The Midnighters, and loads more ... over 400 groups by the end of 1962.

**The worlds famous barber in Penny Lane**

**Strawberry Fields**

# liverpool

Most famous of all the venues in Liverpool (and possibly the world) was the Cavern at 10 Mathew Street — where The Beatles are said to have played 292 times. A trad-jazz/skiffle stronghold, it first succumbed to The Beatles in March 61. Public Health officials shut it down in February 66. It reopened from July 66 to May 73 and was then redeveloped. A new building, Cavern Walks describes itself as Liverpool's ultimate shopping and entertainment experience!

Other Merseybeat venues included the Blue Angel Club at 108 Seel Street (operated by sometime Beatles manager Allan Williams, who is said to have thrown Judy Garland out for not paying for her drinks). Formerly the Wyvern, it was the scene of the famous Larry Parnes audition where The Beatles were selected to back Johnny Gentle; the Casanova Club in Dale Street; the Black Cat Club above Sampson & Barlow's Restaurant in London Road (later the Peppermint Lounge); the Iron Door Club at 13 Temple Street; St George's Hall in Lime Street; Silver Blades Ice Rink in Prescot Road; the Locarno and Grafton Ballrooms in West Derby Road, Liverpool 6; Knotty Ash Village Hall, East Prescot Road, Liverpool 14; Blair Co-op Hall in Walton Road; the Holyoake Hall in Smithdown Road; the Pavilion Theatre in Lodge Lane; and the Rialto Ballroom, where the enterprising Oriole Records recorded ten groups in May 63.

Popular coffee bars and clubs included the Jacaranda at 23 Slater Street; the Zodiac (later the Scorpion) at 98 Duke Street; the Odd Spot at 89 Bold Street; Streates in Mount Pleasant; the Lantern at 144 Aigburth Street; the Castle at 70 South Castle Street. One of the city's first black clubs was the Colony at 80 Berkley Street, featuring Beatles' friend Lord Woodbine.

A Hard Day's Night had its Northern premiere at the Odeon in London Road, as did Give My Regards To Broad Street ... on the same day that Paul McCartney was given Freedom Of the City.

The Empire Theatre in Lime Street was the major package tour venue. The Beatles supported Little Richard here in October 62 and played their last Liverpool concert in December 65. They also did their Juke Box Jury show from here.

Popular pubs were Ye Cracke in Rice Street, the Philharmonic in Hope Street, the White Star in Rainford Gardens, and — most famous of all — the Grapes in Mathew Street. Cavern disc jockey Bob Wooler has been a regular here since December 60.

The Merseybeat newspaper was published from an office at 81a Renshaw Street.

Top musical instrument shops were Frank Hessy's at 62 Stanley Street, Bradley's at 26 Lord Street, and Rushworth's in Whitechapel.

Favoured tailors included Eric's at 9 Commutation Row and Duncan Classic Tailors at 29 London Road.

In July 64, when the Lord Mayor welcomed back the Beatles from their triumphant US tour, a quarter of a million fans lined the route from Speke Airport to the Town Hall in Water Street.

The individual Beatles were incorporated into street names on the Kensington Fields Estate, built by Wimpey Homes in 1981.

Hessey's guitar shop

What is now 'The Jacaranda' was The Blue Angel

© Global Anter Archive

© Global Anter Archive

# liverpool

The old NEMS shop

The Dooley Statue

The Grapes

Other pupils at the Institute included Don Andrew and Colin Manley (Remo Four), Les Chadwick (Pacemakers), Stu James (Mojos). Plans are now afoot to turn it into a Fame-type academy of the performing arts.

Cilla Black went to St Andrews Secondary Modern and Anfield Commercial College.

The Everyman Theatre in Hope Street was a favourite poetry venue. Adrian Henri later formed the Liverpool Scene (famous for The Entry Of Christ Into Liverpool), while Roger McGough formed Scaffold (number one in 68 with Lily The Pink). Willy Russell's play John Paul George Ringo & Bert had its world premiere here in 1974.

The Spinners were kingpins of the folk scene, but Paul Simon played a gig at the Cross Keys pub in 1964.

Bob Dylan played at the Odeon in 1965 and 1966. Scenes in Don't Look Back

(65) show him chatting to fans outside the venue. A live recording of his 66 concert with the Band became a popular bootleg — but one track, Just Like Tom Thumb's Blues, appeared officially as the b-side of his single I Want You.

Hundreds of groups sprang up following the success of the Beatles, but after 1963 the only new ones to make the charts were The Mojos, The Escorts, Tommy Quickly, and The Cryin' Shames.

Milked dry by the recording industry, Liverpool spent the next 12 years in the doldrums. The only rock groups to make any sort of progress were Liverpool Express, Arrival, Supercharge, Nasty Pop, and Afraid of Mice.

Then, in the late 70s, came the second deluge — centred on Eric's Club in the very same Mathew Street, right opposite the site of the Cavern. On the wall above the door was Arthur Dooley's statue (erected in 1974) to remind bands and fans of their heritage.

Between its opening in October 76 and its police closedown in March 80, Eric's rejuvenated Liverpool. Pistols and Clash gigs inspired local lads; Madness made their provincial debut there in June 79; Devo made their UK debut there in July 79.

First local group was Deaf School (containing future producer Clive Langer and Bette Bright); first punk band was Big In Japan (containing future entrepreneur and Timelord Bill Drummond and Holly Johnson). The floodgates were opened by Echo & The Bunnymen, The Teardrop Explodes, Wah, the Yachts, Pink Military, Orchestral Manoeuvres In The Dark, and less successful outfits like The Spitfire Boys (with Budgie and Paul Rutherford) and The Mystery Girls (with Pete Burns and Julian Cope).

The first wave also included Dalek I Love You, White & Torch, Those

# liverpool

The old Iron Door dub

Liverpool Art School

Naughty Lumps, Ellery Bop, Nightmares In Wax, Hambi & The Dance (with Wayne Hussey).

First local labels were Zoo, based in Whitechapel and Inevitable, at 4 Rutland Road, Liverpool 17.

A favourite meeting place was (and is) Probe Records in Rainford Gardens. There Geoff Davies would bombard incipient bandleaders with weird and wonderful sounds. Pete Wylie, Pete Burns, Julian Cope and Paul Rutherford all worked behind the counter at various times, and Gary Dwyer (later the Teardrops drummer) was employed as a bouncer when it got overcrowded!

The Grapes became top boozer with the new generation as well as the old, and the cafe in Aunt Twacky's Bazaar (just across the road) was always teeming with guys anxious to become famous. It was here that the creative nucleus of the late 70s scene (Jayne Casey, Bill Drummond, Holly Johnson, Paul Rutherford, etc) first met each other. It was later turned into the Armadillo Tea Rooms.

Pete Wylie, Ian McCulloch and various others shared a flat in Penny Lane.

The early 80s saw more quirky bands with strange names ... The Icicle Works, Frankie Goes To Hollywood, Modern Eon, A Flock Of Seagulls, China Crisis, The Lotus Eaters, The Room, Pale Fountains, Dead Or Alive.

Eric's had now re-opened as Brady's. Other gigs were Plato's Ballroom, held weekly at Pickwicks in Fraser Street (off the London Road); the Royal Court in Roe Street, which had once been the province of Laurence Olivier and Margaret Rutherford but had now fallen prey to the punk horde; the Warehouse in Wood Street; and the System (the old Iron Door Club modified) where Club Zoo became groovy for a while.

Frankie Goes To Hollywood made their debut at Pickwicks, supporting Hambi & The Dance.

Another famous band haunt was Brian's Cafe in Stanley Street — a greasy spoon so atmospheric that from ten yards away, people could tell that you'd just been there!

The mid 80s brought The Reverb Brothers, Here's Johnny, Black, It's Immaterial (their hit Driving Away From Home was about a journey down the M62 to Manchester, where they used to live), Doctor (of The Medies) and Rolo McGinty (leader of The Woodentops).

Current faves include The La's, The Christians, 16 Tambourines, The Reynolds Girls, Benny Profane, and Up And Running.

Both Deep Purple (March 76) and Deaf School (April 78) played their last gig at the Empire. (The former later reformed).

Following John and Stu into Liverpool Art College were the instigators of Deaf School and The Yachts, Bill Drummond (Big In Japan), Budgie (The Banshees), and John Campbell (It's Immaterial).

Architecture students at the Uni included Chris Lowe (Pet Shop Boys) and Jarvis Whitehead (It's Immaterial).

Vic Christian, the original keyboard player in The Christians, quit rather than give up his job as music teacher at Quarry Bank Grammar, where Holly Johnson was a pupil . . . and that brings us full circle!

# liverpool

(L) former registry office
64 Mount Pleasant

(r) 3 Gambier Terrace, flat for
Sutcliffe & Lennon

(below) 7 Percy Street, flat for
Stuart Sutcliffe

Mersey cash-in time

More Mersey Mania

Deaf School

Echo & The Bunnymen

The Christians

# liverpool

Penny Lane: the shelter in the middle of the roundabout...

Liverpools finest

Site of the original Mersey Beat newspaper office

Razamataz Club, (Blue Angel)

(below) Mathew Street, home to The Cavern

# GREATER MANCHESTER

## ALTRINCHAM

Current home of Manchester's most illustrious agency, Kennedy Street Management — who looked after Herman's Hermits, Wayne Fontana, 10cc, Sad Cafe, etc.

## BOLTON

Howard Devoto was a student at the Institute of Technology, where his prototype Buzzcocks made their ill-received debut in April 76.

## BURY

Birthplace of Peter Skellern, 14.3.47;

## CHEADLE HULME

In 1963, John Mayall lived in a tree house, 30 feet above the ground, in Acre Lane. He had a record player up there ... I'm not sure about a loo.

Birthplace of Then Jerico's Jasper Stainthorpe, 7.12.61.

## CHORLTON

The Oaks was a prime punk venue for a while, presenting the likes of Slaughter & The Dogs and The Heartbreakers.

## CHORLTON-CUM-HARDY

As children, the Bee Gees lived in Keppel Road.

## CORONATION STREET

Pop stars with Corrie pedigrees include Peter Noone (Herman's Hermits), Chris Sandford, Davy Jones (Monkees), Tony Blackburn (can this be true?), Lyn Paul (New Seekers), Clive Hornby (The Dennisons) and Jilted John.

## DAVYHULME

Herman's Hermits, then known as The Heartbeats, were discovered by future manager Harvey Lisberg at a church hall here.

## DIGGLE

Barclay James Harvest got their act together in a remote farmhouse near Saddleworth Moor.

## HULME

Tony Wilson's Factory club opened in a Hulme tower block in May 78, with Joy Division, Big In Japan, Durutti Column and others. The Factory label's numerical prefix FAC was used not only on records, but badges and posters too.

FAC 1 was the poster advertising the first club gig.

## LEIGH

Birthplace of Georgie Fame, 24.6.43. He went to Windermere Road Secondary Modern until he left at 16 to work in a local cotton factory.

Also the birthplace of Mike O'Neal, keyboard player who led Nero & The Gladiators in the early 60s and played in Heads Hands & Feet a decade later.

## MANCHESTER

Quite impossible to list everyone who was born here, but here are a few: Freddie Garrity, 1940 (& the Dreamers); Roy Harper, 12.6.41; Eric Stewart, 20.1.45 (10cc); Wayne Fontana, 28.10.45 (Mindbenders); Davy Jones, 30.12.45 (Monkees); singer Peter Noone, 5.11.47 (Herman); Robin and Maurice Gibb, 22.12.49 (Bee Gee twins); Stuart Adamson, 11.4.58 (Big Country); Mick Hucknell, 8.6.60 (Simply Red); Johnny Marr, 31.10.63 (The Smiths).

The best 60s R&B club was the Twisted Wheel at 30 Brazennose Street. John Mayall was resident there in 1962/3 but every group worth its salt played there.

Other 60s venues were the Oasis in Lloyd Street, where The Deltas changed their name to The Hollies (after seeing holly in the Christmas decorations, December 62) and where Wayne Fontana was spotted and signed (Dave Lee Travis was the disc jockey there); Mr Smiths in Brazil Street; the Three Coins in Fountain Street; and the Manchester Cavern.

# greater manchester

Roger Eagle

In the post-beat/pre-punk era came 10cc, Stackwaddy, Gravy Train, Greasy Bear and Sad Cafe.

The city's best psychedelic venue was the Magic Village, started by former Twisted Wheel promoter Roger Eagle. When Mick Hucknell was putting Simply Red together, he stayed at Eagle's house, absorbing his almighty record collection. Eagle later operated the amazing Eric's in Liverpool, and now owns the two International Clubs in Manchester.

The late 70s punk/new wave scene was sparked off by a Sex Pistols gig at the Lesser Free Trade Hall in Peter Street in June 76. Howard Devoto and Pete Shelley were the promoters of that, and a second Pistols gig in July 76, where their own punk group The Buzzcocks made their official debut. Most of the audience also formed bands of their own.

Earliest groups on the scene included The Buzzcocks, Slaughter & The Dogs, The Fall, Warsaw (later Joy Division), Ed Banger & The Nosebleeds, and The Drones.

Hot on their trail were Durutti Column, Magazine, The Passage, Ludus, Pulp, Manicured Noise, The Negatives, Spherical Objects, Dislocation Dance, Jilted John, The Diagram Brothers, V2, The Decorators, Bette Lynch's Legs, The Tiller Boys and John Cooper Clarke — not to mention Alberto Y Los Trios Paranoias.

In the 80s came The Mothmen, The Distractions, A Certain Ratio, Occult Chemistry, Crispy Ambulance, Dislocation Dance, The Freshies, The Smirks, Any Trouble, Flag of Convenience, The Inca Babies, Simply Red, and two thirds of Swing Out Sister.

Groups would also meet in various coffee bars — Guys and Dolls in Kennedy Street being most fondly remembered — and at Barrett's Music Shop, 86 Oxford Road.

In January 64, a converted church in Dickinson Road became the first studio for Top Of The Pops.

In August 64, two policewomen fainted during riots at a Stones gig at the New Elizabethan Ballroom in Bellevue, and in March 65 a hysterical girl fell from the dress circle during a Stones gig at the Palace Theatre.

The 60s group scene threw up national stars in the shape of The Hollies, Herman's Hermits, Freddie & The Dreamers, and Wayne Fontana & The Mindbenders.

Hundreds more failed to make any national impression — like Graham Gouldman's Mockingbirds, or Paul Young's Toggery Five.

# greater manchester

Latest wave of groups include King Of The Slums, The Sun And The Moon, Happy Mondays, James, Baby Ford, and Easterhouse (who perversely named themselves after a council estate in Glasgow!)

The Bee Gees made their world debut at the Gaumont Theatre in December 56.

Lol Creme's dad had a shop in Shude Hill, where his early group the Sabres used to rehearse.

Van Der Graaf Generator formed at Manchester University; Carmel went to Manchester Poly; John Mayall attended the Regional School of Art.

Ian Curtis (Joy Division) and Clive Gregson (Any Trouble) used to meet on training courses at the Employment Exchange in Aytoun Street when both were studying to become Disablement Officers. Ian worked at the Dept of Employment offices in Macclesfield, Cheshire (now the Job Centre) and Clive at the Labour Exchange in Hyde.

Best late 70s city centre club was the Electric Circus, in Collyhurst Street. Warsaw made their debut there in May 77; Magazine made their's on the night it closed in Autumn 77.

Next to open was Rafters in an Oxford Road cellar. At an audition here in Spring 78, Joy Division failed to impress Stiff execs, but they did impress Factory boss Tony Wilson (who signed them) and club DJ Rob Gretton (who became their manager).

In late 77, Morrissey (Smiths) and Billy Duffy (The Cult) made their public debut at the Ritz in Whitworth Street, when they were both in The Nosebleeds. The Smiths made their debut at the same venue in October 82 (supporting London poseurs Blue Rondo a la Turk).

A popular late 70s watering hole was the Ranch, a gay bar often "littered with Bowie casualties" in Little Lever Street. The Buzzcocks played an early gig there.

First local label of note was Rabid, started in 77 by flyposter king Tosh Ryan. Most stylish was Factory, started by Tony Wilson in late 78.

The Hacienda club (FAC 51) was a self-styled post-industrial fantasy venue, opening in May 82, at 11-13 Whitworth Street in West Manchester.

New Order made their debut at the Beach Club (a Wednesday night take-over of Oozit's Club in Shude Hill) in July 80.

Strangeways Here We Come was a famous Smiths' title; The Ballad of Strangeways was a song by Donovan, who found himself temporarily confronted by prison bars after a misunderstanding in 1964.

The Bard of Salford, John Cooper Clarke directed one of his most biting diatribes at Beasley Street, a remote backwater in Gorton, and he mentions tacky Oxford Road in Salome Maloney.

Meanwhile, Chris Sievey of the Freshies committed to vinyl his plaintive declaration I'm In Love With The Girl On The Manchester Virgin Megastore Check-out Desk!

I wonder where she is now?

## OLDHAM

Birthplace of all four members of Barclay James Harvest: Wooly Woolstenholme, 15.4.47; John Lees, 13.1.48; Mel Pritchard, 20.1.48; Les Holroyd, 12.3.48. Also funny man Bernard Cribbins, 29.12.28 (two top ten hits in 1962!); bass player Ray Jones, 20.10.39, (Dakotas); drummer Chris Curtis, 26.8.41 (Searchers).

Home of late 80s garage-rock indie band The Inspiral Carpets.

## OPENSHAW

Mindbenders/10cc guitarist Eric Stewart went to the Technical High School.

## RADCLIFFE

Hitless for two years, the once sensational rocker Johnny Kidd was killed in a car collision on the way to a cabaret gig in October 66. Another passenger, his bass player Nick Simper, went on to play in the first line-up of Deep Purple.

## ROCHDALE

Birthplace of disc jockey Andy Kershaw, 9.11.59.

Blue Zone were late 80s hopefuls.

## SALFORD

Birthplace of singer Allan Clarke, 5.4.42 (The Hollies); drummer Tony Mansfield, 28.5.43 (Dakotas); guitarist Fritz Fryer, 6.12.44 (Four Pennies); bassist Karl Green, 31.7.47 (Hermits); singer Elkie Brooks, 25.2.48 (Vinegar Joe, solo); Mark Smith, 5.3.57 (The Fall); Dave Ball (Soft Cell); John Cooper Clarke (the Bard of Salford).

Passing through Salford Grammar School were Graham Nash (Hollies) and Ian Curtis (Joy Division). Elkie Brooks went to Sedgley Park County Primary and North Salford Secondary Modern, where Graham Gouldman and Kevin Godley were also pupils.

New wavers included the Salford Jets. Craig Davies is a late 80s hopeful.

# greater manchester

## STALYBRIDGE

Any Trouble auditioned for Stiff Records at the Commercial Arms.

## STOCKPORT

Birthplace of bassplayer Eric Haydock, 3.2.43 (Hollies).

Opened in 1968, Strawberry Studios at 3 Waterloo Road was soon the hottest studio in Greater Manchester. Co-owners were Graham Gouldman, Eric Stewart and Peter Tattersall. The first hit was Neanderthal Man by Hotlegs, who eventually mutated into 10cc. Late one night, as Paul McCartney was leaving, he found a girl standing at the adjacent bus-stop crying – and promptly took out his acoustic and rattled off a few songs to cheer her up.

Local bands include The Purple Gang (psychedelic types), The Elite (punk/new wave). Sixties beat group The Toggery Five were named after a clothes shop in Mersey Square ... "all the top groups visit the Toggery for their stage and leisure wear"!

A short-lived psychedelic club was the Sinking Ship in Royal Oak Yard, Underbank.

New Order's Gillian Gilbert was a pupil at Stockport Tech.

## STRETFORD

Birthplace of Steven Morrissey, 22.5.59. He went to St Mary's Secondary Modern

**Strawberry Studios**

**Memories of a festival**

and Stretford Technical College.

Peter Noone went to Stretford Grammar.

## WIGAN

The small mining village of Bicker-shawe was the setting for a rock festival in May 72. The Kinks, Grateful Dead and Captain Beefheart were headliners.

## WITHINGTON

20 Cotton Lane housed the city's first independent labels, Rabid (featuring Jilted John and John Cooper Clarke) and Razz (featuring the idiosyncratic Chris Sievy & The Freshies).

## WYTHENSHAWE

Birthplace of Lyn Paul, 16.2.49 (New Seekers: she made her singing debut at Wythenshawe Labour Club).

John Mayall was a youth club leader here, which provided adequate facilities for his group the Blues Syndicate to rehearse.

Cult guitarist Billy Duffy (born 12.5.61) was educated at Brookway High School. Johnny Marr used to watch his school group rehearse, picking up guitar hints.

# MERSEYSIDE

(excluding Liverpool)

## A I N T R E E

Birthplace of drummer Pete Gill, 1964 (Frankie Goes To Hollywood).

The Institute (in Longmoor Lane, next to the Black Bull) and the Orrell Park Ballroom in Orrell Lane were popular early 60s venues.

First wave Merseybeat group Faron's Flamingos sprang from here.

The Scaffold thanked us very much for the Aintree Iron . . . what was it exactly?

In July 88, Michael Jackson played Aintree Racecourse in what was the biggest ever British concert by a single artist.

## B I R K E N H E A D

Birthplace of Lewis Collins, 26.5.42 (sometime bassplayer in The Mojos; later star of TV series The Professionals).

It was during a package show at the Essoldo Cinema, Argyll Street, in September 58 that Billy Fury talked his way into Marty Wilde's dressing room and impressed his manager (Larry Parnes) enough to win an invitation to London. Within weeks he was a national star! That's the popular myth . . . what actually happened was this: Fury's parents had asked Parnes to return his 78 rpm demo of Playing For Keeps, and Parnes suggested that Billy call round to the gig. He duly went (with his pal Jimmy Tarbuck!) and performed on-stage that same night, joining the tour for the rest of its schedule. He had no job at the time, having just got out of hospital.

The local group venue was the Majestic Ballroom in Conway Street.

Groups often stopped off at Morgan's fish and chip shop on Borough Road, near the Fire Station. Rory Storm was a regular customer, and the proprietor remembers that Sandie Shaw had dirty fingernails!

Many Merseybeat groups bought their instruments and amps at R A Strother & Son, 7 Charing Cross.

Elvis Costello (whose formative years were spent on Merseyside) paid tribute by snapping the run down Clockwork Orange Cafe, in Hoylake Road, on the back of his Oliver's Army sleeve.

Home of idiosyncratic indie faves Half Man Half Biscuit (who took their name from punk group Instant Agony, who were describing Prince Charles). They turned down an invitation to appear on The Tube because Tranmere Rovers were playing at home!

Also celebrationists of the Wirral are Jegsy Dodd & The Sons Of Harry Cross – famous for songs like Downtown Birkenhead, Who Killed New Brighton and I'm The Trendiest Man Who Never

# merseyside

Got Into Atmosphere – Atmosphere being "a horrible disco club for pseudo poseurs" according to one observer.

Another local lad is Bill Steers – member of two hardcore bands, Napalm Death and Carcass.

## BOOTLE

Birthplace of Billy J Kramer, 19.8.43.

Mike Pender and Chris Curtis of the Searchers both went to St Winifred's School.

A popular early 60s gig was the Blue Penguin Club at St Johns Hall.

## BROMBOROUGH

Birthplace of Paul Heaton, 9.5.62 (Housemartins).

## CROSBY

The Jive Hive, held at St Luke's Hall in Liverpool Road, opened for business in May 59. Less popular was the Alexandra Hall in Coronation Road.

## FORMBY

Home of Steve Murray, later known as folkie recording artist Timon, and subsequently (during his dalliance with The Clash) as Tymon Dogg. He's currently half of new age folk duo The Frugivores.

## GARSTON

The Silver Beatles gigged at Garston Baths in Speke Road. Drunken thuggery led to the nick-name Garston Bloodbaths.

Wilson Hall in Speke Road was a Quarrymen venue. It was here that

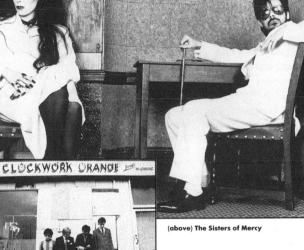

(above) Costello's Army in Birkenhead

George first saw the group and became interested in joining.

## HESWALL

Birthplace of John Peel, 30.8.39 (disc jockey); singer Ian Astbury, 14.5.62 (The Cult).

In the midst of Beatlemania, Paul McCartney bought his father a house in Baskervyle Road.

Home of Andy McCluskey, founder of Orchestral Manoeuvres In The Dark.

The Sisters Of Mercy used the Wirral estuary as a backdrop for promotional shots for their album Floodlands.

(above) The Sisters of Mercy

## HOYLAKE

Cynthia Powell, later Cynthia Lennon, lived in Trinity Road. Her son Julian was educated at Hoylake School.

Also from here were Stan Hugill (world authority on sea shanties) and Paul Kennerley (wrote concept albums – like White Mansions – and married Emmylou Harris).

## HUYTON

Prime Minister Harold Wilson was MP for Huyton. In July 66, he presided over the re-opening of the Cavern.

Beatle Stu Sutcliffe, who died in Hamburg in 1962, is buried at the Parish Church Cemetery in Stanley Road.

Primo 60s gig was the Jive Hive at Hambleton Hall in St Davids Road, Page Moss.

© Waldos archive

© WEA Records (U.C.)

# merseyside

## KIRKBY

Birthplace of Hal Carter, who left the area to work as Marty Wilde's roadie and later managed Billy Fury.

The area was immortalised on the b-side of the first single by Teardrop Explodes ... Kirkby Workers Dream Fades!

Both born here, China Crisis mainmen Eddie Lundon and Garry Daly met at St Kevins Comprehensive ... while Will Sergeant lived at nearby Melling.

From acorn beginnings, Amazon Recording Studios in Stopgate Lane, Simonswood has attracted everyone from The Smiths to Wet Wet Wet, Dusty Springfield to New Order. Owner Jeremy Lewis started with a 4 track in the cellar of his Woolton home (recording Nasty Pop and Deaf School) and then sold his car to buy this place in the mid 70s. He also started (with Pete Fulwell) the Inevitable label and took proteges China Crisis and Dead Or Alive to Virgin ... who didn't want Dead Or Alive!

## LITHERLAND

During the early 60s, the Town Hall in Hatton Hill Road was one of the most popular venues on Merseyside. The Beatles' gig on 27.12.60 (fresh back from Hamburg) was widely seen as the turning point in their career.

## MAGHULL

Les Pattinson and Will Sergeant (both Bunnymen) went to Deyes Lane Secondary Modern.

## NESTON

Neston Village Institute was a 60s venue.

## NEW BRIGHTON

The Tower Ballroom on the Promenade held up to 5000 punters. Everyone from Little Richard to The Stones played here until fire destroyed it in 1969.

When big enough to fill one of Liverpool's largest venues, Elvis Costello chose to play the Grand in New Brighton instead ... for nostalgic reasons, no doubt.

## NEWTON LE WILLOWS

On leaving Selwyn Jones High School, Rick Astley worked for his father at the Parkside Garden Centre in Southworth Road.

## PORT SUNLIGHT

Birthplace of singer Pete Burns, 5.8.59 (Dead Or Alive).

Hulme Hall in Port Sunlight Village (created for his workers by soap magnate Lord Leverhulme) got the Beatles for 30 quid in October 62 — just as Love Me Do carried them into the chart for the first time.

## PRESCOT

Before going to the Art College, Stu Sutcliffe went to Prescot Grammar.

## ST HELENS

The Plaza Ballroom in Duke Street started featuring local groups in 1959.

Before joining Frankie Goes To Hollywood, Paul Rutherford was at St Helens Art School.

## SEAFORTH

Birthplace of disc jockey Kenny Everett, 25.12.44.

Lathom Hall in Lathom Avenue was a merseybeat stomping ground.

## SOUTHPORT

Birthplace of Dora Bryan, 7.2.24 (hit 1963 top twenty with All I Want For Christmas Is A Beatle); guitarist Ollie Halsall, 14.3.49 (Patto, Kevin Ayers, etc); Berni Flint (hits in 1977); Marc Almond, 9.7.57 (Soft Cell). He went to Starbeck Infants, King George V Grammar, and Southport Art College.

Annual pantomimes have always been star-studded affairs ... ever since Vince Eager played Simple Simon in Mother Goose (1960).

The Beatles and their rivals regularly played the Cambridge Hall in Lord Street and the Floral Hall on the Promenade.

Comedian Alexei Sayle (a chart star in 1984) went to Southport School of Art.

Noted merseybeat singer and guitarist Kingsize Taylor now has a butcher's shop in Crown Buildings, Birkdale.

## SPEKE

Local lad George Harrison made his public debut at Speke British Legion Club in Damwood Road, with the Rebels in 1956. At age 6, he and his family had moved into a council house at 25 Upton Green.

As a child, Paul McCartney lived at 72 Western Avenue and went to Stockton Wood Road Primary. His family later moved to 12 Ardwick Road. He and George rode the same school bus to the Liverpool Institute.

# m e r s e y s i d e

The Teardrop Explodes Kirkby ode

The Undertakers below Liverpool's Anglican Cathedral, which held a memorial service for John Lennon in March '81 & in which Echo And The Bunnymen recorded The Beatle's 'All You Need Is Love' for the 'Play At Home' T.V. series

Stuart Sutcliffe (R) with influential girlfriend Astrid

## W A L L A S E Y

Birthplace of Les Maguire, 27.12.41 (the Pacemakers); Jackie Lomax, 10.5.44 (the Undertakers);

As a child, Paul McCartney lived briefly at 92 Broadway.

The Beatles played the Grosvenor Ballroom several times in the early 60s.

Most famous local Merseybeat group was The Undertakers, led by Jackie Lomax.

## W E S T  K I R B Y

In February 62 The Beatles played the Macdona Hall on the corner of Banks Road and Salisbury Avenue (above the Thistle Cafe) – their first booking under Brian Epstein's management.

Home of Paul Humphries, who founded Orchestral Manoeuvres In The Dark with schoolfriend Andy McCluskey.

# MIDDLESEX

**(all within Greater London boundary, but with Middlesex postal address)**

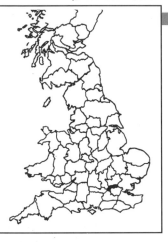

## ASHFORD

Marc Bolan's T Rex cohort Steve Peregrine Took attempted to kick his heroin habit at the Ashford Hospital in London Road.

## BRENTFORD

In the early 60s, Rod Stewart was an apprentice at Brentford football club ... but only briefly!

## CRANFORD

Ian Gillan made his first public appearance at St Dunstans Youth Club, fronting The Moonshiners.

## EDGWARE

Birthplace of drummer Dave Mattacks, March 48 (Fairport Convention); singer Jenny Haan (Babe Ruth); singer Billy Idol, 30.11.55.

## ENFIELD

Birthplace of John Dalton, 21.5.43 (Kinks); Lenny Davidson, 30.5.44 (Dave Clark Five); Johnny Almond, 1946 (Mark Almond).

Cliff Richard worked as a credit control clerk at Ferguson's TV and radio factory until August 58, when (against all advice) he gave up his day job to become a rock'n'roll star!

## GREENFORD

It was at the Oldfield Hotel in Oldfield Lane that Keith Moon first heard and blagged his way into the Who.

In his song Hoover Factory, Elvis Costello sang of the scrolls and in-scriptions which decorate that edifice on the Western Avenue.

## HAMPTON

Birthplace of guitarist Brian May, 19.7.47 (Queen); guitarist Colin Earle (Mungo Jerry).

Future Yardbirds Jim McCarty and Paul Samwell-Smith first met at Hampton Grammar, where Brian May was also a pupil.

Home of 60s beat group The Others, who often appeared at the Thames Hotel R&B club.

## HARROW

Birthplace of Mike Vernon, 20.11.44 (producer); guitarist Andy Roberts (Liverpool Scene).

Former pupils of Harrow Art School include Charlie Watts (Rolling Stones), Malcolm McLaren, Marco Pirroni (Adam's chief Ant), The Models (punkers), Blancmange (electro poppers).

Former pupils of Harrow County Grammar School include Episode Six, who lost their impetus when two of them (Roger Glover and Ian Gillan) joined Deep Purple in 1969, Kimberley Rew (guitarist/songwriter in Katrina & The Waves) and Jamie Stewart (bass-player in The Cult).

Harrow public school frowned on the pursuit of popular music, but five pupils sought fame and fortune as the Band of Angels. Singer Mike D'Abo found both when he replaced Paul Jones in Manfred Mann and guitarist John Gaydon was later manager of Roxy Music and ELP. Another Harrow pupil was Chris Blackwell, founder of Island Records.

Aspiring politician/rock'n'roll star Screaming Lord Sutch was a local lad, working as a plumber's mate before his dreams got the better of him.

Local R&B group The Bo Street Runners won the Ready Steady Go talent contest in 1964, and Wainwright's Gentlemen featured Ian Gillan on vocals. After he left, they evolved into The Sweet.

During the mid 70s, the Tithe Farm in Eastcote Lane was part of the Pub Rock circuit, presenting the likes of Brinsley Schwarz and Graham Parker – but changing tastes have reduced it to a disco.

## HAYES

Birthplace of drummer Honey Lantree, 28.8.43 (Honeycombs); bass player Frank Allen, 14.12.43 (Searchers); 50s rocker Larry Page (then known as the Teenage Rage – later manager of the Kinks and Troggs); bass player Steve Priest, 23.2.50 (Sweet).

## HEATHROW AIRPORT

Weeping fans waved off the US bound Beatles in Feb 64; revolted travellers reeled as the Sex Pistols puked and swore in Jan 77.

# middlesex

Northwood Hills pub – Rockin' Reg's old haunt

Hoover –

Pinner Parish Church sways to 'Girls on Film'

Ritchie Blackmore worked as an aircraft radio mechanic in the early 60s.

Lemmy's first bass was bought at a London Airport auction. He acquired it for £27.50.

## HESTON

Birthplace of guitarist Jimmy Page, 9.1.44.

Ritchie Blackmore (Deep Purple) attended Heston Secondary – now Lampton Comprehensive.

## HILLINGDON

Birthplace of Ron Wood, 1.6.47 (Rolling Stones); Steve Luscombe, 29.10.54 (Blancmange).

## HOUNSLOW

Birthplace of Ian Gillan, 19.8.45 (Deep Purple); Ian McLagen, 12.5.46 (Small Faces).

Housed in a room above the A1 Car Showrooms, opposite the bus station, was hot R&B club The Attic, which became the Ricky Tick in 1966 – presenting the likes of Cream, Hendrix, Pink Floyd, etc.

During the late 60s, Dave Cousins of The Strawbs ran an Arts Lab at the White Bear pub in Kingsley Road. His attempts to bring mixed-media events to the suburbs went unheeded by a hippie audience interested only in loud progressive rock and more Paki black.

Depeche Mode's video of See You was shot in McLary's Easi-Coin Launderette and Woolworth's, both in the High Street.

## ISLEWORTH

Birthplace of 50s coffee bar rocker Vince Taylor – the subject of a Golden Earring single and an inspiration to David Bowie.

## KENTON

Kevin Rowland lived in Kenton as a teenager.

## NORTHWOOD

Elton John started his career as a pub pianist at Northwood Hills Hotel in 1964.

## PERIVALE

Birthplace of Chris Thomas, 13.1.47 (producer); keyboard star Rick Wakeman, 18.5.49 (Strawbs/Yes).

## PINNER

Birthplace of Elton John, 25.3.47, who was educated at Pinner County Grammar.

Simon LeBon attended West Lodge Infants and Primary School, and sang in the choir at Pinner Parish Church.

# middlesex

## PONDERS END

Birthplace of Dave Peacock, 24.5.45 (Chas And). He went to Elmer Road School and actually recorded a track (on an early Chas & Dave album) called Ponders End Allotments Club! How obscure can you get?

## RUISLIP

Local groups include The Paranoids (punks).

Ron Wood was educated at Ruislip Manor.

## SHEPPERTON

In 1977, The Who purchased a chunk of Shepperton Studios for rehearsal, storage, filming, etc.

## SOUTHALL

Birthplace of bassplayer Nick Simper, 3.11.46 (Deep Purple); and jazz singer Cleo Laine, 28.10.27, who met her future husband, Johnny Dankworth after a gig at Southall British Legion Club in 1951.

During the 50s/60s, the town's main venue was the Dominion — now a Sikh temple.

Future manager Ken Pitt first saw Manfred Mann at the Hamborough Tavern in 1963. The pub continued to present bands until a 4 Skins gig in July 81, when it was burned to the ground during race riots which erupted between local Asians and NF skinheads/pinheads.

Eel Pie Island

**Fairport drummer dies in M1 crash**

FAIRPORT CON-VENTION drummer Martin Lamble, and an American girl known as Jeanie The Tailor were killed when the group's van overturned and crashed on the M1 at Mill Hill on Monday morning.

The group were on the way back to London after a gig at Mother's Club in Birmingham.

LAMBLE... died instantly

Martin (19) and Jeanie, whose real name was Franklin, girl friend of Fairport guitarist Richard Thompson, both died instantly. Group members Simon Nicol and Tyger Hutchins were all taken to hospital in Barnet with cuts and bruises. Richard suffered cracked ribs in the crash. Road manager Harvey Bramham was also seriously injured.

Singer Sandy Denny escaped injury because she was not travelling in the group bus. She had made the journey from Birmingham with boyfriend Trevor Lucas.

© Global Antar Archive

Reggae group Misty emerged from Southall in 1978.

## STAINES

The Town Hall was a popular gig in the 60s.

## STANMORE

Fairport Convention were taken to the Royal National Orthopaedic Hospital after their van careened off the M1 in May 69. The others survived, but doctors were unable to save either drummer Martin Lamble or their friend Jeannie Franklyn, who made clothes for rock stars. Jack Bruce dedicated his first album to her memory — Songs For A Tailor.

## SUDBURY

In 1960, the first line-up of Screaming Lord Sutch & The Savages rehearsed in the back room of the Swan public house.

## SUNBURY ON THAMES

In its eighth year (August 68), the National Jazz Blues & Rock Festival was held at Kempton Park racecourse. Arthur Brown was the star, but 74 fans were injured when a catwalk roof collapsed.

## TEDDINGTON

When he was discovered and turned into a star, Matt Monro was a bus driver on the number 27 route between Teddington and Highgate.

# middlesex

When Tony James and Mick Jones were forming their punk group London SS, they lived at opposite ends of that very route — a two and a half hour ride, just to rehearse and formulate plans.

## TWICKENHAM

Birthplace of guitarist Vic Briggs, 14.2.45 (Animals).

The hotel on Eel Pie Island (approached by the footbridge at the end of Water Lane) contained a dance hall which was first used for a jazz club in 1956. By the early 60s, it had become one of the hottest R&B venues in the London area — where the Stones, Jeff Beck, the Who, etc could wail into the night. Already beaten up, it gradually disintegrated and finally burned down in 1971. Now covered in town houses.

It was (so the story goes) on Twickenham station, following an Eel Pie gig, that Rod Stewart was approached by Long John Baldry to join him in fronting the Hoochie Coochie Men (January 64).

In late 69, Genesis played their second ever gig at Eel Pie Island (then briefly known as Col Barefoot's Rock Garden) and their third at Twickenham Technical College in Egerton Road. They got paid five quid and fifty quid respectively.

Operational base of The Strawbs (originally The Strawberry Hill Boys), The Muleskinners (with future Small Face Ian McLagen), hot R&B combo The Downliners Sect, and No Sweat (who failed to make it despite a contract with local resident Pete Townshend's Eel Pie label).

Both Hard Day's Night and Help were filmed at Twickenham Studios, and additional scenes were shot in nearby Ailsa Avenue.

Teenager Ritchie Blackmore's first group had a residency at Vicki Burke's Dancing Studio in King Street. He left them to join another Twickenham group, Mike Dee & The Jaywalkers.

The Crown at 174 Richmond Road housed an epochal folk and blues club where the likes of the Levee Breakers, Bert Jansch and Davy Graham played.

## UXBRIDGE

Denham was the birthplace of R&B pioneer Cyril Davies, 1932.

Local bands include The Lurkers (1976) from Ickenham. They plotted in the Coach & Horses pub.

Genesis made their hesitant public debut at Brunel College in late 69.

## WEALDSTONE

One of the hottest R&B venues of the mid 60s was the Railway Hotel, near Harrow and Wealdstone station. It was here that The Who were accidentally discovered by future manager Kit Lambert, who just happened to be driving past one evening in late 64 and thought he'd investigate the long queue. The promoter was Pete Townshend's Ealing Art School pal Richard Barnes, who later wrote a book on The Who.

## WEMBLEY

Birthplace of Keith Moon, 23.8.46 (the Who). He lived in Chaplin Road, went to Alperton Secondary School, and joined the Sea Cadets in Linthorpe Road.

Mari Wilson went to Preston Manor Grammar.

Two of the London area's largest venues are next door to each other — the Arena (formerly the Empire Pool) and the outdoor Stadium.

The Arena has presented rock shows since the 50s — usually multi-starred packages. As the pop audience expanded, single acts have been able to fill it amply — for example David Bowie (6 nights in May 76).

The Stadium has resounded to Little Richard (72 ... Malcolm McLaren was a programme seller), Elton John and The Beach Boys (Jun 75), Live Aid (July 85), Wham's farewell concert (June 86), four nights of Genesis (June 87), three of Madonna (August 87), Nelson Mandela's 70th birthday tribute (June 88), seven nights of Michael Jackson (July 88) and many more!

The Rediffusion Studios in Empire Way were used for the last series of Ready Steady Go, and The Stones filmed their Rock & Roll Circus there in December 68. (It's never been screened).

## WEST DRAYTON

Home base for Cliff Bennett & the Rebel Rousers and Ron Wood's R&B group, The Birds.

## WHITTON

During the late 70s, Elvis Costello lived here and Yardbirds singer Keith Relf died here — of electrocution in May 76.

In 1971, Madness saxplayer Lee Thompson broke into Whitton Hospital and made off with a bag containing 130 quid — resulting in a thirteen month sentence.

# NORFOLK

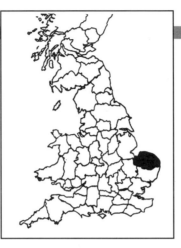

## DISS

The notorious Singing Postman had a ditty about a Pretty Little Miss From Diss!

Early 70s progressive band the Global Village Trucking Company were based here.

## EAST DEREHAM

When pre-hit Pink Floyd played here in April 67, uncomprehending dick-head punters threw beer bottles at them.

## FELTWELL

Katrina & The Waves were based here. Two of the group's parents live on the US air base.

## GREAT YARMOUTH

Birthplace of trad jazz and skiffle pioneer Ken Colyer, 1928.

The only local band of note appears to have been 60s beatsters The Sons Of Fred — remembered for their name rather than their music.

Madness shot their House Of Fun video at Great Yarmouth Funfair.

## KINGS LYNN

Birthplace of drummer Roger Taylor, 26.7.49 (Queen).

Home base for The Boz People, led by Boz Burrell, later of King Crimson and Bad Company.

Blow Monkeys' leader Dr Robert grew up here. (He spent his youth here, anyway).

## NORWICH

Fifties rocker Tony Sheridan was educated at Thorpe St Andrew.

Scores of local groups during the 60s, but none made it out of East Anglia . . . Mr Toad, Kiss, The Moving Finger, The Versions, The Plastic Dreamboat, The News, etc!

Passing through the University of East Anglia were the Higsons and half of Haircut 100. Robyn Hitchcock alluded to the former in his song Listening To The Higsons, which included the classic couplet "The Higsons come from Norwich, they eat a lot of porridge".

Billy Bragg was arrested and charged with criminal damage at a CND demo at the Bawburgh military base.

Home base of 80s faves Serious Drinking.

## SNETTERTON

In his motor racing debut on the circuit here, Andrew Ridgeley came 20th.

# NORTHAMPTONSHIRE

## BYFIELD

Home of Sandy Denny, singer with Fairport Convention — who used to rehearse in the village hall at nearby Aston Le Walls.

## FOTHERINGHAY

The Fairport Convention song Fotheringay was written after Sandy Denny had visited the castle where Mary Queen Of Scots was beheaded in 1587. She never got the spelling right, not even when she left Fairport to form a group called Fotheringay.

## KETTERING

Birthplace of Jim King, founder member of Family.

## NORTHAMPTON

Birthplace of guitarist Harvey Hinsley (Hot Chocolate); guitarist Tony Poole, 28.7.50 (leader of 70s band Starry Eyed And Laughing); keyboard player Richard Coles, 23.6.62 (Communards).

A local resident during the mid 60s, Ian Hunter led The Apex to nowhere in particular. In 1967, he moved to London to join Freddie "Fingers" Lee's rock'n'roll band and two years later he emerged as the star front man of Mott The Hoople.

The Fairport Convention song Close To The Wind describes events leading up to the last public mass hanging in Britain.

The Sex Pistols played an early gig at Northamptonshire's cricket ground.

Rockabilly revivalists The Jets scored a string of early 80s hits. From St James End, they regularly played the St James Working Man's Club and drank at the Welcome in Grafton Street.

In the early 80s, various local musicians and art school bods from groups like The Submerged Tenth and The Craze channelled their energies into Bauhaus, who made waves nationally until leader Peter Murphy left to become a screen star.

Hollies singer Allan Clarke lives in a village just south of Northampton, and another chart star with local connections is Des O'Connor, who worked in Church's shoe factory until becoming a redcoat.

Eighties indie faves include The Telltale Hearts and their offspring, The Headskaters.

## ROTHWELL

Birthplace of Carry On star Jim Dale — once a 6.5 Special rocker . . . reached the 1957 top three with Be My Girl.

## WELLINGBOROUGH

Birthplace of Bauhaus singer Peter Murphy. The group made its debut at the Cromwell pub on New Year's Eve 1978.

**Jim King of Family**

**Sandy Denny at home**

© Global Antar Archive

# NORTHUMBERLAND

## BLYTH

Birthplace of Graham Bell (Skip Bifferty, Bell & Arc).

## CRAMLINGTON

Between September 74 and July 76, Sting taught at St Pauls, a primary school.

## HOLY ISLE

Site of the first establishment of Celtic Christianity in England, this was formerly called Lindisfarne — a name which the Newcastle group resurrected.

## WARK

Home of Kathryn Tickell, the country's leading player of the Northumbrian pipes.

St Pauls primary school vacated by Sting

(L) Holy Isle: Lindisfarne

© Global Anter Archive

© Global Anter Archive

# NOTTINGHAMSHIRE

## MANSFIELD

First big local group was Shane Fenton & The Fentones. The guy who later became Alvin Stardust was in fact the second Shane . . . the first one died.

Previously known as Ricky Storm & The Storm Cats, The Mansfields were mid 60s faves. Split up when drummer Ric Lee joined Ten Years After.

It was at the Granada in October 62 that Little Richard first introduced a bogus heart attack routine into his act . . . . falling from the top of his piano as if dead.

Home of new wavers B-Movie.

## NOTTINGHAM

Birthplace of guitar maestro Alvin Lee, 19.12.44 (Ten Years After); saxplayer Elton Dean, 1945 (from whom Reg Dwight took his name); drummer Ian Paice, 29.6.48 (Deep Purple); singer Graham Russell, 1.6.50 (Air Supply);

Corinne Drewery, 21.9.59 (Swing Out Sister).

Formed in 1961, the Jaybirds were billed as "the biggest sounding trio in the country". They became Ten Years After in November 66, releasing a dozen hit albums and touring the States 28 times before their demise in March 74.

In a different league altogether were the town's other big success, Paper Lace – two of whom were born in Nottingham: Philip Wright, 9.4.48; and Chris Morris, 1.11.54. They disappeared after three 1974 hits.

Other local breakouts include Plummet Airlines (made waves on mid 70s London pub circuit), Fatal Charm and Medium Medium (new wave), and One Million Fuzztone Guitars (80s indie).

In February 72, Paul McCartney & Wings turned up unannounced at the university and asked if they could do a gig. They could and did . . . a low profile world debut!

David Coverdale's Whitesnake made their world debut at the Sky Bird Club in February 78.

In November 77, a copy of the Sex Pistols album, Never Mind The Bollocks, displayed in the window of Virgin Records in King Street, caused offence to a policewoman. A subsequent court case found Virgin not guilty to obscenity charges.

Corinne Drewery

Alvin Lee, once fastest guitar in the west

# OXFORDSHIRE

## ABINGDON

Birthplace of Barron Anthony, 15.6.40 (Barron Knights); Carl Fysh, 25.1.63 (Brother Beyond).

## ASTON TIRROLD

During the late 60s, Joe Cocker and Traffic occupied adjacent cottages on the Downs. The sleeve photos on the first two Traffic albums were shot here.

## BANBURY

Birthplace of Gary Glitter, 6.6.44;

The back page of the Daily Sketch revealed how thugs known as the Swallow Gang attacked 60s star Danny Storm for autographing local girls' knickers!

## BARFORD ST MICHAEL

Location of Wormwood Studios, made famous by Fairport and Jethro Tull.

## BICESTER

Deep Purple drummer Ian Paice grew up in Bicester.

Led by the newly arrived Fish, Marillion made their world debut at the Red Lion pub in the Market Square in March 81.

## CHINNOR

Birthplace of bassplayer Adam Clayton, 13.3.60 (U2).

## CHIPPING NORTON

Founded by Mike Vernon and operated by his brother Richard, the town's celebrated recording studio at 28-30 New Street has turned out hits for Level 42, Duran Duran, Howard Jones, The Proclaimers and scores more.

## CROPREDY

Sometime home of Fairport Conventionals Simon Nicol, Dave Swarbrick and Dave Pegg, who quaffed ale at The Brasenose – pictured on the sleeve of their album Nine. They played their "final" gig here on 4.8.79, and placed the village firmly on the folk-rock map with annual reunion concerts. The title track of their 1988 album Red And Gold discusses the civil war battle which took place here in 1644.

## DIDCOT

Pete Townshend and Karen Astley were married at Didcot Register Office in May 68.

## HENLEY ON THAMES

When rockers make it big, they look at houses in the Henley area. Among those who bought are George Harrison, Tony Visconti, Kenny Lynch, Tony Hicks (Hollies), Mick Ralphs (Bad Company), Joe Brown, and Dave Edmunds.

## OXFORD

Birthplace of Legs Larry Smith, 18.1.44 (Bonzo Dog Band); singer Kip Trevor, 12.11.46 (Black Widow); Pennie Leyton, 1958 (Belle Stars).

Despite its luxuriant literary heritage, the city of dreaming spires is a rock'n'roll dead zone. The biggest group appears to have been Mr Big, remembered for their 1977 top five hit Romeo. Six More Prophets were a mod band and the Half Human Band were weird.

In the 50s, local lad Roy Young (from St Ebbe's ... his mother is thought to have worked at Joe's Cafe in Between Towns Road, Cowley) made a splash by covering Little Richard hits on 6.5 Special while Mal Ryder from Wolvercote (leader of Mal Ryder & the Spirits) went to Italy to become a massive star.

Lonnie Donegan's smash hit Does Your Chewing Gum Lose Its Flavour On The Bedpost Overnight? was recorded live at the New Theatre (later the Apollo) in December 58.

Eric Clapton, then in R&B group the Roosters, played his first professional gig at the Carfax Assembly Rooms in early 63. The Beatles also played there in early 63, supported by local group the Maddisons.

The Carfax was the prime local venue, situated in Cornmarket.

# oxfordshire

In June 64, The Rolling Stones interrupted a US tour and spent £1500 on air fares to honour a longstanding booking at Magdalen College. Their fee ... £400! Support group was again The Maddisons, who by this time had gone fully pro as The Falling Leaves.

The Forum was a jazz club cum R&B venue in the High Street in the early 60s.

In March 64, at the zenith of their media popularity, The Beatles were persuaded to attend a charity dinner at Brasenose College — organised by future MP and author Jeffrey Archer! It was here that George Harrison examined the lavish fare and offered to trade his autograph for a jam butty!

David Bowie made his debut as a mime artist in Lindsay Kemp's Pierrot In Turquoise at the New Theatre (now the Apollo) in December 67.

The Eagles made their UK debut at Oxford Polytechnic, where the art school lecturers have included Humphrey Ocean, formerly in Ian Dury's group Kilburn & The High Roads, and Chris Dawsett, once in John's Children.

Most famous Oxford University student was Rhodes scholar Kris Kristofferson, who studied English at Merton. He was also a light middleweight boxing blue in 1959, but quit the sport on medical advice.

Other University students include Paul Jones, Paula Yates, June Tabor, Mike Ratledge (Soft Machine), Kit Lambert (manager of The Who), Simon Park (he of the Orchestra), Paul Gambaccini, Andrew Lloyd Webber, Jack Good (television producer), Johnny Rogan (rock author).

Before she set her sights on Bob Geldof, Paula Yates went out with John Otway, who she met when he played the Oranges And Lemons pub in St Clements Street. It was a brief affair ... she stood him up on their second date. (Who can blame her?)

At Oxford Crown Court in November 75, Bay City Roller Les McKeown was found guilty of assaulting two photographers and causing criminal damage after a gig at the New Theatre. He was fined £750 and sentenced to three months, suspended.

In tragic decline at 30, Bee Gee's brother Andy Gibb died at the John Radcliffe Hospital (March 88).

## SHILLINGFORD

Birthplace of Bonzo Dog Band leader and noted eccentric Viv Stanshall, 21.3.43.

## SHIPTON ON CHERWELL

In March 71, Virgin Records boss Richard Branson purchased the Manor House for £30,000 and turned it into a recording studio. His first signing, Mike Oldfield, spent a year there making Tubular Bells, which fortunately became a massive seller and the cornerstone of the Virgin empire.

**Fairport at The Brasenose**

## THAME

UK residence of the Bee Gees, whose road crew are often to be seen quaffing in the local hostelries.

## UFFINGTON

The White Horse, carved into the hillside off the A 420 was the inspiration for the XTC album English Settlement.

## UPPER HEYFORD

Thirty years before the jets took off for Libya, US Air Force serviceman Johnny Duncan was stationed here. He took advantage of the skiffle boom to reach the top three with Last Train To San Fernando ... then went home to become a country & western star.

## WALLINGFORD

The Springs Hotel, a mock Tudor affair built in 1874, was the late 70s home of Deep Purple singer Ian Gillan. It was he who installed the guitar-shaped swimming pool.

## WATCHFIELD

The site of an August 75 free festival featuring 150 groups (none of which I can recall).

## WOODSTOCK

Not the site of the famous festival (that was in New York State), but Barry Manilow did play at Blenheim Palace in 1984. The gig was a commercial disaster by all accounts.

© Global Antar Archive

# SHROPSHIRE

## LUDLOW

Birthplace of saxplayer Dick Heckstall Smith, 26.9.34 (Graham Bond Organisation/Colosseum).

## OSWESTRY

Birthplace of drummer Alan Whitehead, 24.7.47 (Marmalade).

## SHREWSBURY

Birthplace of singer Ian Hunter, 3.6.46 (Mott The Hoople); drummer Simon Kirke, 28.7.49 (Bad Company).

It was his rejection by a girl called Irene Wilde in Barker Street bus station that made 16 year old Ian Hunter determined to become a rock'n'roll star. (Where are you now, Irene?)

John Peel went to Shrewsbury School (as indeed did Richard Ingrams and William Rushton).

Home of splendidly named new wave group Quality Fish.

T'Pau singer Carol Decker did an art foundation course at college here, and in the summer holidays worked as a lifeguard, teaching toddlers to swim at Shrewsbury Baths.

## TELFORD

In September 48, 14 year old Brian Epstein entered Wrekin College at Wellington.

## WELLINGTON

Carol Decker moved here with her family at the age of 5. Later she went to Wellington Girls' High School.

© Global Anter Archive

**A very old shot of John Peel**

# SOMERSET

## GLASTONBURY

One of the hippie era's great celebrations was the Glastonbury Fayre of June 71. The Pink Fairies, Hawkwind (unveiling Stacia for the first time) and David Bowie were among the entertainers.

## MELLS

A large rambling farmhouse housed a commune which included psychedelic group Magic Muscle and folksinger Keith Christmas.

## MIDSOMER NORTON

Birthplace of Anita Harris, 3.6.44.

## MINEHEAD

The rest of Status Quo first met Rick Parfitt at Butlins in summer 65. Rick was in the Highlights, a one boy/two girl trio. They shared dressing rooms with wrestlers who fixed their fights upfront.

## SHEPTON MALLET

In June 69, some 300,000 fans hit town for the curiously named Bath Festival, held at the Bath and West Showground. Attractions included Led Zeppelin, who were also headliners a year later, along with Pink Floyd, Jefferson Airplane and Country Joe.

Worthy farm at Pilton became the June setting for the annual Glastonbury CND Festival, which always featured interesting acts. (For example: New Order, Aswad and Judy Tzuke in 81; Madness in 86; Elvis Costello in 87).

## STRATTON ON THE FOSSE

Echo & The Bunnymen drummer Pete de Freitas went to Downside Public School.

## TAUNTON

Home of early 70s Transatlantic label group Marsupilami.

## YEOVIL

Birthplace of guitarist Jim Cregan, 9.3.46 (Cockney Rebel, Rod Stewart).

Supertramp lived at Southcombe Farm in late 73, writing Crime Of The Century . . . wherever that is.

The original pyramid stage for the Glastonbury Festival, featuring Traffic, Family & Magic Michael

# Rolling Stone Keith arrested

### By CHRIS HOUSE

ROLLING STONE Keith Richard was today arrested on suspicion of having drugs, 48 hours before the start of the group's sell-out concert at Earl's Court.

Police found a "substance" in his Bentley after the car crashed on the M1 at Newport Pagnell.

Police said Richard appeared to have fallen asleep at the wheel.

The car left the road, went through a barrier and ended up in a field.

A passing motorist called police on one of the motorway "SOS" phones.

Guitarist Richard, 33, was unhurt.

### £50 bail

A Thames Valley police spokesman said that one of the officers called to the scene noticed "a substance in the vehicle and Mr. Richard was arrested on suspicion of being in possession of drugs."

He was taken to Newport Pagnell police station where, it is understood, he was detained for about two hours.

He was then released on £50 bail.

The police spokesman said: "We will not know if there will be any charges until laboratory tests have been carried out and the substance identified."

A lawyer representing the star said today: "The car was badly damaged but neither Mr. Richard nor any of his passengers were hurt.

**KEITH RICHARD on stage in Stafford last night.**
*Picture by DAVID THORPE*

"He wil return to the police station when the results of the analysis are known."

The Stones are currently on a sell-out tour of Britain.

Last night they appeared at New Bingley Hall in Stafford where they were given a rapturous reception by 10,000 fans.

*JOHN BLAKE, who was with the Stones at Stafford, writes:*

After a spectacularly successful show the Stones threw a backstage party for dozens of people who had helped them—including more than 20 local police officers and detectives.

Keith sat quietly in a corner most of the time.

And fellow Stone Ronnie Wood told me: "Keith hasn't been to bed for four days. It's amazing he's still able to stand."

# GARY'S BIG AIR SCARE

**By SUN REPORTER**

POP star Gary Numan came in on a wing and a prayer when his private plane ran out of fuel, it was revealed yesterday.

The singer was forced to land on a busy road . . . even though he **SHOULD** have had enough petrol left to fly on for another 1½ hours.

## First

His single-engined Cessna could have dropped at any moment towards the end of its journey from the south of France to Southampton last year, according to a report.

The RAF Institute of Aviation said that Gary had given orders for re-fuelling in France — and that the empty tank "had not been satisfactorily explained."

Aircraft-mad Gary, dubbed the Biggles of the pop world, was flying back from a Cannes music festival with his dad and a friend when the near-disaster happened.

Gary's biggest hit – page 37

# Bill Haley's COLUMN
## as told to NOEL WHITCOMB
# THE WELCOME of MY LIFE!

*KING' HALEY and kisscurl*

**F**ANTABULOUS—that's the only word for it—fantabulous.

I'd heard we were going to get a welcome. And we have enjoyed some pretty crowded receptions in the past. But never in my life have I seen anything like the razzmatazz of a welcome we got at Southampton yesterday.

We were amazed and overjoyed. In act—you really rocked and rolled us ! It had all been so quiet on the ship that—even though Noel had warned me here would be what he called "A 'erby Day turn-out"—we weren't really prepared for the fantastic scenes we saw.

If this was Derby Day—that must be some horse race !

We had assembled with our baggage by the ship's gangway ready to disembark when I got my first surprise. There was a mighty roar that I thought must be the ship's hooter. Then suddenly I realised it wasn't. THEY were shouting "Haley" from the shore.

From that moment on it was unbelievable—sheer hellzapoppin.

### Dig that Car !

When we got out of the Customs shed I thought we were never going to make the car—there were so many people on top of it.

We certainly nearly had to dig that car—it sure was buried ! Then, when we thought we'd seen everything—the real onslaught began.

Noel muttered that this must be the biggest thing since the Charge of the Light Brigade — and I wouldn't argue about that. I figure the Light Brigade must have had it easy compared with us.

A vast concourse of people with bands, banners, streamers, stickers, badges, balloons—they all whirled together into a fantastic kaleidoscope of colour and noise as we suddenly started floating towards the train.

And I do mean floating ! My feet didn't touch the ground for fifty yards —I was just carried along on the tide of people.

I lost my gloves, the buttons off my overcoat, and a little case with my overnight gear in it. But that didn't bother me. They made good souvenirs for some of the fans.

What did worry me considerably is that I thought for a moment I'd lost Cuppy, my wife.

She's not used to this sort of thing, and it can be pretty frightening for a girl. Fortunately she was all right—

# STAFFORDSHIRE

## BURSLEM

Birthplace of bassplayer Ian Kilminster – better known as Lemmy from Motorhead.

## BURTON UPON TRENT

Birthplace of Joe Jackson, 11.8.55.

## CANNOCK

Birthplace of drummer Ric Lee, 20.10.45 (Ten Years After).

The town's first star was Tanya Day, early 60s chanteuse.

Trapeze were formed locally in 1968.

Hottest export of the late 80s was Balaam & the Angel.

## HANLEY

Birthplace of vocalist Biff Byford, 15.1.52 (Saxon).

Victoria Hall was the start of the Kalin Twins/Cliff Richard package tour of October 58.

The Place in Bryan Street was one of the first and most famous rhythm & blues clubs in Britain, presenting everyone from John Mayall to Derek & The Dominoes. "If it's going to happen, it'll happen at the Place first" said the posters.

## LICHFIELD

Local blues group The Broom Dusters split up in 1967, when leader Jeremy Spencer helped form Fleetwood Mac.

## NEWCASTLE UNDER LYME

The town's most celebrated group was The Cyril Dagworth Players, featuring David (Isn't She Lovely?) Parton.

Nearby Madeley was the venue for the Hollywood Rock Festival of May 70 (so called because of adjacent thicket of holly trees), which featured Traffic, Colosseum, Quintessence and the UK debut of The Grateful Dead.

One of Britain's first folk festivals was held at Keele University in 1965. Former Keele students include Jem Finer of The Pogues.

Bridge Street Arts Centre was one of the best venues in the area. Now an aerobics centre.

## ROCESTER

Birthplace of drummer Graeme Edge, 30.3.42 (Moody Blues).

## STAFFORD

Birthplace of Pete Haycock, 4.4.52 (founder of Climax Blues Band, the city's most famous group ... he still lives here); Miranda Joyce, 26.7.62 (Belle Stars).

Bingley Hall was a major gig in the 70s; Keith Richards crashed his car driving home from there in May 76, and Bowie filled it for three nights in June 78. Rush played there in July 79; Police in December 80. In September 81, it was the venue for the Futurama Festival headlined by Simple Minds.

## STOKE ON TRENT

Birthplace of Mike Wilsh, 21.7.45 (Four Pennies); singer Sylvia Tatler (The Silkie); Jem Finer, 20.7.55 (The Pogues).

First local group to make it out were The Marauders, who scored a minor hit with That's What I Want in August 63. Hipster Image were produced by Alan Price, but failed to make it.

The Sutherland Brothers are from the council estate in Blythe Bridge, and still live in the area. Iain has a recording studio in Longton, while Gavin (who went to Moorside School and wrote Rod Stewart's hit Sailing) leads local band The Rockets.

Any Trouble guitarist Chris Parks went to Stoke Poly; the rest of the group were either at college or school here too. Most of their early gigs were in the Potteries.

Kevin Godley (10cc) went to Stoke Art College.

Local punks Discharge attracted national notoriety.

## TAMWORTH

Birthplace of guitarist Dave Clempson, 5.9.49. He made waves leading the local Bakerloo Blues Line, which split up when he joined Colosseum. He became even more famous in Humble Pie.

# SUFFOLK

Stafford continued...............

Former leader of the Teardrop Explodes, Julian Cope grew up here ... his albums are peppered with local references.

## UTTOXETER

Iain Sutherland was educated at Uttoxeter Grammar.

**The Bible from Bury**

## BURY ST EDMUNDS

Boo Hewerdine from The Bible used to work in the warehouse at Andy's Records.

## IPSWICH

In March 58, Buddy Holly & The Crickets played the Gaumont, and in Jan 60, the same venue saw the start of the Gene Vincent/Eddie Cochran package tour.

Local 60s groups included The Sullivan James Band (Parlophone) and Nix Nomads (HMV).

Brian Eno was a student at Ipswich Art School.

In the early 80s, Nik Kershaw worked in the DHSS office while playing in semi-pro groups like Half Pint Hog and Fusion.

## WOODBRIDGE

Birthplace of Brian Eno, 15.5.48 (Roxy Music, etc); Nick Lowe, 25.3.49 (Brinsley Schwarz, Rockpile, solo).

**The Brothers Sutherland**

**Julian Cope caught in a Polesworth cemetry near Tamworth**

© Chrysalis Records

© Global Antar Archive

# SURREY

(including boroughs in the Greater London area, but with Surrey postal addresses)

## ALBURY

In September 73, Bad Company held their first rehearsals at Albury village hall, not far from Guildford.

## ASHSTEAD

Birthplace of Cream lyricist and bizarro popster poet Pete Brown, 25.12.40.

## CAMBERLEY

Birthplace of lyricist Richard Stilgoe, 28.3.43.

Graham Parker grew up in Deep Cut and called his first group The Deep Cut Three. Their big gig was Black Down Youth Club. Next hot local group was The Members, who fingered the area in their 79 hit The Sound Of The Suburbs.

The town's major export was Bros — late 80s teen heart throbs who lived on the Heatherside estate and went to Collingwood County Secondary in Kingston Road. Their plans for world domination were hatched in various pubs, including the Wheatsheaf, the White Hart and the Kings Head. They were also said to frequent the Monday night disco at the Civic Hall and Pantiles night club on the London Road.

## CARSHALTON

Cliff Richard lived here for 18 months and attended Stanley Park Road Primary School. Because of his tan, acquired during his childhood in India (born Lucknow, 14.10.40), schoolmates called him Nigger.

Mud got together in Carshalton in February 66.

## CATERHAM

Just prior to joining The Damned, Rat Scabies was appearing in the Yorkshire Theatre Company's production of Puss In Boots.

## CHERTSEY

It was here, on the Thames, that former Bonzo Dog Band leader Vivian Stanshall lived on a houseboat . . . before it sank with all his possessions in 1984.

Keith Moon lived here in the early 70s, at Tara House — where his Rolls Royce Silver Cloud ended up in the lake. Kevin Godley purchased it from him in 1974.

The video for Ten Pole Tudor's Wunderbar was shot in Thorpe Park.

## CHESSINGTON

On moving from Dublin to England, The Boomtown Rats took over a mansion said to have been a gift from Henry VIII to one of his mistresses.

The video for Give Me Your Heart Tonight by Shakin' Stevens was filmed at Chessington Zoo.

## CHIDDINGFOLD

It was here that The Stranglers lived while plotting to ride the punk boom to glory.

## COBHAM

In June 70, Moody Blues singer Ray Thomas bought a palatial residence for £16,000!

## CROYDON

Birthplace of Matthew Fisher, 7.3.46 (Procol Harum); Kirsty MacColl, 10.10.59 (sang with local punk group Drug Addix before going solo on Stiff).

It was in Croydon in 1952 that 16 year old Christopher Craig shot policeman Sidney Miles: the subject of Elvis Costello's song Let Him Dangle.

Eden Kane's first public appearance was at Croydon Youth Club in 1959.

The Star Hotel at 296 London Road, Broad Green was part of the Crawdaddy R&B circuit in the 60s.

The Greyhound pub in Park Lane was a major gig during the 70s, when the likes of David Bowie and Genesis played there. The Electric Light Orchestra made their debut there in 1972 and on their hit Saturday Gigs, Mott The Hoople imply that playing there was the turning point of their career.

Punk entrepreneur Malcolm McLaren and punk designer Jamie Reid both went to Croydon Art School, as did Kinks leader Ray Davies and blues producer Mike Vernon. Ian Dury's first band, Kilburn & The High Roads, made their debut there in December 71.

Fairfield Hall has long been a prestigious concert venue. It was here that Rat Scabies, employed as a porter, first

# surrey

**Elstead**

**The Fairfield Hall with its famous toilets**

## EAST MOLESEY

Birthplace of Kinks drummer Mick Avory, 15.2.44.

## ELSTEAD

In the early 70s, Stephen Stills lived here – in a haunted mansion previously owned by Peter Sellers and Ringo Starr.

## EPSOM

Birthplace of Petula Clark, 15.11.33; producer Glyn Johns, 15.2.42.

As a schoolboy, Jimmy Page lived in Miles Road.

In January 66, George Harrison and Patti Boyd were married at Epsom Register Office.

Geoff McClelland and Chris Dawsett, founders of John's Children, met up at Epsom Art School. Richard Butler of The Psychedelic Furs was a later pupil.

## DORKING

Simon Napier Bell agreed to manage John's Children after seeing them play at a barbecue at Burford Bridge (summer 66).

Having dropped out of school, Genesis moved into a cottage in Dorking (owned by their roadie's parents) to write their first Charisma album Trespass.

## ESHER

In July 64, George Harrison paid twenty thousand pounds for Kinfauns, a noble residence on the Claremont Park Estate. It was here that he was busted for possession of cannabis possession in March 69.

met Captain Sensible, working as a toilet cleaner. Both resolved to improve their situations and formulated plans to launch The Damned.

Strength are late 80s hopefuls on Arista.

## EAST HORSLEY

The Psychedelic Furs got started here – at Richard and Tim Butler's home.

## EWELL

Elvis Costello's pub-rock group Flip City played their last gig at North East Surrey College of Technology – supporting Climax Blues Band in Dec 75.

surrey

**The Wooden Bridge Hotel**

## FARNHAM

Pink Floyd drummer Nick Mason was educated at Frensham Heights public school.

## GODALMING

Pupils at Charterhouse public school sidelined academic pursuits to form Genesis in 1967. Their first producer was another Charterhouse graduate, Jonathan King.

Splendidly named Charterhouse pupil Rivers Job (originally in school group The Anon with Mike Rutherford) went on to play bass in the Savoy Brown Blues Band.

## GREAT BOOKHAM

Birthplace of Roger Waters, 9.9.44 (Pink Floyd).

## GUILDFORD

Birthplace of Tony Blackburn, 29.1.43 (at Mt Alvernia Nursing Home); Mike Rutherford, 2.10.50 (Genesis).

Local bands include The Stormsville Shakers (60s), Camel (70s progressive), The Stranglers (originally known as The Guildford Stranglers) and The Vapors (80s).

Rather less famous are myriad late 70s hopefuls like House, The Famous Rondini Brothers, Poker and Head Waiter.

Local residents include Jackie Lynton (Savoy Brown), Mel Collins (King Crimson), Philip Goodhand Tait (songwriter) and Ray Dorset (Mungo Jerry).

Led Zeppelin made their world debut at the University of Surrey on 15.10.68.

Eric Clapton, who lives nearby, often started or finished his UK tours at Guildford Civic Hall — primarily so that his granny could come and see him. His very first group, The Roosters, used to rehearse at the Wooden Bridge Hotel in 1963.

In 1978, The Sex Pistols and The Stranglers were both banned from playing at the aforementioned Civic Hall.

The promotional video for Eurythmics' Sweet Dreams Are Made Of This was shot in fields just outside the town.

## HERSHAM

Truculent local punk Jimmy Pursey put the last syllable of his town into Sham 69.

The funeral of pop manager and multi-millionaire Gordon Mills took place at St Peters Church.

## surrey

### HORLEY

Birthplace of saxplayer Dick Morrissey, 9.5.40 (If, Morrissey Mullen).

### KEW

The Boat House was a popular early 60s gig.

### KINGSTON UPON THAMES

Birthplace of Richard Butler, 5.6.56 (Psychedelic Furs leader).

Kingston Art School alumni include Sandy Denny, Jimmy Page, John Renbourn, Keith Relf and Eric Clapton. Angela Bowie and Jona Lewie studied at Kingston Poly.

Plans to form The Yardbirds (originally The Metropolis Blues Quartet) were hatched in the bar of the Railway Hotel, Norbiton.

Sandy Denny made her debut at The Barge, a floating folk club moored at Townsend Wharf. It was a gig here that led directly to John Martyn getting signed up by Island.

### LEATHERHEAD

Most celebrated local group were John's Children, whose manager (Simon Napier Bell) actually bought them a club ... the Bluesette, a converted nissen hut in Bridge Street. Group members included Andy Ellison (later of Jet and Radio Stars) and Marc Bolan.

In January 78, Police cut their first album at Nigel Gray's Surrey Sound Studio at 70 Kingston Road. It cost £2000 and made millions.

Surrey Sound

### MITCHAM

The Game were 60s schoolkids managed by Kenny Lynch. Rather more successful was another local bunch, Mud.

### MORDEN

The Yardbirds made their first recordings at R.G.Jones Studio in February 64.

### REDHILL

Birthplace of organist Roy Lines, 25.11.43 (original line-up of Status Quo).

### REIGATE

Manfred Mann singer Mike D'Abo was born at nearby Bletchworth, 1.3.44.

Home of Third Ear Band leader Glen Sweeney. His 50s skiffle group, The Anacondas, had a residency at the Bridge House.

### RICHMOND

Birthplace of singer Keith Relf, 22.3.43 (Yardbirds).

During the late 50s, the focal point for the area's large art school/beatnik contingent was L'Auberge coffee bar, next to the Odeon.

It was during their Sunday residency at the Crawdaddy Club, held at the Station Hotel, that The Rolling Stones were discovered by future manager Andrew Oldham — in April 63. Shortly afterwards, club owner Giorio Gomelsky moved the Crawdaddy to the clubhouse of Richmond Athletic Club on the A 316. The Yardbirds, T-Bones and Authentics were early favourites. (The Station Hotel was revamped as The Bull And Bush).

Eric Clapton came to join The Yardbirds in October 63, when they were rehearsing at the South Western Hotel (opposite the Station Hotel ... now Drummonds).

The first five annual National Jazz Blues & Rock Festivals (precursors to Reading Festival) were held at the Richmond Athletic Ground — 1961 to 1965. The first two were all jazz; Cyril Davies and The Stones crept onto the third; ten R&B groups made the fourth; by 1965 R&B held sway.

In September 72, Ron Wood paid a reputed £140,000 for The Wick on Richmond Hill — previously owned by film star John Mills.

Home base for 80s innovators The Lemon Kittens.

### RIPLEY

Eric Clapton was born (30.3.45) and raised at 1 The Green. He went to Ripley Primary and St Bedes Secondary Modern.

### SURBITON

Birthplace of Yardbird Chris Dreja, 11.11.46, who attended Hollyfield Road Secondary Modern.

# surrey

The Red Lion, Sutton, Scene of very early Stones gigs

Petula Clark went to St Bernard's School.

The Toby Jug at 1 Hook Rise, Tolworth was a prestige gig during the 60s and early 70s. Captain Beefheart played there in 68 and Bowie started his Ziggy Stardust tour there in February 72. For a while, John Lennon's father Fred was a barman there.

## SUTTON

Birthplace of Clark Datchler, 27.3.64 (Johnny Hates Jazz).

Roulettes guitarist Peter Thorp and jazz-rock saxplayer Dick Morrisey were educated at Sutton High School.

Some of The Rolling Stones earliest gigs were those they promoted themselves at the Red Lion pub.

## WALLINGTON

Birthplace of guitarist Jeff Beck, 24.6.44.

Wallington Public Hall in Stafford Road housed the Kazoo Club, a 60s venue whose resident group was Peter Frampton & The Herd.

## WALTON ON THAMES

Birthplace of Gary Taylor (The Herd).

## WEYBRIDGE

Home base for The Nashville Teens — heroes of Tobacco Road, whose punitive recording contract gave them less than one penny per record sold!

In June 64, John Lennon paid twenty grand for Kenwòod, and a year later Ringo paid 37 grand for Sunny Heights — palatial houses in St Georges Hill. Other residents on this exclusive estate have included Cliff Richard, Tom Jones, Gordon Mills (Tom's manager), and Mike Read ... while Gilbert O'Sullivan lived in nearby Byfleet.

## WINDLESHAM

Birthplace of Wham! founder Andrew Ridgeley, 26.1.63.

## WOKING

Birthplace of Art Sharp, 26.5.41 (Nashville Teens); rocker and author Ian Whitcomb, 10.7.41 (who hit the US top ten with You Turn Me On in 1965); Mark Wynter, 29.1.43; Billie Davis, 22.12.45 (60s poppet and Jet Harris escort); Martin Stone,11.12.46 (Chilli Willi); Rick Parfitt, 12.10.48 (Status Quo ... in Church Street); Peter Gabriel, 13.2.50; Bruce Foxton, 1.9.55, Paul Buckler, 6.12.55, and Paul Weller, 25.5.58 (all three in The Jam).

The Jam all attended Sheerwater Comprehensive. Weller attended Maybury Primary and lived in Stanley Road, where the group used to rehearse. Buckler went to Goldsworth Primary and lived in Church Street. Foxton went to Sheerwater Junior and lived on the Maybury estate. Strategies were discussed at the Princess and the Wheatsheaf, and early gigs were at Sheerwater Youth Club.

Badfinger star Pete Ham hung himself at his Woking home in April 75.

## VIRGINIA WATER

Elton John, Gary Numan, Five Star and bandleader Ted Heath are among pop stars to have purchased mansions in the locality.

Holloway Sanitorium was the setting for two chart topping videos ... Goody Two Shoes by Adam & The Ants and Total Eellpse Of The Heart by Bonnie Tyler.

# EAST SUSSEX

## BODIAM

Adam & The Ants filmed their Ant Rap video at Bodiam Castle.

## BRIGHTON

Birthplace of drummer Steve Ferrone, 25.4.50 (Average White Band).

1956 saw the first local skiffle groups – The James Boys and The Checkers – followed by the first wave of rock'n'roll groups: Bobby Sansom & The Giants, Ray DuVal & The Downbeats, Gene Coburn & The Chimes, Count Downe & The Zeros.

Sixties groups included The Motion, The Untamed and The Web.

A profusion of venues/meeting places included the Whiskey A Go Go coffee bar in Queens Square, the Starlight Rooms under the now demolished Montpelier Hotel in Montpelier Road, the Box disco above the Wimpy Bar in Western Road, the California and Zodiac coffee bars in West Street, Tiffanies coffee bar opposite the Kemp Town Odeon, the Mallaca in Duke Street, Jimmy's in Steine Street, and the Zodiac in St James Street.

The Hippodrome in Middle Street (going since the 40s) presented The Beatles and Stones before becoming a television studio and then a bingo and social club. Sixties package shows also visited the Essoldo Cinema in North Street, and the Top Rank opened in 1965.

In May 64, mods and rockers had some of their bloodiest skirmishes on the seafront. Mods used to go to the Florida Rooms (adjoining the Aquarium), which housed the Cadillac Club. They would pick up girls and throw them in the sea! Pilled up, they would swagger through the allnighters, before zooming back to London on their Vespas.

The Dome was a hot 60s venue. In May 65, Britain's one and only National Festival Of Song was held there. Kenny Lynch won, Lulu came second, and the event lost £1500.

In the early 60s, Brighton beach was a favourite destination for London's coffee bar cowboys, beatniks and CND devotees ... including the likes of Long John Baldry, Rod Stewart and Wally Whyton. Twenty five years later, that same strand provided the setting for the amorous interlude recounted in Marillion's Three Boats Down From The Candy – the Candy being the only one with its name painted on the side.

In the early 80s, Brighton beach also provided a stage for Pookiesnackenburger, a bunch of local buskers who soon graduated to Covent Garden piazzas and a Stiff recording contract.

It was while tickling the ivories in a Brighton seafront bar called Harrison's that local bank clerk Keith Emerson was spotted by a representative of R&B group Gary Farr & The T Bones, who persuaded him to jack in his job and join them in their quest for fame. The group never found it, but Emerson did – a few years later when he started The Nice and ELP.

The T-Bones were managed by Gary's brother Rikki, who also operated the Perfumed Garden club at the Florida Rooms. He later mounted the Isle of Wight festivals.

In 1974, the Eurovision Song Contest was held at the Dome ... Abba won with Waterloo.

Despite its size and status, Brighton has produced few bands of national repute. The Piranhas looked set to establish themselves in new wave terms but ultimately succeeded only with novelty revivals of Tom Hark and Zambesi. The Amazorblades, The Depressions, and The Lambrettas cut a few records ... but what of Peter & The Test Tube Babies, The Parrots, Spoons, Krakatoa, Lodestone, Beggars Death, Joby & The Hooligans, The Chefs, Wrist Action, Nicky & The Dots, No Exit, The Vandells, and The Dodgems?

Vi Subversa and her Poison Girls made it to London.

The Jam played their last gig at the Brighton Centre in December 82. Bruce Springsteen, The Who and other major league acts also played this 5000 seater.

Other local venues include the Dome, the Poly, the Sussex Sports Centre in Queens Square, the Hotel Metropole, the university, the Zap Club, the New Regent in West Street, the Buccaneer in Madeira Drive, and the Alhambra – a great seafront pub/punk rock gig, now demolished.

The punk scene centred on the Resource Centre in North Road, a shabby converted church hall. The Stranglers (including local lad Dave Greenfield) used to rehearse here.

Sherry's Disco in West Street presented Culture Club before revamping as the Pink Coconut.

Several bands got started at the university of Sussex at Brighton, but few turned pro ... late 60s blues group

## east sussex

Cotchford Farm & ill placed swimming pool

Luxford House, Crowborough

Jellybread did, and so did Affinity (early 70s jazz rock), but the hottest success was Billy Idol — former philosophy student (it says here!)

Jellybread keyboard player Pete Wingfield became versatile singer, session man and producer.

The Darts were originally students from the Poly, as was Harvey Goldsmith, whose first promotion was Deep Purple and Jellybread at the college's Cockroft Hall in 1969.

Attrix Records was based in Sydney Street in the late 70s and Creation boss Alan McGee moved here from East Kilbride. One of his acts is Brighton band Pacific.

Local resident Anne Nightingale worked on the Brighton Argus before graduating to Radio One.

## BURWASH

When The Who made it big, Roger Daltrey bought Holmshurst Manor in East Burwash — a Jacobean mansion set in 35 acres.

## CROWBOROUGH

Luxford House was a country house owned by Charisma boss Tony Stratton Smith. It was here that Genesis wrote and rehearsed their Nursery Cryme album, and that guitarist Bert Jansch recorded with producer Mike Nesmith.

## EAST HOATHLEY

Birthplace of keyboard player Tony Banks, 27.3.50 (Genesis).

## EASTBOURNE

Birthplace of Leapy Lee, 2.7.42.

It was in Eastbourne that Tony Stratton Smith first saw Genesis, soon to become the flagship of his Charisma label.

Ultravox shot their video for Reap The Wild Wind at nearby Beachy Head.

## ETCHINGHAM

Local residents Ashley Hutchings and Shirley Collins formed the Etchingham Steam Band in 1974 — precursor to The Albion Band.

## east sussex

The Half Moon, Plumpton

## HALLAND

In September 67, Rolling Stone Charlie Watts bought Peckham's, a 13th century farmhouse with a 40 acre spread. His previous residence had been The Old Brewery House at Southover.

## HARTFIELD

In the early hours of 3.7.69, the unconscious body of former Rolling Stone Brian Jones was recovered from the swimming pool of his country residence, Cotchford Farm – once owned by Winnie The Pooh author A.A. Milne. He was dead by the time medical assistance arrived.

## HASTINGS

Birthplace of Suggs, 13.1.61 (Madness).

The video for David Bowie's 1980 chart topper Ashes To Ashes was shot here with extras recruited from Blitz in Covent Garden.

The Teenbeats were local late 70s mods.

## HOVE

Ringo Starr and Maureen Cox had their honeymoon in Hove.

## NEWHAVEN

Birthplace of drummer Nigel Glockler, 24.1.53 (Saxon); Eric Goulden, 18.5.54 (better known as Stiff recording artiste Wreckless Eric).

## PLUMPTON

In its ninth and tenth years, the National Jazz Blues & Rock Festival moved to Plumpton Racecourse. In August 69, The Nice were accompanied by a 40 piece orchestra, and the landlord of the Sun on Plumpton Green complained to the press that punters had stolen every glass in the place. Though it began as a jazz festival, practically all trace of jazz had been phased out by 1970.

In 1972, Jimmy Page bought the 18th century manor house, set in 50 acres. One of the few times he played locally was in September 77 when he and Ron Wood jammed with Arms And Legs (led by the unknown Joe Jackson) at the Half Moon pub.

## RYE

Southern residence of the McCartney family.

# WEST SUSSEX

## BOGNOR REGIS

Birthplace of Shadows rhythm guitarist Bruce Welch, 2.11.41.

David Bowie and Elton John first met at Bognor's Shoreline Club in June 66. Elton was in Bluesology, backing Long John Baldry, and support group was David Bowie & the Buzz.

Elaine Paige's father was an estate agent in Bognor.

Staa Marx carried local hopes for new wave recognition.

## CHICHESTER

In June 67, Mick Jagger and Keith Richards found themselves in the dock at West Sussex Quarter Sessions defending drugs charges (see West Wittering). They were found guilty but jail sentences were quashed after widespread indignation.

## CRAWLEY

Robert Smith, Lol Tolhurst and Michael Dempsey all went to Notre Dame Middle School and St Wilfred's Comprehensive, where they formed The Cure — originally known as Easy Cure. They had their first rehearsal at St Edwards Church Hall in Jan 76 and made their debut in nearby Worth in Dec 76.

## EAST GRINSTEAD

Cutting Crew leader Nick Van Eede went to Imberhorne School, having been born in the Ashdown Forest on 14.6.58.

## FULKING

Nothing happened here — I just like the name.

(above) The caravan site at Selsey Bill

(below) Paul Weller, on holiday, about to write the fabulous Eton Rifles

## HORSHAM

Home of aptly named 60s group The Beat Merchants.

## SELSEY BILL

Paul Weller wrote Eton Rifles while on holiday in his parents' caravan.

## SHOREHAM BY SEA

Birthplace of Leo Sayer, 21.5.48.

In the early 60s, Rod Stewart was among a bunch of beatniks who used a derelict barge, moored on the estuary, as a refuge ... much to the consternation of the local establishment, always anxious to oust them.

## WEST WITTERING

In February 1967, 15 police officers burst into Redlands, the country home of Keith Richards. They arrested the owner, and his guest Mick Jagger, on charges relating to drug possession and use. In July 73, Redlands was badly damaged by fire.

Local group The Mars Bars were late 80s hopefuls.

## WORTHING

The Mexican Hat Club was the place to be in the 60s; The Otis Men were the hippest band.

The hippie festival Phun City was held at Ecclesden Common in July 70. MC5 topped the bill in their UK debut.

Several London pub-rock bands recorded in Pebble Beach Studios at 12 South Farm Road.

# TYNE AND WEAR

## BLAYDON

I seem to remember that one of Eric Burdon's relatives wrote Blaydon Races.

## DUNSTON

Birthplace of singer Brian Johnson, 5.10.47 (Geordie, AC/DC).

## GATESHEAD

Birthplace of Animals drummer John Steel 4.2.41.

## GOSFORTH

Mark and David Knopfler both went to Gosforth Grammar. The Dire Straits song Down To The Waterline is about the Tyne.

Sting's band Last Exit had a 1976 residency at the Gosforth Hotel.

## JARROW

Birthplace of singer John Miles, 23.4.49 (mid 70s hits).

## NEWCASTLE UPON TYNE

Birthplace of Hank Marvin, Britain's most influential guitarist ever, 28.10.41. He lived at 138 Stanhope Street, and was educated at Todds Nook School, Snow Street School and Rutherford Grammar — where he met Bruce Welch. The pair of them united in The Railroaders Skiffle Group, before moving to London to seek fame and fortune in April 58.

Also the birthplace of Chas Chandler, 18.12.38, and Eric Burdon, 4.5.41 (both of The Animals); Lee Jackson, 8.1.43

(The Nice); singer Alan Hull, 20.2.45 (Lindisfarne); drummer Paul Thompson, 13.5.51 (Roxy Music).

As a schoolboy, Bruce Welch lived in a flat above Nazam's Fish and Chip Shop at 126 Elswick Road.

The Newcastle Empire hosted a string of rock'n'roll stars, from Charlie Gracie on up. Guitarist Bert Weedon made his variety debut there in 1959 ... at age 38!

The Odeon was another package tour venue: The Stones, Bo Diddley and the Everly Brothers played there in 1963.

Meanwhile, the City Hall's stage has seen everyone from Buddy Holly (March 58) to Bad Company, who made their debut there in March 74. It was here also that Andy Summers impersonated the indisposed Mike Oldfield for a performance of Tubular Bells in Autumn 75. Ironically, the support group was Sting's Last Exit.

Students passing through Newcastle University have included Bryan Ferry and John Porter (they formed soul/R&B group The Gas Board here and were later reunited in Roxy Music), Wilko Johnson (Dr Feelgood), and John Walters (once trumpeter in the Alan Price Set, now Radio One producer and jovial chatterbox).

Lee Jackson went to St Mary's Technical School — the very place that Stewart Copeland first saw Sting, playing with Last Exit in December 76.

A vibrant club/pub scene has always thrown up interesting groups: The Animals put Newcastle on the international map in 1964, while The Von Dykes (with Lee Jackson, later in The Nice) and The Junco Partners (with producer Bob Sargeant) found only localised success. The Gamblers (originally seen as Animals rivals) became Billy Fury's backing group after the Tornados. The Chosen Few contained Alan Hull (later of Lindisfarne), Mickey Gallagher and John Turnbull (later in Ian Dury's Blockheads); they had residencies at the long-gone Manhole and Key clubs. Popluar in the late 60s were Skip Bifferty, led by Graham Bell. And whatever became of Shorty & Them?

The most famous 60s venue was the Club A Go Go. Home of The Animals, it presented every group from the Yardbirds to Hendrix. No alcohol was served in the Young Set room, but they had booze and gambling until 3am in the Jazz Lounge, where The Animals would play for up to five hours a night. That and sister club the Downbeat were owned and operated by Mike Jeffries — later manager of The Animals and Hendrix.

In the early 70s came Geordie, who made national waves. Their singer Brian Johnson was reduced to doing vacuum cleaner ads when AC/DC revitalised him.

Later in the 70s came a whole raft of new bands ... The Young Bucks, Penetration, The Carpettes, Neon, and Last Exit — led by Sting.

The early 80s saw the arrival of Punishment Of Luxury (arty farty progressive), Blind Fury, Raven (both HM),

# tyne and wear

Wavis O'Shave, Arthur 2-Stroke, Erogenous Zones, and The Noise Toys. Later in the decade came Pop Dick & Harry, The Skywalkers, The Blues Burglars, The R&B Rockers, The Bats, and The Tribe Of Toffs, who reached the 1989 top twenty with their novel John Kettley Is A Weather Man.

Look out for Bob Smeaton & The Loud Guitars, Ian McCallum, The Dead Flowers, Soviet France, And All Because the Lady Loves, and Dum Dum Score.

Currently happening places include the Bridge Hotel in Castle Square (home of the Jumping Jive Club); the Mayfair in Newgate Street; the Playhouse Theatre in the Haymarket; the Cornerhouse in Heaton Road (pub); the Jewish Mother in Leazes Lane (blues/R&B pub); the Broken Doll in Blenheim Street (pub with good R&B); the Riverside in Melbourne Street (club and studio complex)... and loads more; the whole city appears to be jumping!

Owned by AC/DC man Brian Johnson, Lynx Studio is the town's hottest. Producer Dave Brewis was/is also in The Kane Gang (who made their debut at local Tiffany's in December 83), early stars of the Kitchenware label, which operates from St Thomas Street Workshops. Their first signing was the local Hurrah! in 1982.

Many songs have been written about the locality. Lindisfarne's Fog On The Tyne was the biggest selling album of 1972. The Nice recorded an album inspired by the Five Bridges spanning the Tyne.

In January 88, the Bucks Fizz tour bus crossed onto the wrong side of the Great North Road and crashed headlong into a lorry. Singer Mike Nolan was badly hurt.

## NORTH SHIELDS

Birthplace of guitarist Hilton Valentine, 22.5.43 (Animals ... he lived at 56 Church Street); bass player Rod Clements, 17.11.47, and drummer Ray Laidlaw, 28.5.48 (both Lindisfarne); Neil Tennant, 10.7.54 (Pet Shop Boys).

A good current venue is the Wolsington House.

## SOUTH SHIELDS

In May 57, Hank Marvin's Crescent City Group won the North East Skiffle competition, held at the Pier Pavilion.

The Angelic Upstarts grew up on the Brockley Whims estate. Their stage set resembled a dungeon and gigs were terrifying.

## SUNDERLAND

Birthplace of guitarist George Bellamy, 8.10.41 (Tornados); guitarist Mick Grabham, 1948 (Procol Harum); guitarist Dave Stewart 9.9.52 (Longdancer, Tourists, Eurythmics).

Tommy Steele made his variety debut at the Empire Theatre in November 56.

Bryan Ferry's first group, The Banshees were based here. (Avid fan Siouxsie adopted the name!)

Battleaxe were early 80s heavy metal heroes.

## TYNEMOUTH

Birthplace of guitarist Simon Cowe, 1.4.48 (Lindisfarne); guitarist Andy Taylor, 16.2.61 (Duran Duran); Johny Brown (singer with the Band of Holy Joy).

Sting lived on the Marden Farm estate and was married to actress Frances Tomelty at St Oswins Roman Catholic Church, Front Street, in May 76.

## WALKER

On the b-side of their first single, The Animals covered an American hit by Timmy Shaw, Gonna Send You Back To Georgia. They recorded it as Gonna Send You Back To Walker — a Newcastle suburb!

## WALLSEND

Birthplace of harmonica player Ray Jackson, 12.12.48 (Lindisfarne); Gordon Sumner, better known as Sting, 2.10.51 (Police).

Sting lived in Gerald Street and then in a flat above his father's dairy business in Staion Road. He was educated at St Cuthberts Grammar in Benwell Hill.

The town's oldest pub is also the best current venue — The Ship In The Hole.

## WASHINGTON

Birthplace of Roxy Music leader Bryan Ferry, 26.9.45.

Home of late 80s cult band Martin Stephenson & The Daintees.

## WHITLEY BAY

The Dire Straits song Tunnel Of Love was inspired by fond memories of Spanish City, a seaside funfair.

The Tygers of Pan Tang were late 70s heavy metal grinders ... guitarist John Sykes became a star in Thin Lizzy and Whitesnake.

# tyne and wear

**The Nice 5 Bridges**

**Lindisfarne; Newcastle**

© Global Antar Archive

© Global Antar Archive

**The Spanish City Pleasureland inspired
Dire Straits 'Tunnel of Love'**

# WARWICKSHIRE

## LEAMINGTON SPA

Birthplace of bass player Arthur Grant, 14.5.50 (Edgar Broughton Band).

In the mid 80s, local band Mummy Calls were signed by Geffen, given a huge deal, but split after a couple of singles.

Nearby sleepy Harbury is the home of Rather Records. Swell Maps lived & rehearsed at 'Meadow Bank' in Hall Lane, home for guitarist Nikki Sudden's parents.

Other local groups included The Cult Figures, The Shapes, Bingo Little, The Defendents & Steve Treatment (all late '70's).

## NUNEATON

Birthplace of Peter Becker (Eyeless In Gaza).

When The Rolling Stones played the Co-op Hall in November 63, a contingent of fans threw cream buns at them — covering Charlie Watts, who was not amused!

## RUGBY

Clifton Hall, owned by madcap rock manager Reg Calvert, became an early 60s teen paradise/commune for his stable of would-be stars — including Buddy Britten, Mike West, Tracey Martin, The Fortunes and Gullivers Travels. A bemused Jerry Lee Lewis accepted an invitation to stay overnight.

Local groups include The Mighty Avengers, who cut Jagger/Richard songs produced by Andrew Oldham; Pinkerton's Assorted Colours, who flickered through the charts in 1966; and The Flying Machine (what was left of the Pinkertons), who scored one big US hit.

Home of current indie faves, Spacemen 3.

## STRATFORD-UPON-AVON

Screaming Lord Sutch represented the National Teenage Party in a 1963 by-election — the first of many vain attempts to become a Member Of Parliament. He drew a ton of publicity but only 209 votes.

## TANWORTH-IN-ARDEN

Singer Songwriter Nick Drake lived here with his family.

## WARWICK

Birthplace of brothers Edgar, 24.10.47, and Steve Broughton, 20.5.50 — founders of hot late 60s underground/progressive group The Edgar Broughton Band.

the Flying Machine of Rugby

Swell Maps in their Harbury Kitchen

# WEST MIDLANDS

## A S T O N

Birthplace of guitarist Tony Iommi, 19.2.48; drummer Bill Ward, 5.5.48; singer Ozzy Osbourne, 3.12.48; bass-player Geezer Butler, 17.7.49 — all of whom formed Black Sabbath in 1969. Ozzy lived at 14 Lodge Road. Also the birthplace of guitarist Trevor Burton, 9.3.49 (The Move).

## B I L S T O N

Birthplace of drummer Don Powell, 10.9.46 (Slade). He went to Villiers Road Primary, and then Etheridge Secondary Modern.

Slade regard the Trumpet in the High Street as their local pub.

## B I R M I N G H A M

Birthplace of bass player John Rostill, 16.6.42 (Shadows); songwriters/singers John Carter, 20.10.42, and Ken Lewis, 3.12.42 (Ivy League); keyboard player Mike Pinder, 12.12.42 (Moody Blues); singer Carl Wayne, 18.8.44 (The Move); drummer Bev Bevan, 24.11.44 (The Move); drummer Nick Mason, 27.1.45 (Pink Floyd); guitarist Roy Wood, 8.11.46 (The Move); drummer Mike Kellie, 24.3.47 (Spooky Tooth); bass player Overend Watts, 13.5.47 (Mott The Hoople); bass player Dave Pegg, Nov 47 (Fairport Convention); guitarist Jeff Lynne, 30.12.47 (Idle Race, Move, ELO); bassist Clint Warwick, 25.6.49 (Moody Blues); Steve Winwood, 12.5.48 (Spencer Davis Group, Traffic); Carl Palmer, 20.3.51 (Atomic Rooster, ELP); Andy Cox, 25.1.56, Dave Wakeling, 19.2.57, and Ranking Roger, 21.2.61 (all of the Beat); John Taylor, 2.6.60, and Nick Rhodes, 8.6.62 (both Duran Duran); Roland Gift, 28.5.62 (Fine Young Cannibals); Michael Ball, 27.6.62.

Lol Creme (10cc) and Dave Swarbrick (Fairport) both went to Birmingham College of Art.

Local hero Steve Gibbons has been leading bands since the late 50s. First Brum group to record was Jimmy Powell & The Dimensions (62) and the first to hit the top ten was The Applejacks with Tell Me When (March 64).

Among the millions of bands to get going in the 60s were Big Bertha, The Fortunes, Raymond Froggatt, The Idle Race, The King Bees, Judas Priest, Gerry Levene & The Avengers, Locomotive, The Rockin' Berries, Mike Sheridan & The Nightriders, The Uglys, Carl Wayne & The Vikings, Pat Wayne & The Beachcombers, The Meddy Evils, etc etc etc. Far too many to mention.

Most popular 60s acts were the Spencer Davis Group, who had a residency at the Golden Eagle (obliterated for a car park); The Moody Blues, who used to hang around Jack Woodroff's music shop hoping an agent would come in and offer them a gig; and The Move, who got together at the Cedar Club in Constitution Hill — one of the city's primo haunts.

After gigs, many groups would meet at the Alex Fleur de Lys mobile pie stall at the end of Hill Street, opposite the Alabany Hotel and just along from the Crown pub where Denny Laine & The Diplomats were resident. The Move formed after initial discussions over pie and chips.

In the 70s came E.L.O. (71), Wizzard (72), City Boy, Suburban Studs, Magnum (77), The Beat, Dexy's Midnight Runners, Duran Duran (78), the Au Pairs, the Prefects (79), and more.

In the 80s came UB 40 (80), The Bureau, Nikki Sudden, Orphan, The Maisonettes, Fashion (82), Terry & Gerry, Red Shoes (83), Felt, Swans Way (84), Jaki Graham (85), Great Outdoors, The Boatyman, Fuzzbox, Scarlet Fantastic (86), Hollywood Beyond (87), The Hudson Giants, Dandelion (88), and more.

Schooled in Brookfields after emigrating from St Kitts as a wee lass, Joan Armatrading moved to London to find fame and fortune in 1971.

Venues come and go. At different times the Odeon in New Street and the Town Hall were happening — but the National Exhibition Centre spelt the demise of most large halls. In the 60s, it was essential to play the Ma Regan circuit — run by the venerable woman herself.

Prime 60s blues venue was Henry's Blueshouse at the Crown Hotel in Station Road. Booker was Jim Simpson, later manager of Black Sabbath, owner of Big Bear Records, publisher of Brum Beat.

The Railway pub on Curzon Street was hot in the 70s, when Steve Gibbons was one of the few singers keeping the local scene alive ... but it's now a Mexican restaurant.

Barbarella's in Cumberland Street (now buried under some convention centre site) was the groovy club throughout the 70s, when its cheesy red lighting and sticky carpeting even in-

# west midlands

spired an album track by The Photos. Duran Duran did their earliest gigs there. When it closed down, the new romantic set moved on to the Underworld, the Cedar Club and Hawkins Wine Bar before settling at the Rum Runner (which had been going since the 60s). Housed under Don Berrow's betting shop in Broad Street, it became world famous as Duran Duran's home base and as such remains a shrine for fans, despite having been bulldozed and redeveloped. Simon LeBon's debut with the group was at the Hosteria, a wine bar in Hurst Street.

Rebecca's in Lower Severn Street was a popular new wave venue: the famous Police line-up of Sting/Copeland/Summers made their debut there in August 77. Dexy's Midnight Runners played there when they were still Lucy & The Lovers.

The oldest recording studio in Birmingham is Zella, housed in a rented church hall in Ampton Road. Everyone from The Move to The Maisonettes worked there. Probably more famous is UB 40's studio, the Abattoir (a converted slaughter house) at 92 Fazeley Street, on the canal. Rich Bitch, at 505 Bristol Road, Selly Oak is also currently hot, with the likes of Fuzzbox and Ruby Turner recording there.

Before he zapped into view with Sigue Sigue Sputnik, Martin Degville had a clothes stall in the Oasis Street market. It was known as Degville's Dispensary and Boy George was an occasional sales assistant.

ELO recorded Birmingham Blues; Mott The Hoople cut Birmingham (contrasting Brum with its Alabama namesake).

## BLOXWICH

Ambrose Slade used to play Mossley Youth Club and Noddy Holder used to quaff ale at the Three Men In A Boat in Stephenson Avenue on the Beechdale estate.

## BRIERLEY HILL

Screaming Lord Sutch wiped his nose on the brand new stage curtains at the Town Hall, causing the caretaker to throw a dramatic wobbler.

Brierley Hill Youth Club was a regular venue for The 'N Betweens (later Slade).

## CASTLE BROMWICH

Birthplace of Roger Taylor, 26.4.60 (Duran Duran).

The Bel Air Club was a 60s venue.

## COVENTRY

Birthplace of Frank Ifield, 30.11.37; Hazel O'Connor, 16.5.55.

In May 64, the headmaster of Woodlands Comprehensive suspended eleven boys for sporting Rolling Stones hairstyles. He reinstated them when they compromised with neater Beatles' styles.

The town's first hit group was The Sorrows, who hit with Take A Heart in 65. Five years later, lead singer Don Fardon reached the top three with Indian Reservation. In the mid seventies, Fardon was the landlord of the Alhambra pub, just behind Sainsbury's.

Less successful 60s groups included The Sovereigns, Rufus' Rebels, The Sabres, The Toreadors, and The Peeps (obviously a Lady Godiva allusion).

In June 68, John Lennon and Yoko Ono planted two acorns outside Coventry Cathedral.

Chuck Berry's biggest (and worst) hit, My Ding A Ling, was recorded live at the Lanchester Arts Festival in 1972.

Coventry was the home of the neo-ska 2-Tone sound which swept Britain soon after its inception in February 79. Originators were The Specials (77) and Selecter (79). Fast behind were The Swinging Cats (79). Fun Boy Three and Roddy Radiation & The Tearjerkers were both Specials' descendents.

As a local talent showcase, the General Wolfe on Foleshill Road is still a focal point on the scene. The Dog & Trumpet (next to HMV!) is another good place to see bands.

Horizon Studios in Warwick Road was the home of the 2-Tone sound, while Paul Sampson runs Cabin Studios on London Road.

All but forgotten Coventry groups include The Flys and God's Toys.

More memorable (and more recent) are King, The Primitives, The Giraffes, The Pink Umbrellas, and Julianne Regan from All About Eve.

Among pupils at Coventry Drama school were Paul King (King) and Loz Netto (Sniff & The Tears).

Pupils at Coventry Art School included Specials organiser Jerry Dammers and Hazel O'Connor.

Before becoming lead singer in Selecter, Essex-born Pauline Black was studying biochemistry at Lanchester Poly. She also worked in the radiography unit at Coventry Hospital.

As lead singer in The Reluctant Stereotypes, Paul King played his first gig at the Climax, a pub in the Arcade (January 80).

The Specials' 1981 hit Ghost Town was a sad commentary on the city's decline.

# west midlands

## DIGBETH

A popular venue since the 60s, the Barrel Organ is still going. The Civic Hall presented bigger acts.

Ozzy Osbourne worked in a slaughter house here, killing "a minimum of 250 cattle a day".

## DUDLEY

JBs in King Street has been described as the best rock club in the Midlands. Robert Plant has used it for press gigs and video shoots. Some of the audience are reputed to have stood on the same spot for 15 years!

Local group The Montanas were poised for national breakthrough in the 60s ... but it wasn't to be.

Graduate Records, based at 1 Union Street, released singles by Eazie Ryder, The Venigmas, The Chefs, The Last Gang, The Circles, and Mean Street Dealers before zooming into the top five with UB 40's King/Food For Thought in March 80.

Birthplace of Lennie Henry, 29.8.58!

## EDGBASTON

In the 60s, the Cecilia coffee bar at Five Ways, just around the corner from Ladywood police station, was a meeting place for impressionable teenagers, arty types, layabouts and potential pop stars. Steve Gibbons & The Dominettes often played there.

Toyah Wilcox was educated at the Church of England College for Girls.

Steve Gibbons lived in Yew Tree Road.

## ERDINGTON

Mothers Club was one of the most famous progressive/underground venues in Britain. The Pandora achieved only local notoriety.

## HANDSWORTH

Local residents Steel Pulse called their 1978 debut album Handsworth Revolution.

Ozzy Osbourne lived here with other members of his first group The Music Machine.

Also local were The Equators, The Beat and Fine Young Cannibals (formed early 85).

The Beat's record label Go Feet had offices at 116 Hamstead Road.

The Plaza Ballroom was a popular 60s venue ... part of the Ma Regan circuit.

## KINGS HEATH

Birthplace of Toyah Wilcox, 18.5.58.

UB 40 played their first gig at the Hare And Hounds in February 79 and recorded their first album in a makeshift studio in Bob Lamb's house at 68 Cambridge Street. Duran Duran also cut their first demos there. Lamb then moved to a custom built studio in Highbury Road, where the likes of Slade, Ruby Turner and Stephen (Tin Tin) Duffy have recorded albums.

The Ritz Ballroom was the local gig during the 60s — another Ma Regan venue.

## KINGSTANDING

Steve and Muff Winwood spent much of their spare time listening to records in Matty's record shop (now Rumbelow's) in Hawthorn Road.

## KINVER

During the 70s, Roy Wood lived at Gothersley Hall in nearby Stourton.

## MOSELEY

Birthplace of bass player Ace Kefford, 10.12.46 (The Move).

The Fortunes started at Moseley Grammar School, as did Denny Laine & The Diplomats. Other pupils included Bev Bevan (ELO) and Jasper Carrot.

Roy Wood went to Moseley Art College.

The Au Pairs were based in Moseley, as were Dangerous Girls, Fashion, and The Noseflutes.

Blues singer Ruby Turner made her debut at the Fighting Cocks pub, backed by two guitarists.

## NECHELLS

1982 chart toppers Musical Youth all went to Duddeston Manor School. They made their debut at the Pack Horse in Shard End.

## SHARP END

Jeff Lynne went to Alderlea Secondary Modern. Jeff Lynne and Roy Wood plotted E.L.O. in the Packhorse.

## PERRY BARR

Ozzy Osbourne went to Birchfield Secondary Modern.

## SMALL HEATH

Operational base of Carter Lewis & The Southerners, which evolved into The Ivy League, The Flowerpot Men, and First Class.

# west midlands

## SOLIHULL

The Applejacks were hot in 1964 — Tell Me When was their big hit. They had a girl bassplayer . . . unheard of!

Before moving to Sheffield and forming the Human League, Phil Oakey was at school here.

The NEC (National Exhibition Centre) is at Bickerhill. Rory Gallagher was the first rock act to play here, followed by Rod Stewart and hundreds more. Now one of the country's major venues.

When she fronted The Lazers, Carol Decker sang outside the entrance to the NEC — promoting the Brum Beat album. Locals smiled when she vowed to headline there some day.

Hottest local group of the late 80s — The Fanatics.

## SPARKHILL

Bev Bevan's mother used to run a record store in Stratford Road.

## STOURBRIDGE

Hottest mid 60s band was Sounds Of Blue, with Christine Perfect and Stan Webb.

Most top 60s bands played at the Town Hall, where the stage was so close to the audience that undoing the singer's trousers became a local ritual.

Diamond Head were big on the 80s heavy metal scene.

The Belfry Hotel was a major circuit gig in the 70s when everyone from Bowie to Mott The Hoople played there.

Hottest late 80s bands are Pop Will Eat Itself and The Wonder Stuff.

## SUTTON COLDFIELD

Birthplace of singer Rob Halford (Judas Priest).

The Move made their debut at the Belfry, a prime venue of the national circuit in the 60s but now a night club and golf course.

## WALSALL

Birthplace of singer/guitarist Noddy Holder, 15.6.46 (Slade). He lived in New Hall Street and went to Blue Coats Infants, followed by T.P. Riley Comprehensive.

Judas Priest singer Rob Halford grew up in Lichfield Street.

The Moody Blues played their earliest gigs in an upstairs room at the Stork Hotel — then an R&B club, now a Berni Inn.

In August 68, Jimmy Page travelled to West Midlands College of Higher Education in Gorway Road to check out a singer for his new group . . . Robert Plant, then leading local hopefuls Hobstweedle. He got the job! At the time, Plant was living at 21a Bloxwich Road . . . and a local agent had just told him that he "would never make it as a professional singer as long as he'd got a hole in his arse".

Paul Ffenech, guitarist with The Meteors, caused an affray and was caught with an offensive weapon at a Walsall gig in late 85. He got sent down for nine months.

## WARLEY

Christine McVie's father lives in Lightwoods Hill, Bearwood — and still gives violin lessons.

The Kings Head in Bearwood was a popular 60s gig.

## WEST BROMWICH

Birthplace of Robert Plant, 20.8.48. He moved to Walsall when he was 16.

Spencer Davis first encountered Steve and Muff Winwood at the Golden Lion pub. The Adelphi was another 60s haunt.

Paul Lockey, a teacher at Charlemont Junior School, was in The Band Of Joy with Robert Plant and John Bonham during the late 60s.

## WEDNESBURY

Home of Thank Your Lucky Stars panelist Janice Nichols who made "I'll give it five" a 60s cliche.

Slade drummer Don Powell went to Wednesbury Technical College.

## WILLENHALL

In their early days as the 'N Betweens, Slade regularly played St Giles Church Youth Club.

## WINSON GREEN

Birthplace of singer Wendy Wu, 29.11.59 (Photos).

Ozzy Osbourne was incarcerated in Winson Green prison for six weeks, for non-payment of fines.

## WOLVERHAMPTON

Birthplace of guitarist Brian Pendleton, 13.4.44 (Pretty Things); bass player Jim Lea, 14.6.49 (Slade); singer Kevin Rowland, 17.8.53 (Dexy's Midnight Runners).

# west midlands

Slade guitarist Dave Hill went to Warstones Primary, Springdale Infants, and Highfields Secondary Modern.

Before they became Slade, The N'Betweens played local pubs the Connaught, the Woolpack and the Ship And Rainbow. Jim Lea had actually been born in a pub, the Melbourne Arms (long since demolished). Noddy Holder joined the group after long negotiations in Beatty's coffee bar in the High Street.

Finders Keepers were another local group. Things were looking good when Scott Walker produced them ... but they split when Glenn Hughes and Mel Galley went off to form Trapeze. There were also The Californians, The Wolves (Pye) and Zuider Zee (CBS).

Wolverhampton Poly in Wulfruna Street has put on gigs since the 60s. Motorhead made their local debut in the refectory, on a stage made of dining tables taped together, and when Sonny Terry & Brownie McGhee played, Sonny was so inebriated he had to be carried onstage.

The Catacombs was a popular venue, as was the Lafayette Club in Thornley Street. The Pistols and the Pretenders played there, and local group Magnum were always called when groups pulled out. There wasn't a glass or neon tube left in the place after The Angelic Upstarts took on some local facist thugs. Police were called and were not amused to find a pig's head with a copper's helmet on it ... an Upstarts' stage prop. Closed down and became a casino.

The Keys To The Highway is a blues club which opened at the Queens Head, but moved to the Ship And Rainbow. Everyone from Champion Jack Dupree to Robert Plant has sung there.

Henry's Blues House (Birmingham) – now just a dreary pub

The Hosteria, Hurst Street, Birmingham

Another perennial meeting place was the Milano coffee bar in Darlington Street.

Hottest late 80s group was The Mighty Lemon Drops, who started in Spring 85 and made their debut in the upstairs room of the Opposite Lock. Others include Neon Hearts, The Wild Flowers, Arcana, Dogs D'Amour, and The Sandkings.

Robert Plant and Bev Bevan remain staunch Wolves fans, despite all their tribulations.

## YARDLEY

Denny Laine (Move, Wings) and Dave Pegg (Fairport) went to Yardley Grammar.

The Twitch Club was the place to go during the mid 60s beat boom.

# west midlands

© Esperanza

**Robert Plant**

**Plants old house in Walsall**

**West Midlands College of Higher Education
where Page met Plant**

# WILTSHIRE

## CHIPPENHAM

The car taking Gene Vincent and Eddie Cochran from Bristol to Heathrow spun out of control and crashed into a concrete lamp post on the A4. (This was Easter Sunday 1960 – before the construction of the M4 motorway). Vincent survived after hospitalisation but Cochran died of multiple head injuries. Also travelling in the car was Cochran's fiancee Sharon Sheeley, who escaped with minor injuries.

Dave Dee was the policeman entrusted to look after Cochran's possessions, including his guitar, until arrangements were made to ship them back to California.

## ENFORD

Birthplace of Trevor Davies 27.11.44 and Ian Amey 15.5.44 – better known as Dave Dee's pals Dozy and Tich.

## MARLBOROUGH

Singer songwriter Nick Drake was a pupil at Marlborough School.

## NORTH WRAXALL

After his hits, Curt Smith from Tears For Fears purchased a 16th century pad here.

## SALISBURY

Birthplace of David (Dee) Harman 17.12.43, John Dymond 10.7.44 and Michael Wilson 4.3.44, who with a couple of mates from Enford formed the city's most famous popsters – Dave Dee, Dozy, Beaky, Mick and Tich. Reached commercial peak with chart

topping Legend Of Xanadu in 1968, but soon went off the boil. Once a police cadet, Dave Dee became a record company executive while his cohorts kept at it ... until, tired of buzzing round Britain in a van, they bought their own night club in Spain. There sun-baked revellers recall their mis-spent youth to the strains of Hold Tight and Bend It.

Kerry Minnear of Gentle Giant also came from round here.

Thin Lizzy leader Phil Lynott died at the city's General Infirmary in January 86. Aged 36, he was suffering from pneumonia, heart failure, kidney mal-

**The end of Eddie Cochran (Chippenham)**

function and liver deterioration. The last song he wrote was called I'm Still Alive.

## STONEHENGE

Scene of myriad summer solstice festivals – usually involving Hawkwind and usually thwarted by the police.

## SWINDON

Birthplace of Rick Davies, 22.7.44 (Supertramp instigator); Justin Hayward, 14.10.46 (saviour of The Moody Blues/victor in the War Of The Worlds); drummer Terry Chambers, 18.7.55, and bass player Colin Moulding (both of XTC).

After paying dues in such bands as The Helium Kidz, Breeze, Dice and Star Park, the aforementioned Chambers and Moulding united with friends Andy Partridge and Barry Andrews to form XTC, who rode the new wave to a Virgin contract and subdued global acclaim. Moulding went to Headlands School, Andrews to Park Comprehensive – after which both secured day jobs as dustmen.

XTC gained much local exposure as their manager also owned the town's grooviest night club, The Affair.

Andrews later jumped ship and formed Restaurant For Dogs, then Shriekback.

Other local bands include The Stadium Dogs.

Gilbert O'Sullivan and Rick Davies went to Swindon Art College.

## TROWBRIDGE

Birthplace of Bob Day, 21.2.42 (half of The Allisons, our 1961 Eurovision representatives).

# NORTH YORKSHIRE

## BLAKEY

Home of jazz-rock trio Back Door, who broke out in 1972.

## FILEY

In summer 60, Billy Gray & The Stormers were resident at Butlins Holiday Camp. Their bass player was Chas Hodges, later half of Chas & Dave.

## HARROGATE

Local 60s R&B group The Beat Preachers included subsequent disc jockey Stuart Colman.

## RICHMOND

Screaming Lord Sutch fought the Richmond by-election in February 1989. He polled 167 votes ... even less than he mustered in his first attempt 26 years earlier!

## RIPON

The video for OMITD's hit Joan Of Arc was shot at Fountains Abbey.

## SCARBOROUGH

First local group to record was The Ineas, who cut One Night Stand.

Robert Palmer went to the Boys High School, then the Art College, where he formed The Mandrakes. After a long apprenticeship with The Alan Bown Set, Dada and Vinegar Joe, he made it as a solo star.

Between June 66 and August 67, the pirate station Radio 270 broadcast from a converted Dutch lugger moored three miles off Scarborough.

The Penthouse and the Candlelight were two nationally famous hippie/underground era clubs. Everyone from Family to Hendrix to T.Rex to Colosseum played at one or the other.

In April 80, the appearance of several neo-mod bands and the film Quadrophenia sparked off a brief mod revival, complete with beach hooliganism. Scarborough took the main impact, with 217 arrests.

On his 1970 album Fully Qualified Survivor, Michael Chapman recorded Postcards From Scarborough.

Without any doubt, Scarborough's most famous resident besides Professor Laurie Taylor, is Dr Rock aka Charles White — chiropodist and rock biographer to the legendary. His official

**Michael Chapmans ode to Scarborough**
© Global Anter Archive

biography of Little Richard was published in the UK in 1984 to considerable acclaim and the great man himself flew over to London to attend the launch party at The Hippodrome and tell the world how wonderful his biographer was. Charles White has recently embarked on a biography of Jerry Lee Lewis. As Dr Rock he can be heard on Stuart Coleman's wonderful show on Capitol Radio in London and on his own show for BBC York.

## SELBY

Coffee bar rocker Keith Kelly (hits in 1960) went to Selby Art College before moving to York to start his career in the John Barry Seven.

## SKIPTON

Birthplace of guitarist Charlie Whitney, 24.6.44 (Family).

In the 60s, the town's most popular venue was the Clifford Hall, where gigs inevitably ended in bloody fights. The Silver Beatles are said to have played there.

## WHITBY

Birthplace of Arthur Brown, 24.12.44.

Marillion guitarist Steve Rothery grew up here, having been born in West Melton on 25.11.59. (Where the hell is West Melton?)

## YORK

John Leyton spent nine months in repertory at the Theatre Royal, where he was spotted by Robert Stigwood and turned into a pop star.

Vicky Aspinall (The Raincoats) studied at York University.

Most popular late 80s band was Zoot & The Roots.

# north yorkshire

(Above) Doc rock, Scarborough based author of rock 'n' roll biographies

(L) Genius John Barry

(Below) Family's Charlie Whitney

Birthplace of John Barry, 3.11.33. After a rock'n'roll apprenticeship in the 50s, leading the John Barry Seven, he wrote film scores — the most famous being The James Bond Theme. His father owned two cinemas in town — the Rialto and the Clifton.

# SOUTH YORKSHIRE

## BARNSLEY

Home of 60s Pye group First Gear, heavy metal band Saxon, and gothic marauders Danse Society.

## CONISBROUGH

Birthplace of balladeer Tony Christie, 25.4.44.

## DONCASTER

Birthplace of Steve Hogarth, new singer in Marillion.

Having renounced rock'n'roll for religion five years earlier, Little Richard made his UK debut (October 62), singing gospel to a puzzled audience at Doncaster Gaumont. Anxious promoter Don Arden convinced him to revert to manic rock'n'roll for the rest of the tour.

Doncaster Baths was a big gig in the 60s, presenting the likes of Shane Fenton and Johnny Kidd.

To beat local bans, imposed in 1977, The Sex Pistols appeared at Doncaster Outlook as The Spots. Sheffield band Vice Versa made their debut at the Outlook Club, supporting Wire.

Late 70s progressive/heavy metal groups Bitter Suite and Ponders End battled for national recognition. Their lead guitarist John Parr eventually found it in 1985 when St Elmo's Fire zipped up charts around the world.

Early 80s groups included B-Troop, Richard & The Taxman, The Diks, and The Shy Tots.

Vinyl home of The Darling Buds, Treebound Story and Screaming Trees is independent label Native Records, based at 36 Beckett Road.

## ROTHERHAM

Birthplace of comedian Dougie Brown, 7.8.40. For twelve years, he played in rock group The Imps ... high spot was playing on the 6.5 Special.

Local venues include the Travellers Rest in Main Street, the Florence Nightingale in Moorgate, Elliots in the Westgate Centre, the ball Inn at Bramley, the Sub Club in Main Street, and the Madhouse in Nelson Street.

The Windmill Club at Rotheram Football Club had punk nights with the likes of Generation X, 999 and The Doctors of Madness.

Future Comsat Angels Steve Fellows and Mick Glaisher were schoolfriends in Rotheram.

Perversely named local group Phil Murray & The Boys From Bury put the town on the indie map with Rainy Night In Rotheram.

Hottest current band is Screaming Trees.

## SHEFFIELD

Birthplace of 60s star Dave Berry,6.2.41 (in the mining village of Beighton, where the first line-up of his Cruisers also came from); singer Joe Cocker, 20.5.44; guitarist Chris Spedding, 17.6.44; singer Paul Carrack, 22.4.51 (Ace, Squeeze, Mike & The Mechanics); guitarist Michael Vaughan, 27.7.50 (leader of Paper Lace); drummer Pete Thomas, 9.8.54 (Elvis Costello's Attractions); singer Martin Fry, 9.3.58 (ABC); singer Joe Elliott, 1.8.59 (Def Leppard); singer Bruce Dickinson (Iron Maiden); Gloria Robakowski (studio singer for Rick Astley and ABC; soloist as Romana).

Dave Berry was the first local star; he went to Woodhouse Secondary School and now lives in Dronfield. The star of his late 60s Cruisers was guitarist Frank White, the first guy in England with a twin necked guitar. He still has a residency at the Pheasant Inn on Sheffield Lane Top. White used to live in Bilton Road, Dornall and was the only English guy to record for the Californian Fantasy label.

Next up was Joe Cocker, who lived in Tasker Road, Crookes, and led several locally popular groups before moving to London to make it. With him went loyal henchman Chris Stainton (who lived in Woodseats) and keyboard player Tommy Eyre (who became Wham's musical director). Cocker worked for the East Midlands Gas Board (as indeed did Mark White from ABC) and at the wholesale newsagents near the station.

Other 60s groups included The Sheffields (no hits) ... but that was about it for ten lean years!

University students include Geoff Downes (Buggles, Asia), Jamie West-Oram (The Doll, The Fixx), Martin Fry (ABC), Bridget St John (singer songwriter).

First of the experimental synth bands was Cabaret Voltaire, who were years ahead of their time and debuted in May 75. On their heels came The Human League, who cut their first vinyl utter-

## south yorkshire

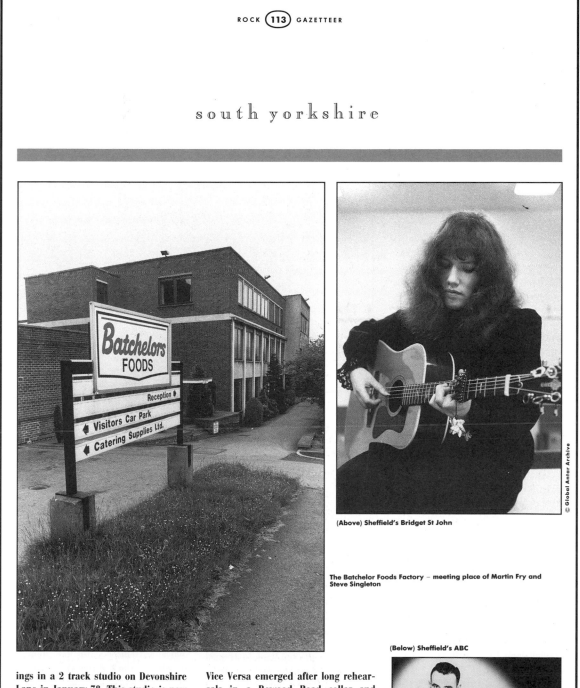

The Batchelor Foods Factory – meeting place of Martin Fry and Steve Singleton

(Above) Sheffield's Bridget St John

© Global Antar Archive

(Below) Sheffield's ABC

© Phonogram Records

ings in a 2 track studio on Devonshire Lane in January 78. This studio is now owned by producer Steve Singleton, founder of ABC (see below).

The late 70s new wave swell also inspired Artery, Clock DVA, The Comsat Angels, I'm So Hollow, Musical Janeens, 2.3, The Flying Alphonso Brothers, Stunt Kites, Vendino Pact, and They Must Be Russians – who celebrated their city on Doom And Decay The Sheffield Way!

Vice Versa emerged after long rehearsals in a Bowood Road cellar and moved to London and the big-time as ABC. Martin Fry joined after going to interview them for his fanzine Modern Drugs. (He and Steve Singleton first met at the Batchelors food factory).

Clock DVA, I'm So Hollow, Stunt Kites and Vice Versa all made their debut on Neutron Records, launched by Steve Singleton and Mark White from Vice Versa.

# south yorkshire

The St Aidens Church Hall in Sheffield — the birthplace of Peter Stringfellow's empire

The Limit Club on West Street was the cool place to be at the zenith of late 70s activity. The Human League, the Cabs, Siouxsie, Simple Minds and U2 all played there.

Also popular was the George IV on Infirmary Road.

The 80s have thrown up Pulp (whose singer Jarvis Cocker — no relation — sang from a wheelchair after falling from a window), Treebound Story (with Frank White's nephew Richard Hawley on guitar), The Sharp Cuts (who made New Faces!), The Toy Shop, Funky Worm, and two members of Living In A Box.

In the 60s, the city's most illustrious venues were the Esquire Club at the Leadmill, 9 Leadmill Road. A pillar rose from the stage to hold up the roof. Resident R&B/soul groups were Vance Arnold (Joe Cocker) & the Avengers and the Scott William Combo; Club 60 on Shalesmoor — a Cavern style place in the cellar of an old pub; the Mojo Club at Pitsmore — run by London's trendiest nightclub operator Peter Stringfellow. The Small Faces made their world debut here in July 65.

A Sheffield lad, Stringfellow's first venture was the Black Cat Club at St Aiden's Church Hall on City Road. From there he moved to the Blue Moon (another vestry hall in The Wicker), and then the Mojo which became one of the most famous provincial clubs of the R&B era.

Now council funded, the Leadmill has been converted to a rock venue/arts centre and still presents the likes of Fairground Attraction, Tom Tom Club, and Texas.

Other local venues have included the Uni, the Poly, the Groovy Fishtank (held at Take Two in Staniforth Road), the Black Swan (otherwise known as the Mucky Duck and, for awhile, the Compleat Angler), the Top Rank in Arundel Gate, the Rockingham Arms in Wentworth, and the Broadfield pub, which has presented every local group from Def Leppard to the Human League. Not to mention Penny's Disco (which served fresh fruit), the Bee Hive and the Hallamshire on West Street, Cafe Piccolo's, the Crucible Theatre's cafe and bar, and the Fiesta Club in Arundelgate which once put on the Jackson 5!

Marples in Fitzallan Square was a key turn of the 80s venue, as were the Lyceum Theatre and the Penthouse.

It was at futurist night club/disco the Crazy Daizy in the High Street that Phil Oakey spotted two gyrating schoolgirls (Suzanne Sulley and Joanne Catherall) and invited them to "come and tour the States as dancers with the Human League" — which of course they did.

Until it was replaced during alterations in 1984, the stage of the City Hall was notorious for its slope. A lighting gantry toppled over and almost crushed Marillion during an early 80s concert.

In August 69, Deep Purple played at the University, supported by Middlesbrough band the Government, led by David Coverdale. Jon Lord was so impressed that he took Coverdale's phone number ... four years later, he became Deep

# south yorkshire

Old Gravell Throat, Joe Cocker

Julie Stewart ex singer with the defunct Funky Worm

Purple's singer.

The Clash made their world debut at the Black Swan supporting The Sex Pistols in August 76. ABC made their world debut at the Psalter Lane Art College.

The biggest band ever to come out of Sheffield are Def Leppard, who made their debut at Westfield School in July 78. They also used to play at Dialhouse Working Man's Club, and the Wapentake Bar (where they also indulged in under-age drinking).

Local musicians Ray Stewart (The Mainliners) and John Fleet (The Cruisers/Joe Cocker) are now radio personalities on Radio Hallam and BBC Sheffield respectively.

The city has been immortalised on such waxings as Sheffield Steel by Joe Cocker and West Street by the Naughtiest Girl Was A Monitor.

Phil Oakey and Martyn Ware (Heaven 17) met at Myers Grove School; Oakey marked time as a porter at the Children's Hospital on Western Bank and now lives in Ecclesall.

Bruce Dickinson (Iron Maiden) and Paul Heaton (Housemartins) went to King Edwards School in Glossop Road, where Jilted John was once head boy!

Steve Singleton (ABC) and Joe Elliot (Def Leppard) both attended Hunters Bar Middle School where they formed a band together.

Tom Bailey was a teacher at Brook Comprehensive before hotfooting it back to Chesterfield to start the Thompson Twins.

The Human League and The Comsat Angels (now called The Head Hunters) have studios in the Red Tape complex. Western Works was the home of Cabaret Voltaire.

Bruce Springsteen filled United's Bramall Lane football ground in July 88; Tony Christie runs a night club at Wednesday's ground, Hillsborough.

Sheffield based producer Robert Gordon has cut hits with Pop Will Eat Itself, Krush, Treebound Story, and Yazz — at Fon Studios. The Fon label is based at Sheldon Row in The Wicker.

A-ha did their first demos at Vibrasound Studios, The Wicker.

In the early 60s, a promising group called The Beatles were one of many to play the Azena Ballroom in Whites Lane, Gleadless . . . now a supermarket.

Guitarist John McLaughlin was born on 4.1.42 . . . somewhere in Yorkshire!

# WEST YORKSHIRE

## BATLEY

Birthplace of Robert Palmer, 19.1.49, who went professional with the Alan Bown Set in 1968 and finally cracked the top ten with Addicted To Love eighteen years later.

## BRADFORD

Birthplace of Mike Sagar, 27.9.40 (early rock'n'roller); Kiki Dee, 6.3.47; Susan Fassbender (Twilight Cafe); not to mention David Hockney and Denis Healey.

The Beatles opened their first national tour at the Gaumont in February 63. Helen Shapiro was top of the bill.

In the mid 60s, Ian Matthews (Fairport Convention and Matthews Southern Comfort) was an apprentice at Bradford City FC.

Eighties groups include The Radio 5, New Model Army (hit big in 85, wearing clogs made in Hebden Bridge), Southern Death Cult (fronted by Ian Astbury who lived in Forrest Road and later led The Cult to stardom), Getting The Fear (SDC descendants), Baby Tuckoo (heavy metal), Joolz (punk poet), Psycho Surgeons, Somebody's Brother (R&B). Zodiac Mindwarp also hails from Bradford.

All the local groups rehearse in the Flexible Response, a studio in Church Lane.

When Liverpool punk band Big In Japan played at the Royal Standard, the promoter told them he "wouldn't be letting any Pakis in". The band were so incensed that Bill Drummond pissed in the teapot they'd just emptied ... and got caught by said promoter. He took them to court but lost the case because of his racist remarks!

Slammer are the first UK thrash band to sign direct to a major label. Great things are prophesied for them.

## BRIGHOUSE

PJ Proby worked as a farm labourer somewhere in the locality.

In November 77, The Brighouse and Rastrick Brass Band reached the top three with Floral Dance.

Jane Harrison, the classical singer who won Opportunity Knocks in 1988, was born here.

## GUISELEY

Marc Almond was educated at Aerborough Grammar.

## HALIFAX

Birthplace of 6.5 Special star Don Lang.

Home of 60s beat group The Quare Fellows. (Too literary for their own good, by the sound of it).

The Spurs are just about the only late 80s band from here.

## HUDDERSFIELD

Ultravox keyboard player Billy Currie studied at Huddersfield Poly.

Two members (Mark Price and Tim Bicheno) of All About Eve are from Huddersfield.

Local late 80s groups include The Instigators (noisy), Roberta Junk (poppy), Arrin (folky) and The Stinging Jellyfish (defy description!)

## LEEDS

Birthplace of guitarist/singer Michael Chapman, 24.1.41; guitarist Lek Leckenby, 14.5.46 (Herman's Hermits); singer Stevie Wright, 20.12.48 (Easybeats).

Sixties groups include Jan Dukes de Gray, and R&B group The Cresters (still going strong).

Hottest 60s venue was the Three Coins in Albion Walks. Their All Nighters presented the likes of John Lee Hooker, Carl Perkins and the city's own Blue Sounds.

Jon King and Andy Gill both studied art at Leeds University, but were more interesting in starting up the Gang of Four, who played their first gig at Leeds Corn Exchange in May 77.

Other Leeds University students include drummer Bill Bruford (Yes, King Crimson), Fad Gadget, Ted Key (Housemartins).

Soft Cell (who met there) made their debut at a Leeds Polytechnic party in 78. Scritti Politti (who formed at the art college) also made their debut in 78.

The Queens Hall was the setting for Futurama, the annual sci-fi rock festivals. Playing the first, in September 79 were the unlikely bedfellows Joy Division, PIL, the Fall and Hawkwind.

# west yorkshire

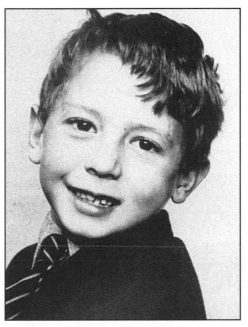

**Marc Almond**

Late 70s/early 80s bands include the Delta 5, Girls At Our Best, Icon, The Xpellaires, The Mekons, Music For Pleasure, and Sisters Of Mercy — who made it to the national stage after years of toil.

Local heavy metal band Praying Mantis made their debut at Fford Green Hotel in June 81.

Queen started their first major tour at the Town Hall in November 73, supporting Mott The Hoople.

The Warehouse at 19 Somers St was a popular early 80s gig. ABC made their first foray out of Sheffield to play there in 1980; Frankie Goes To Hollywood made their first foray out of Liverpool to play there in July 82.

Current faves are The Wedding Present who in 1989 moved from their own Reception label to RCA.

## NORMANTON

Local groups include the new wave Donkeys, who excited a little national interest.

## OSSETT

Home of Black Lace, bare-faced perpetrators of Agadoo.

**Leeds Town Hall immortalised on this Gang of Four Single sleeve**

## OTLEY

In April 58, rock'n'roller Wee Willie Harris was fined five quid by Otley magistrates for using a car with inefficient brakes. Surely something more exciting must have happened here!

## TODMORDEN

Birthplace of keyboard wizard Keith Emerson, 1.11.44 (Nice, ELP); saxplayer John Helliwell, 15.2.45 (Supertramp).

Also the birthplace of orchestra leader Geoff Love, who recorded hits as Manuel & his Music Of The Mountains.

## WAKEFIELD

The big local star is Bill Nelson, who led Global Village, Be-Bop Deluxe and Red Noise while establishing his solo identity. His earliest recordings were made right here in town at Holyground Studio.

During the 80s, Stranger Than Fiction made ripples and Strangeways attracted press attention. Played at the Unity Hall and the Technical College but couldn't progress.

# NORTHERN IRELAND

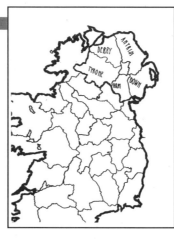

## ANTRIM

### BALLYMENA

The Flamingo Ballroom was where the action was; The Gentry were 60s residents.

Local lad David McWilliams almost had a UK hit with The Days Of Pearly Spencer, which was played to death on Radio Caroline.

### BELFAST

Van Morrison was born in Hyndford Street on 31.8.45. He went to Orangefield Secondary and left to join The Monarchs, a show band. In 1963, he joined The Gamblers, who became Them — one of best of the UK R&B boomers. They played their earliest (and some say finest) gigs at the Maritime Hotel, operated by the Sailors' Friendly League. Van's songs are peppered with local references ... to Cyprus Avenue, Sandy Row, etc.

Also the birthplace of crooner Ronnie Carroll, 18.8.34; guitarist Eric Bell, 3.9.47 (Thin Lizzy); singer Ernie Graham, 14.6.46 (Eire Apparent, Clancey); guitarist Gary Moore (Thin Lizzy, solo).

In 1957, establishment opposition to rock'n'roll resulted in Bill Haley playing to a half empty Hippodrome Theatre. His film Don't Knock The Rock was banned.

In May 64, a Rolling Stones concert was terminated after 12 minutes — due to a superabundance of fainting, hysterical girls and an imminent riot.

Sixties groups included The Mad Lads (R&B), The Belfast Gypsies (Them descendants), and The Wheels.

Most famous 60s club gig was the Spanish Rooms, as mentioned in the autobiographical song Story Of Them ... "made the scene at the Spanish Rooms on the Falls".

The Maritime Hotel became Club Rado and bands like the Interns, the Wheels and Taste all had residencies there.

Other popular 60s haunts were Sammy Hustons and Clarkes.

Fruupp made many forays over the Irish Sea during the early 70s progressive rock era.

Formed in 1977, Stiff Little Fingers were the hottest punk/new wave band.

Other late 70s/80s acts included Protex, Rudi, Ruefrex, The Starjets, Big Self, Friction Groove, Sweet Savage, Victim, The Outcasts, Xdreamysts, Mama's Boys, Jake Burns & The Big Wheel, and singer/songwriter Andy White.

Most influential local indie label was Good Vibrations, formed by Terry Hooley and operating from 102 Great Victoria Street. The Derry based Undertones got their start on it in 1978.

Songs about the city include Belfast Boy by Simple Minds, Michael Caine by Madness, plus any number by local writers.

## CARRICKFERGUS

The title of a folk ballad which several rock singers have found attractive — notably Bryan Ferry.

## ARMAGH

### PORTADOWN

Operational base for psychedelic group The People, who became Eire Apparent. Managed by future Stiff boss Dave Robinson and produced by Jimi Hendrix, they looked like happening. Guitarist Henry McCullough later joined Joe Cocker; singer Ernie Graham went solo; drummer Davy Lutton was in T Rex; bassist Chris Stewart was later in Poco.

## COUNTY DOWN

### DOWNPATRICK

Birthplace of Ian Mitchell, 22.8.58 (Bay City Rollers).

### WARRENPOINT

Birthplace of Clodagh Rodgers, 5.3.49.

## LONDONDERRY

### LONDONDERRY

Birthplace of Dana, 30.8.52. Left Thornhill Convent of Mercy to top the 1970 chart with All Kinds Of Everything.

Home of imaginative late 70s garage rockers The Undertones and (when they split in 1983) their descendants: Feargal Sharkey and That Petrol Emotion.

# northern ireland

Them

© Global Antar Archive

## TYRONE

### STRABANE

**Birthplace of Paul Brady, 6.5.47. Emerged as potent singer/songwriter after apprenticeship in The Johnstons.**

EIRE APPARENT

Eire Apparent

© Global Antar Archive

THE UNDER TONES ARE SHIT PISH COUNTY WANKERS

The Undertones

© Global Antar Archive

# EIRE

This is supposed to be a gazetteer of Great Britain — but a brief word about Eire. (For a much fuller picture, read Irish Rock by Mark J Prendergast).

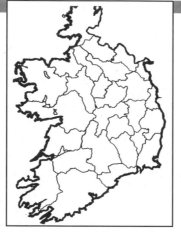

## DUBLIN

Some observers contend that Irish rock began with Bluesville, an early 60s R&B outfit started at Dublin University by true blue Englishman Ian Whitcomb. He went off to America to become a solo star while the rest of the group evolved into the pioneers of the London pub rock scene, Bees Make Honey.

Early venues included the Number Five Club and the Caroline Club, operating in a converted cinema in the south coastal region of the city.

Most important 60s group was Skid Row, led by Brush Shiels (born Dublin, 1952) and containing at various times Phil Lynott (born in English West Midlands, 20.8.49, but raised in Dublin) and Gary Moore (born in Belfast).

Lynott left to form Orphanage with Brian Downey (they'd both gone to CBS Crumlin and Clogher Road Technical School), which became Thin Lizzy with the arrival of Belfast born Eric Bell. In January 73, they became the first band from Eire to crack the UK singles chart — with Whisky In The Jar. (Unless you count the folksy Dubliners, with Seven Drunken Nights).

Skid Row had already reached the UK album chart, briefly in October 70.

Strabane-born Paul Brady was at the University of Dublin when he joined The Johnstons in 1967.

Folk rock group Dr Strangely Strange formed in a house on Mount Street in 1969, around the time that Tir Na Nog were signing to Chrysalis.

Horslips introduced Celtic rock in the early 70s.

The Boomtown Rats changed their name from The Nightlife Thugs during the interval of their debut gig, on Halloween 75, at Bolton Street College of Technology — where Johnnie Moylett,

Gerry Cott and Pete Briquette had been studying architecture. Bob Geldof was living in a flat in Clyde Road, and Gary Roberts was at Trinity College.

The city's most popular 70s rock club was Moran's, in the basement of Moran's Hotel.

In February 79, Dark Space was Dublin's first punk festival, held at the Project Arts Theatre. Bands included U2, Protex, Rudi, The Attrix, Virgin Prunes, The Vipers and Ireland's first reggae outfit, Zebra.

The Virgin Prunes made international progress on Rough Trade; The Radiators From Space signed with Chiswick; and U2 went with Island — hitting the UK chart with their album Boy in August 81. They formed at Mount Temple School, where all were students. Adam Clayton and The Edge were from England, but Bono (born 10.5.60 at Rotunda Hospital) and Larry Mullen (born 31.10.61) were Dubliners.

U2's powerful Sunday Bloody Sunday could refer to the shooting of thirteen civilians in January 72 ... or it could be about an incident in 1920 when English soldiers gunned down several people at a football match in Croke Park — which, incidentally, was the venue for U2's biggest ever Dublin concert, in June 85.

In the 80s came Blue In Heaven, Cactus World News, The Stars of Heaven, The Fat Lady Sings, Hot House Flowers, and half of My Bloody Valentine.

Meanwhile, tax exiles like Spandau Ballet and Howard Jones relaxed in Dublin's fair city.

Ian Whitcomb: birth of Irish rock

## eire

Bob Geldof 1972

The Radiators From Space

U2's early stab at the world

Tir Na Nog

The Virgin Prunes

# eire

## HOWTH

In Tua Nua formed here in 1982.

## SLANE, MEATH

In Tua Nua signed with Island the same week they supported Bob Dylan at Slane Castle in summer 84.

## NEWBRIDGE, CO KILDARE

Birthplace of Christy Moore, who founded Planxty in 1970.

Thin Lizzy made their debut here in April 70.

## WICKLOW

Birthplace of Sonny Condell, 1.7.49 (leader of Horslips).

The sleeve of their album Kip Of The Serenes shows Dr Strangely Strange on the banks of the River Dargle.

## ARKLOW

Van Morrison sang about the Streets Of Arklow. When his mid- 60s R&B band Them had split up, Van lived in Dublin . . . at the flat of Dave Robinson — later roadie for Jimi Hendrix and the boss of Stiff Records.

## WEXFORD

Born in Buenos Aires, 15.10.47, Chris de Burgh moved here when his family bought a dilapidated castle for conversion to a restaurant and hotel in 1960. Attended Dublin University before being discovered at a London party.

Kip of the Serenes, Wicklow

Birthplace of Pierce Turner, late 80s breaker on the Beggars Banquet label.

## WATERFORD

Birthplace of omnipresent 70s chart artist Gilbert O'Sullivan, 1.12.46.

Sinead O'Connor quit boarding school here and fled to Dublin to emerge as a fine singer.

## LISMORE

Birthplace of Patrick Campbell Lyons, 1943 (instigator of flower power champions Nirvana).

## CORK

Rory Gallagher formed his blues trio Taste here in summer 66. First group from southern Ireland to reach UK album chart, in February 70.

Microdisney were idiosyncratic late 70s new wavers.

## TIPPERARY

Born in Kent, Shane McGowan grew up here — but moved to London to form punk band The Nips and the wild folk-rocking Pogues.

## LIMERICK

Birthplace of Terry Wogan, 3.8.38.

Progressive/underground group Granny's Intentions formed here. Got signed to Deram but made marginal headway in UK.

## GALWAY

Home of seminal folk-rock group Sweeney's Men, who got together in summer 66 (Johnny Moynihan, Terry Woods, etc).

Home of singer/songwriter Mary Coughlan, who broke through with her 1985 album Tired And Emotional.

## BALLYSHANNON, DONEGAL

Birthplace of guitarist Rory Gallagher, 2.3.48.

## GWEEDORE, DONEGAL

All five members of Clannad (formed in 1970) were from this tiny village . . . as was late 80s star Enya — born 17.5.61. (Two of her uncles are in Clannad).

# SCOTLAND

## BORDERS

### EYEMOUTH

In February 63, shocked town council-lors demanded a written apology after Screaming Lord Sutch appeared on stage with a lavatory seat around his neck.

### GALASHIELS

Birthplace of bassplayer Neil Murray (Whitesnake, Vow Wow).

Local group Blewitt used to play at the Golden Lion in the early 80s. Their singer was Fish, later of Marillion.

Jessie Rae, he of the Viking helmet and broadsword, lives on a farm at nearby St Boswells.

Jessie Rae

© WEA Records (U.K.)

The Golden Lion, Galashiels

The house once occupied by ex Whitesnake, Vow Wow & current Black Sabbath bass guitarist Neil Murray & his brother Andy: Marketing Director at WEA (US) and leader of The Stiff All Stars

### HAWICK

Operational base of the Duncan McKinnon Agency — one of the biggest bookers of the 60s. Handled all the Larry Parnes acts and scheduled The Beatles first foray over the border.

# scotland

## CENTRAL

### BATHGATE

Home of 60s beat group The Golden Crusaders — signed to a punitive EMI contract after a two day audition which drew almost every unsigned group in Scotland.

### FALKIRK

Later the owner of several record stores, Bruce Findlay started here — operating the only import service in Scotland.

Childhood home of Robin Guthrie (see below).

### GRANGEMOUTH

Elizabeth Frazer and Robin Guthrie started the Cocteau Twins here in late 1980.

### STIRLING

Riots followed Queen's gig at the University in March 74. Two of their road crew were attacked and two punters were stabbed.

© Lizzard Sound Archive: photo Jacki Hogg

Rockwriter Brian Hogg scribbles down the collective wisdom of Bruce Findlay on a note pad in the Zoom offices 1978

## THE GOLDEN CRUSADERS

★ ★ ★

The Golden Crusaders, tonight's pre-match entertainers, are rated one of the outstanding beat groups in Britain, and on Friday they will be in London for their fourth appearance on television.

Six members of the group belong to West Lothian, and the other comes from Motherwell. The Crusaders started up four years ago, and it's two years since they decided to become full-time professionals. And the teenagers have taken the Crusaders to their hearts. For in addition to their T.V. shows, the group have cut two records.

This is the first outdoor performance by the group, whose manager is Colin Meiklem. Bobby Johnston (bass guitar) is the leader and the other members are —Brian Johnston (rhythm and organ), Billy Colquhoun (baritone sax), Jack Taylor (tenor sax), John Lee (drums), Brian Sheridan and Denis Murphy (vocalists).

© Lizzard Sound Archives/Hibs Footer Club

## DUMFRIES & GALLOWAY

### ANNAN

Usual start of Scottish tours by Larry Parnes acts. It was here that The Beatles backed Johnny Gentle for the first time and The Big Three backed Duffy Power (both in Spring 60).

### DUMFRIES

The Stagecoach Hotel was a 70s venue presenting everyone from Frankie Miller to The Pirates to Toyah.

### LOCKERBIE

Among the passengers aboard the Pan-Am jumbo which crashed on the town in December 88 was former Cockney Rebel bassplayer Paul Jeffreys.

### NEWTON STEWART

Birthplace of Bill Drummond, leader of Liverpool punk group Big In Japan and the chart topping Timelords.

The Foundations played here once — and that was like the event of the century.

# scotland

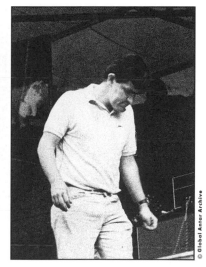

(Top far left) Stuart Adamson of Big Country
(Top left) Bonny Barbara Dickson
(bottom far left) Jackie Leven of Doll By Doll
(bottom left) The Mark 5
(above) The late Ian Stewart as a tour manager, 1969

## FIFE

### AUCHTERMUCHTY

The Proclaimers grew up here, going from bedroom group to touring with The Housemartins, who had heard their demo tape.

### COWDENBEATH

Big Country leader Stuart Adamson was educated at Beath High School.

### CROSSGATES

Manchester born Stuart Adamson moved here at six months. His first group, Tattoo, made its debut at Cross-gates Miners Welfare Institute.

## DUNFERMLINE

The town's first major export were 70s mainstream rockers Nazareth, who evolved from local club group The Shadettes.

Nazareth's Manny Charlton was originally in 60s group the Mark Five, who walked from Dunfermline to London to demand a record deal! They got one . . . on Fontana. Was it worth it, one wonders?

Birthplace of Richard Jobson instigator of punk band The Skids, who played their first gig at the Belleville Hotel in August 77. After four years, guitarist Stuart Adamson left to form Big Country with Dunfermline pal Bruce Watson.

Also the birthplace of Barbara Dickson, 27.9.47.

## GLENROTHES

Birthplace of Jackie Leven, leader of late 70s challengers Doll By Doll.

This new town was the inspiration for The Skids song Sweet Suburbia.

The Rothes Arms was part of Fife's late 70s punk/heavy metal circuit.

## KIRKALDY

Birthplace of Craig Logan, 22.4.69 (Bros).

## PITTENWEEM

Birthplace of Ian Stewart, founder of The Rolling Stones who manager Andrew Oldham persuaded to become their roadie instead.

# scotland

Rare pic of My Dear Watson

Aleister Crowley's house above Loch Ness

## GRAMPIAN

### ABERDEEN

Birthplace of drummer Stuart Tosh, 26.9.51 (Pilot/10cc); Annie Lennox, 25.12.54 (Tourists, Eurythmics); Jimmy the Hoover, 31.8.58 (83 chartmaker and teen mag pin-up).

Home of neo-progressive Pallas, current indie politicos The Shamen, and Creation stars The Jasmine Minks.

Annie Lennox went to the High School For Girls.

### BRAEMAR

Birthplace of Gordon Waller, 4.6.45 (Peter And Gordon).

### BUCKIE

Home of 60s group Johnny & The Copy Cats, who became My Dear Watson after the failure of their one and only single.

### CRAIGELLACHIE

Zoot Money & His Big Roll Band played a mid-60s gig at the Town Hall. Why? It's miles from anywhere!

### ELGIN

Base for Albert Bonicci, one of Scotland's biggest agents. He and Andy Lothian had exclusive rights to Brian Epstein's stable.

The Two Red Shoes Club hosted the likes of Cream and the Alan Price Set during the 60s.

### PETERHEAD

Birthplace of Iain, 17.11.48, (at Ellon) and Gavin Sutherland, 6.10.51 (Sutherland Brothers & Quiver).

### SPEYMOUTH

In digs where his landlady would allow him only one bath a week, Derek Dick would make the most of it — lying submerged for at least two hours. "What are you . . . a fucking fish?" asked his mate. The name stuck. From then on, he was Fish — and as such sang with Marillion. (Saved him the embarrassment of revealing his real name).

## HEBRIDES

Pop stars are thin on the ground . . . venues even thinner.

In the late 60s, Cream star Jack Bruce bought Sandray, a 400 acre island at the bottom end of the Outer Hebrides.

Punk group Noise Annoys hail from here.

# scotland

## HIGHLANDS

### ALNESS

Local punks The Tools recorded for the Aberdeen based Oily label.

### AULTGUISH INN

During the blizzards of January 78, Glasgow group The Subs saved a Huddersfield couple whose car had become buried in a snow drift on the A 835. They were so resigned to their fate that they were writing out their will. Subs bass player Derek Forbes was later in Simple Minds.

### GOLSPIE

In July 69, John Lennon was involved in a car crash after visiting his aunt in Durness. His wounds required 17 stitches at the Lawson Memorial Hospital.

### INVERNESS

Jethro Tull singer Ian Anderson is also owner of the Strathaird Salmon Processing factory, which opened in Inverness in 1982.

### LOCH NESS

In 1970, Jimmy Page bought Aleister Crowley's old residence Boleskine, on the south side of the Loch near Foyers.

Alex Harvey made an album for K-Tel called Alex Harvey Presents The Loch Ness Monster.

Ian Anderson of Jethro Tull, some old fish & distinguished guest

The Proclaimers

### SKYE

Gaelic rockers Run Rig were formed here and began gigging in and around the islands. Now based in Edinburgh.

### THURSO

Home of new wavers Radio City.

### NAIRN

Birthplace of guitarist Robin McDonald, 18.7.43 (Billy J Kramer & The Dakotas).

### WICK

It was here, on a cafe juke box that the Alex Harvey Soul Band first heard Shout by the Isley Brothers!

Run Rig from Skye

## ORKNEYS

Can't find a thing!

## SHETLANDS

Birthplace of Ian Bairnson, 3.8.53 (Pilot); bass player Charlie Sinclair (Kilburn & The High Roads).

# scotland

Radio Scotland

Writing On The Wall

## LOTHIAN

### DALKEITH

Fish (Marillion) was raised and educated here.

### DUNBAR

Birthplace of bassplayer Jimmy Bain (Rainbow, Dio, etc).

The original location of the pirate station Radio Scotland was three miles off the coast near Dunbar. It broadcast from the former Irish lightship Comet (built on the Clyde in 1904) from January to May 66, when it sailed to a new mooring in the Firth of Clyde. Stuart Henry was its most famous disc jockey.

On their first foray north of the border, Marillion played at the Goldenstones Hotel.

### EDINBURGH

Birthplace of Stu Sutcliffe, 23.6.40 (Silver Beatles); Mike Heron, 12.12.42 (Incredible String Band); Ian Anderson, 10.8.47 (Jethro Tull); David Paton, 29.10.51, and William Lyall, 26.3.53 (both Pilot); Derek Longmuir, 19.3.52, Alan Longmuir, 20.6.53, Eric Faulkner, 21.10.54, Les McKeown, 12.11.55, and Stuart Wood, 25.2.57 (all Bay City Rollers); Mike Barson, 21.4.58 (Madness); Fish, 25.4.58 (Marillion ... at the Simpson Maternity Hospital — same place as the Rollers!).

First local to tap the teenage market was 6.5 Special star Jackie Dennis — more memorable for his kilt than his 1958 smash La Dee Dah.

No local early 60s groups made it nationally although The Boston Dexters, The Moonrakers, The Athenians and Hipple People tried. In the later 60s East-West and Plastic Meringue were contenders, but only Writing On The Wall (heavy/underground/progressive) acquired any sort of national reputation.

Bert Jansch was a landscape gardener here before taking the Soho folk world by storm in 1964.

The Gamp was a beat-boom venue; the Place featured folk and blues — including a televised concert by Joan Baez. In the underground era, the Place became Middle Earth North and presented the likes of Wishbone Ash and Moby Grape.

On their way home to Glasgow in March 65, The Blues Council were involved in a car crash which killed James Giffen and Frazer Calder. Guitarist Les Harvey survived to join Stone The Crows.

After an apprenticeship at the Top Storey Club, The Bay City Rollers broke nationally in the mid 70s, provoking the most hysterical fan worship since the Beatles. After ten top tenners they

# scotland

Tam Paton: shy and retiring

waned in 1976. Their manager, Tam Paton previously led the resident orchestra at the city's Palais de Danse.

Pilot were also hot in the mid 70s singles chart.

The Rezillos formed at the art college in 76, and became the vanguard of the city's punk/new wave. After them came Boots For Dancing, TV 21, Another Pretty Face, Matt Vinyl & the Decorators, The Valves, The Scars, The Switch, Metropak, The Flowers, Avo 8, Josef K, Paul Haig, Fire Engines, The Delmontes and more.

One of Scotland's first independent labels was Zoom, run by the owner of Bruce's Records, Bruce Findlay. His first release was by The Valves, his second by PVC 2 (aka Slik), his tenth by Simple Minds from Glasgow. He operated from 45 Shandwick Place.

Even more influential was Fast Product, an indie label based at 3 East Norton Place, Abbeyhill. Shrewd owner Bob Last snapped up The Mekons, 2.3, The Human League, The Gang of Four ...

all Yorkshire based, oddly.

Les McKeown and the Longmuir brothers (Rollers) were born at the Simpson Memorial Maternity Hospital. Stuart Wood was born at Chalmers Hospital and Eric Faulkner at the Royal Infirmary.

McKeown went to Forresters High School, Woody to St Augustines Secondary, the Longmuirs to Tynecastle Secondary, and Eric to Liberton Secondary.

Abbeyhill resident Mike Scott left Another Pretty Face to start the Waterboys.

In the late 70s, Fish was singing with Not Quite Red Fox, who rehearsed at the Carlton Theatre in the Royal Mile. One of his subsequent Marillion hits was Heart Of Lothian — inspired by the heart-shaped symbol embedded in the cobblestones nearby.

The Proclaimers were born here but raised in Fife. They're now back, looking out over Leith from time to time.

## GOGAR

Bay City Rollers' manager Tam Paton controlled his empire from his home Little Kellerstain, where in December 81 he was arrested and sentenced for committing indecent acts and screening such dubious films as Tina With The Big Tits.

## HADDINGTON

Birthplace of Bruce Robert Howard, 2.5.61 (now known as Dr Robert of the Blow Monkeys).

## PENICUIK

Home of The Jury, who turned into Writing On The Wall.

## PRESTOPANS

Bay City Rollers' manager Tam Paton worked in the family potato business based here.

# scotland

# STRATH CLYDE

## AYR

Birthplace of Mike Scott (Waterboys).

Brian Poole & The Tremeloes were resident group at Butlins during summer 61.

## AIRDRIE

Birthplace of singer Dean Ford, 31.5.47 (Marmalade); organist Hugh McKenna, 28.11.49 (SAHB).

## BELLSHILL

Birthplace of Sheena Easton, 27.4.59.

## BISHOPBRIGGS

Birthplace of bass player Jack Bruce, 14.5.43 (Cream).

## BRIDGE OF ORCHY

Setting for the video of Nick Heyward's first solo hit, Whistle Down The Wind.

## CAMBUSLANG

Midge Ure was born at 24 Park Street on 10.10.53. His first school was Cambuslang Primary.

## CLYDEBANK

Home of punk group Adultery.

Wet Wet Wet were all pupils at Clydebank High School.

## DALMELLINGTON

Les McKeown's first public appearance was with Threshold at Dalmellington Town Hall.

## DUMBARTON

Birthplace of David Byrne, 14.5.52 (moved to the New World at two and later started Talking Heads); guitarist Jimmy McCulloch (Thunderclap Newman, Wings ... at 13 he was lead guitarist in local group One In A Million, who played at the Ally Pally 14 Hour Dream).

## EAST KILBRIDE

Birthplace of Roddy Frame, 29.1.64 ... instigator of Aztec Camera.

Other local groups include The Stilettos, The Sinister Turkeys, and The Jesus & Mary Chain.

While waiting for Slik to click, Midge Ure was an apprentice at the National Engineering Laboratory.

## GLASGOW

Birthplace of Lonnie Donegan, 29.4.31; Karl Denver, 16.12.34; Alex Harvey, 5.2.35 (SAHB); Mike Patto, 22.9.42 (Boxer); Bert Jansch, 3.11.43 (folk singer); Robin Williamson, 24.11.43 (Incredible String Band); Maggie Bell, 12.1.45 (Stone The Crows); Al Stewart, 5.9.45; Donovan, 10.5.46 (in Maryhill); John Martin, 28.6.48; Mark Knopfler, 12.8.49 (Dire Straits); Hamish Stuart, 8.10.49 (Average White Band); Dougie Thompson, 24.3.51 (Supertramp); Malcolm Young, 6.1.53, and Angus Young, 31.3.59 (both AC/DC); Brian Robertson, 12.9.56 (Thin Lizzy, Motorhead); Edwyn Collins, 23.8.59 (Orange

Juice); Jimmy Somerville, 22.6.61 (Communards); Clare Grogan, March 62 (Altered Images); Owen Paul, 1.5.62 (one hit wonder); also Billy Connolly, B A Robertson and hundreds more we don't have room for!

Glasgow rock began with Scotland's answer to Tommy Steele, Alex Harvey who played skiffle and rock'n'roll before forming The Big Soul Band in 1960. A decade later, he combined with progressive rock group Tear Gas to form SAHB, The Sensational Alex Harvey Band, who made their debut at Clouds in June 72. He died in February 81, aged 46.

First Glaswegian to crack the national teen market was skiffle queen Nancy Whiskey in 1957; first group to break nationally was Lulu & The Luvvers in May 64.

Other mid-sixties groups included the much loved Poets, The Pathfinders, The Beatstalkers, Studio Six, and Dean Ford & The Gaylords, who enjoyed many hits after changing their name to Marmalade (67).

The most popular 60s gig was the Barrowland Ballroom in Gallowgate, which closed down after the infamous Bible John murders.

The progressive/underground era brought Tear Gas, Stone The Crows, The Dream Police, White Trash, and The Incredible String Band, who set the folk world on its head in 1967.

In the early 70s came Middle Of The Road (Chirpy Chirpy Cheep Cheep!), Frankie Miller, The Average White Band, String Driven Thing, and Slik — led by Midge Ure.

A prime venue was Greens Playhouse which was purchased by Frank Lynch (manager of Billy Connolly and Slik) and turned into Clouds Disco and Glasgow Apolio.

# scotland

Another was the Electric Garden in Sauchiehall Street (later known as Shuffles and the Mayfair).

There was no pub circuit as such (they weren't allowed to charge entrance fees) but the Burns Howff on Sauchiehall Street became a popular venue.

The Maryland Club in Scott Street presented the likes of Skid Row and The Groundhogs.

Punk and the new wave saw the arrival of The Zones (ex Slik), The Subs, Simple Minds, Positive Noise, Orange Juice, and the Post Card label — run by Alan Horn from 185 West Princes Street.

Satellite City was a club named after the Bowie song and later the subject of its own song by Orange Juice. Simple Minds made their debut here.

In the 80s came Berlin Blondes, Altered Images (hailed nationally as the best new band of 81), H20, The Alleged, Restricted Code, The Bluebells, Strawberry Switchblade, Hipsway, The Primevals, Lloyd Cole & The Commotions, James King & The Lone Wolves, and Cuban Heels.

Love And Money, Hue And Cry, The Soup Dragons, The Beat Poets, Texas, Tantara Blade, The Pastels, Biff Bang Pow (local connections), The River Detectives, and The Right Stuff are the latest groups to make waves.

Alex Harvey lived in the Gorbals, went to Camden Street Junior and Strathbungo Secondary.

SAHB guitarist Zal Cleminson went to Penilee Secondary.

Former pupils of Eastwood High School include Brian Robertson (Thin Lizzy); Midge Ure went to Rutherglen Academy; Billy McIsaac went to Stow College.

Jim Kerr, Charlie Burchill and Brian McGhee all met at Hollyrood Roman

Early brilliant Alex Harvey

Motherwell's finest hope: The River Detectives

The low-key entrance to Glasgow's Barrowlands

Catholic School in 72 and formed Johnny & the Self Abusers in 77, making their debut at the Mars Bar Club — in a side street off St Enoch's Square. In 1978, they became Simple Minds.

Clare Grogan went to Notre Dame Convent.

No-one appears to have gone to the School of Art in Renfrew Street, a stunning building designed by Charles Rennie McIntosh — acknowledged by

Midge Ure in his song The Gift.

Lloyd Cole & The Commotions got together in Tennants Bar, Byers Road.

Altered Images made their debut at the Countdown pub in August 79.

The instigators of AC/DC were Glaswegian: the Young brothers emigrated to Australia with their family in 1963.

Progressive band Gentle Giant has its roots in the Gorbals, where the Shulman brothers, Ray and Phil were born.

# scotland

## HAMILTON

Birthplace of singer Brian Connolly, 5.10.49 (Sweet).

## HELENSBURGH

Birthplace of Kenny Hyslop, 14.2.51 (Slik, The Skids, Simple Minds). He lived in William Street and went to the Hermitage School.

Also the birthplace of Neil Mitchell, 8.6.65 (Wet Wet Wet ... the rest of whom were born in Glasgow).

## IRVINE

Birthplace of Eddie Reader, singer with Fairground Attraction.

## LARGS

Home of singer/songwriting duo Benny Gallagher and Graham Lyle.

## LENNOXTOWN

The grandly named Lennox Castle maternity hospital saw the births of Onnie McIntyre, 29.5.45 (Average White Band); Lulu, 3.11.48; Jim McGinlay, 9.3.49 (Slik).

## LOCH LOMOND

In 1979, The Boomtown Rats headlined the Loch Lomond Bear Park Rock Festival.

## MOTHERWELL

Midge Ure attended Motherwell Technical College.

## MULL OF KINTYRE

Paul McCartney's rural retreat. He purchased his 183 acre farm, High Park near Machrihanish, in June 66 and bought a further 400 acres in January 71. His eponymous anthem topped the charts for nine weeks in 1977 and was the first single to sell more than two million copies in the United Kingdom.

## PAISLEY

Birthplace of Gerry Rafferty, 16.4.47. He and Joe Egan played in local groups The Censors, Fifth Column and The Mavericks, and were later reunited in Stealers Wheel. Their album Ferguslie Park took its name from the notorious council scheme in Paisley, where once only "problem" families were housed. (Nothing to do with Prince's record label!).

Also the birthplace of Johnny Byrne, 6.1.40 (wrote TV series Tutti Frutti, did sleeves, etc); Ian McMillan, 1947 (Poets, Blue); Chris Glen, 6.11.50 (SAHB).

Chris Glen went to Paisley Academy.

Home of new wavers The Mental Errors, who felt at home in the Bungalow Bar − the town's major punk era venue.

Home of Creation singer Momus, whose track The Bishonen begins "I was born in the town of Paisley in early 1960".

## ROTHESAY, ISLE OF BUTE

Birthplace of Billy McIsaac, 12.7.49 (Slik, Zones). He was born at Victoria Cottage Hospital, lived in Rothesay High Street and went to Rothesay Academy.

## STEVENSTON

Birthplace of Ron Geesin, 17.12.43.

## TROON

Final location of the pirate ship Radio Scotland was three miles off Troon. Closed down in March 67.

## WISHAW

Home of 60s beatsters The Hi-Fis and 76 power-poppers The Jolt.

## DUNDEE

Birthplace of Roger Ball, 4.6.44, and Robbie McIntosh, 6.5.50 (both in the Average White Band, where they were known as the Dundee Horns).

Tommy Steele caused a riot when he played Caird Hall in May 58. It became an important package tour venue in the 60s.

The Bay City Rollers played their first major gig at the J M Ballroom in Spring 70.

The Poor Souls recorded for Decca in the 60s; the Head Boys made some national headway in the late 70s; Billy McKenzie and his Associates never equalled their 82 debut hit Party Fears Two.

Dundee based promoter/agent Andy Lothian also ran his own label ALP, with releases by Alan Gorrie's group The Vikings, The Poor Souls (as above) and Red Hawkes.

# scotland

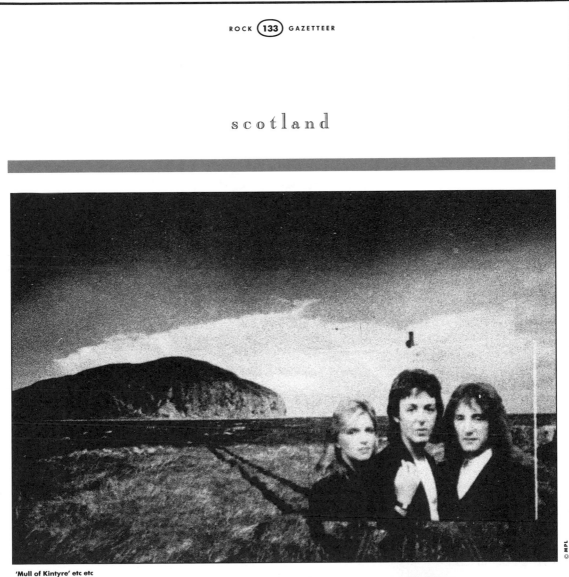

'Mull of Kintyre' etc etc

Scotland's first punk indie label was N-R-G, operating from 17 Union Place.

Home also of new wavers The Scrotum Poles (who weren't going to get far with a name like that), Bread Poultice & The Running Sores (ditto!) and The Visitors.

Most successful late 80s groups are Virgin signing, Danny Wilson — top three with Mary's Prayer — and CBS signing, Deacon Blue.

### KIRRIEMUIR

Birthplace of songer Bon Scott, 9.7.46 (AC/DC).

### MONTROSE

Birthplace of Molly Duncan, 24.8.45 (Average White Band).

### PERTH

Birthplace of Eve Graham, 19.4.43 (New Seekers); Alan Gorrie, 19.7.46 (Average White Band).

Home of Fiction Factory (hot in 84).

Early Average White Band product

# WALES

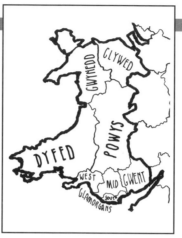

## CLYWED

### FLINT

Ten Years After keyboard player Chick Churchill was born in nearby Mold, 2.1.49.

### PRESTATYN

The Royal Lido was a popular venue in the late 50s/early 60s, when Liverpool bands would descend.

Birthplace of Mike Peters, 25.2.59 (The Alarm).

### RHYL

Home of The Alarm, who moved to London in September 81; and Karl Wallinger, who left the Waterboys to start World Party.

### WREXHAM

Birthplace of drummer Steve Upton, 24.5.46 (Wishbone Ash); guitarist Andy Scott, 30.7.49 (Sweet).

## DYFED

### BRON-Y-AUR

Led Zeppelin rented a cottage on the River Dovey in May 70, to write and rehearse their third album.

### CARDIGAN

Birthplace of David Glasper, 4.11.65 (Breathe).

### LLANELLI

Birthplace of Deke Leonard, guitarist with Man.

The birthplace for Led Zeppelin's 3rd epic

# wales

Mans map of Wales, detail inset. The map was a gigantic pop-out feature of their album 'Be Good To Yourself...'

## MID GLAMORGAN

### CAERPHILLY

Home of splendidly named Roman Jugg, keyboard player in the Damned.

Scritti Politti's Green went to the Boys' Grammar School.

### DERI

Birthplace of singer Julian Cope, 21.10.57 (The Teardrop Explodes).

Roman Jugg

# wales

## SOUTH GLAMORGAN

### BARRY

Home of Bryn Merrick, guitarist with The Damned.

### CARDIFF

Birthplace of Shirley Bassey, 8.1.37; Maureen Evans, 23.3.40 (early 60s hits); singer Ramon Phillips, 23.8.41 (Nashville Teens); Gene Latter (R&B/soul singer); Dave Edmunds, 15.4.44; Shakin' Stevens, 4.3.48 (in Ely); Green Gartside, 22.6.56 (Scritti Politti).

It was at the Capitol Cinema that two of The Kinks, drummer Mick Avory and guitarist Dave Davies, had an onstage fight during their opening number, Beautiful Delilah. Avory fled the building after cutting Davies' head with a cymbal. He was stitched up at Cardiff Royal Infirmary.

First local rock band to take off was Amen Corner in 1967.

Dave Edmunds scored hits with Love Sculpture before going solo with 1970 chart topper I Hear You Knocking.

Budgie made national headway as an early 70s heavy rock trio; Lone Star were mid-70s heavy metal.

New wavers included The Young Marble Giants and Addiction.

Local lad Ian Thomas was the only human drummer on George Michael's album Faith.

Current faves include Papa's New Faith, The Waterfront, Skin Games, Tiger Tailz, The Third Uncles, and Cefl Pren

(Welsh language rockers . . . their name means Trojan Horse, roughly).

### PENARTH

Man's first live album was recorded at the Padgett Rooms.

Home of new wave group The Electric Shavers.

### MAERDY

In late 78, local painter and decorator Kingsley Pugh changed his name by deed poll . . . to Mick Jagger!

**Man fan L.P.**

### MERTHYR TYDFIL

Tom Jones was spotted by future manager Gordon Mills at the Top Hat Club. Then known as Tommy Scott, he was fronting The Senators.

Home of The Bystanders, who became an international 70s cult band as Man.

### PONTYPRIDD

Birthplace of Thomas Woodward, better known as Tom Jones, 7.6.40. He attended Trefforest Secondary Modern before fronting a string of bands. He was often billed as "The Twisting Vocalist from Pontypridd", and on rainy nights did his canoodling in a local phone box. When they switched designs, he arranged for it to be shipped to his Las Vegas home so that he could always be reminded of those halcyon days!

Home of Nick Burton, member of Westworld.

### RHYMNEY

After folksinger Pete Seeger added music to a local poem, The Byrds recorded The Bells Of Rhymney on their first album.

### TONYPANDY

Gordon Mills lived here and worked as a bus conductor. He ended up managing Tom Jones and Engelbert Humperdinck.

### YSTRAD

Birthplace of Andy Fairweather Low, 2.8.48 (Amen Corner).

# w a l e s

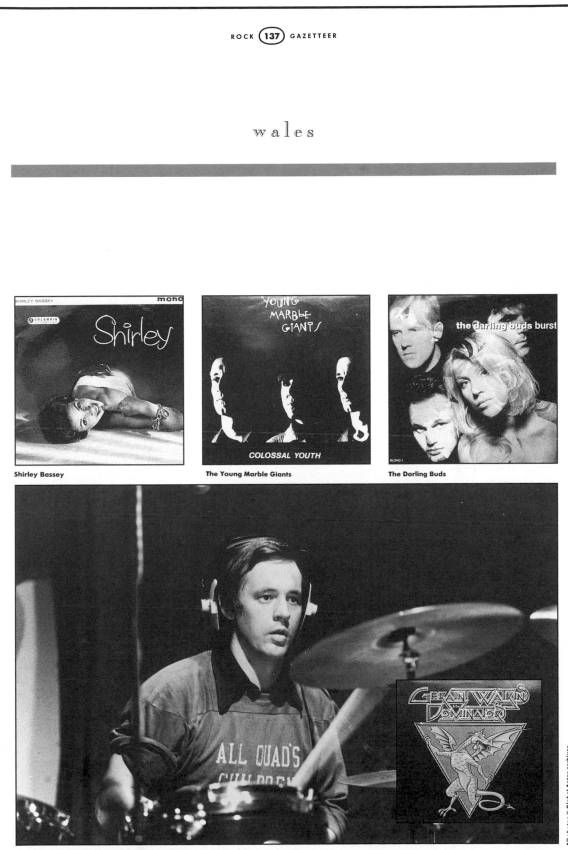

Shirley Bassey

The Young Marble Giants

The Darling Buds

Andy Fairweather-Low drumming for Geraint Watkins patriotic  L.P.

# wales

## WEST GLAMORGAN

### CRYNANT

Birthplace of bassplayer/singer/writer/producer John Cale, 5.12.40 (Velvet Underground and beyond).

### NEATH

Home of the Eyes Of Blue, the Melody Maker's tip for stardom in 1966. It wasn't to be.

### PONTARDAWE

Birthplace of Mary Hopkin, 3.5.50, whose earliest musical training was in the choir at Pontardawe Congregational Tabernacle.

### SKEWEN

Birthplace of Bonnie Tyler, 8.6.53.

### SWANSEA

Birthplace of R&B bandleader Spencer Davis, 17.7.41; Pete Ham, 27.4.47, and Mickey Gibbons, 1949, (both of Badfinger).

Early local groups included The Fleetwoods.

Former Man guitarist Clive John immortalised the place in his 1975 album track Swansea Town.

Local group The Iveys moved to Liverpool to find Apple patronage and fame as Badfinger.

Les Harvey, guitarist with Stone The Crows, was electrocuted on stage at Swansea University in May 72.

The Who filled Swansea Town's football ground in June 76. Little Feat and the Sensational Alex Harvey Band supported.

## GWENT

### ABERGAVENNY

Title of a Marty Wilde single which failed to reach the charts.

### NEWPORT

Birthplace of Steve Strange, 28.5.59, who left town with The Sex Pistols, became roadie for Generation X, and launched the New Romantics movement.

Police made their world debut at the Stowaway Club on Stow Hill in March 77, supporting New York punk star Cherry Vanilla.

Local groups included Racing Cars, who made the charts in 1977; The Beetroots (reggae); and some of Amen Corner and their direct descendants Judas Jump.

Home of late 80s breakers The Senators — and The Darling Buds, who come from Caerleon and played all their early gigs at TJ's Disco in Clarence Place. The same venue incubated The Abs and The Blood Brothers.

Robert Plant plays squash at the Newport Centre.

Van Morrison persuaded the landlord of the Kings Head to start a blues club in 1988 — and Morrison attended a Johnny Mars gig. When he was invited onstage, he left hurriedly never to be seen again!

### ROCKFIELD

Converted from pig farming barns, Rockfield Studio was the brainchild of the Ward brothers, Charles and Kingsley. Investor Dave Edmunds cut their first big hit, I Hear You Knocking, in 1970 — since when everyone from Queen to Del Shannon has recorded there.

## GWYNEDD

### ANGLESEY

The sleeve of Roxy Music's album Siren, featuring Jerry Hall in the title role, was shot on the coast of Anglesey.

### BANGOR

The Beatles, Mick Jagger and Marianne Faithfull were among those seeking spiritual guidance at the Maharishi's transcendental meditation centre in August 67.

The video for The Skids single Iona was shot here ... wrong coast, wrong country, but close.

### PORTMERION

Setting for the television series The Prisoner, and also the video for See Those Eyes by Altered Images.

### PWLLHELI

It was at Butlins Holiday Camp in summer 59 that 16 year old Georgie Fame was discovered by Rory Blackwell, who persuaded him to move to London where he would find fame and

# wales

John Cale

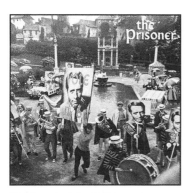

The Prisoner, set in Port Merion

Mary Hopkin

Roxy Music's West coast tribute

fortune as a member of his Blackjacks. Within weeks, he was broke ... but then fate played its hand.

# POWYS

## BRECON

Birthplace of Roger Glover, 30.11.45 (Deep Purple).

## WELSHPOOL

Birthplace of Duster Bennett, 23.9.46 (popular late 60s one man blues band).

## YSTRADGYNLAIS

Birthplace of Steve Alexander, 20.11.62 (Brother Beyond).

Badfinger

# GREATER LONDON
## (by postal district)

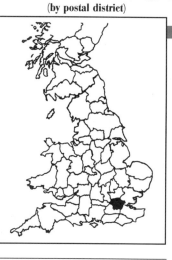

## E 1
## WAPPING, WHITECHAPEL, SHOREDITCH, STEPNEY

Birthplace of Lionel Bart, 1.8.30; Des O'Connor (three top tenners); Kenny Lynch, 20.3.39; rock'n'roller Neil Christian; singer Denis Dalziel, 10.10.43 (Honeycombs); drummer Kenney Jones, 16.9.48 (Small Faces); guitarist Andy Powell, 8.2.50 (Wishbone Ash); Samantha Fox, 15.4.66 (at Mile End Hospital).

Micky Finn & the Blue Men were early R&B/bluebeat merchants from Mile End Road.

In 1964/5, Paul Simon was living at Judith Piepe's house in Cable Street (famous for the Oswald Mosely race riots of 1936). He wrote The Big Bright Green Pleasure Machine in a nearby all-night launderette. Other house guests included Al Stewart and Sandy Denny.

Underground bizarros The Social Deviants lived in Princelet Street.

Robert Wyatt's Shipbuilding video was made at St Katherine's Dock — near Tower Bridge.

## E 2
## BETHNAL GREEN

Birthplace of Laurie London, 19.1.44 (one-hit teen wonder); Helen Shapiro, 28.9.46; Peter Green, 29.10.46 (Fleetwood Mac); Cheryl Baker, 8.3.55 (Bucks Fizz).

The video for Culture Club's Time (Clock Of The Heart) was shot at the Ship And Blue Ball in Boundary Street.

## E 3
## BOW

Birthplace of Steve Marriott, 30.1.47 (Small Faces); Taffy, 14.2.52 (I Love My Radio).

## E 4
## CHINGFORD

Home of 60s group the Druids.

## E 5
## CLAPTON

Helen Shapiro was educated at Clapton Park Comprehensive; she and Marc Bolan both went to Northwold Primary.

## E 6
## EAST HAM

Birthplace of Vera Lynn, 20.3.17 (she went to Brampton Road School); guitarist Bert Weedon, 10.5.20.

Lonnie Donegan grew up here, which accounts for the cockney chirp rather than a Glaswegian growl.

In October 62, Phil Everly took the stage of the Granada (281 Barking Road) at the start of a UK tour — but Don was missing. He was ensconced at the Middlesex Hospital, strung out on speed. He flew home, leaving Phil to complete the tour alone.

The Beatles started their second UK tour at Granada in March 63. Tommy Roe and Chris Montez shared the bill.

## E 7
## FOREST GATE

The Upper Cut in Woodgrange Road, owned by boxer Billy Walker, was opened by the Who in Dec 66. It was hot for a few years, but eventually became a bingo and social club. Jimi Hendrix wrote Purple Haze there.

## E 8, 9
## DALSTON, HACKNEY

Birthplace of Anthony Newley, 24.9.31; Gary Brooker, 29.5.45 (Procol Harum); Marc Bolan, 30.9.47; Leee John, 23.6.57 (Imagination); Phil Collen, 8.12.57 (Def Leppard); Nicola Summers, 13.5.59 (Bodysnatchers), Mel, 11.7.66, and Kim, 28.8.61. Most were born at Hackney Hospital, 230 Homerton High Street.

Formed in November 63, local group The Sherabons eventually found fame as The Honeycombs.

Before his adoption as a punk idol, Sid Vicious studied at Hackney College of Further Education.

## E 10
## LEYTON

Sounds Incorporated made their debut at Leyton Baths in 1961.

Home of The Leyton Buzzards, who eventually mutated into Modern Romance.

# london

Francis Service Station, much rebuilt & cleaned up after The Stones visit (E15)

## E16
## CANNING TOWN

David Essex was educated at Star Lane Primary and Shipman Road County Secondary.

In 1959, 16 year old Georgie Fame was working as a pub pianist at the Essex Arms near Silvertown Bridge when he was "discovered" by Lionel Bart, who sent him along to manager Larry Parnes for an audition.

The Bridge House at 23 Barking Road was an interesting venue. It was here that Blancmange were spotted by Stevo and Depeche Mode were discovered by Daniel Miller of Mute Records. The Blues Band made their debut here in April 79.

## E12
## MANOR PARK

Steve Marriott and Ronnie Lane formed The Small Faces after meeting at the J 60 Music Bar, where the former was employed as a salesman.

## E13
## PLAISTOW, WEST HAM

Birthplace of Ronnie Lane, 1.4.46 (Small Faces).

Operational base of hardcore punks Smak and oi favourites The Cockney Rejects.

The Ian Dury song Plaistow Patricia concerns a junkie whose "tits had dropped and arse had spread", but she still married a wealthy chinaman.

## E15
## STRATFORD

Birthplace of Graham Bonney, 2.6.45; Joe's daughter Sam Brown, 7.10.64.

Fronted by David Essex, The Everons were regulars at the Eagle in Chobham Road. It was here, in 1964, that Essex was discovered by his future manager Derek Bowman.

Refused entry to the loo at the Francis Service Station at 176 Romford Road, three of The Rolling Stones were forced to urinate against a convenient wall. Magistrates fined them five quid each (June 65).

A prime late 60s blues club was the Bottleneck, held at the Railway Tavern in Angel Lane.

## E17
## WALTHAMSTOW

Birthplace of saxplayer Denny Payton, 11.8.43 (Dave Clark Five); guitarist Mick Box, 8.6.47 (Uriah Heep).

In 1961, Ian Dury was a student at Walthamstow School of Art. His tutor was Peter Blake. Dury's first band, Kilburn & The High Roads, played their last gig at the Town Hall in June 76. Support groups were The 101-ers and The Stranglers.

Local groups include Sam Apple Pie (late 60s bluesers) and current psychedelic darlings The Bevis Frond.

# london

Islington's Screen On The Green N1

## EC1
## CLERKENWELL, HOLBORN

Birthplace of Gary Kemp, 16.10.59 (Spandau Ballet) — at Barts Hospital.

Both Steve Marriott and Millie learned stagecraft at the Italia Conti Academy of Theatre Arts at 23 Goswell Road.

Cat Stevens was educated at Hugh Myddleton School and then Northampton Secondary Modern in Old Street.

Spandau Ballet, their manager Steve Dagger and Chris Foreman of Madness all attended Dame Alice Owens Grammar School in Owens Row.

## EC2
## CITY, LONDON WALL, MOORGATE

Among students passing through the Guildhall School of Music in the Barbican are Bernie Watson (John Mayall's Bluesbreakers), Andy Mackay (Roxy Music), producer George Martin, John Cale (Velvet Underground), Peter Skellern, Matthew Fisher (Procol Harum), Ian Mosley (Marillion) and Phil Gould (Level 42).

## N1
## ISLINGTON

Birthplace of drummer Charlie Watts, 2.6.41 (Rolling Stones); singer Tony Hadley, 2.6.60 (Spandau Ballet); bassist Mark Bedford, 24.8.61 (Madness).

It was at the Mildmay Tavern on Newington Green that The Sherabons were spotted by songwriters Howard and Blaikley, who changed their name to The Honeycombs, provided them with Have I The Right, and watched them zip to number one.

The Hope & Anchor at 207 Upper Street was pub-rock mecca for more than a decade. Before he made his name at Stiff, Dave Robinson ran a recording studio here. Among many provincial bands making their London debut in the dank cellar were Joy Division in December 78, Dexy's in June 79, and U2 in October 82. In October 82 also, Frankie Goes To Hollywood made two promotional videos there — Relax and Two Tribes. Arista, who financed the venture, passed on the band. After many financial problems, it closed down in December 84.

Madness played their first gig at a party in the back garden of 8 Compton Terrace (directly opposite the Hope & Anchor) in June 77 and their third at the City and East London College in Pitfield Street in February 78.

The Clash played their first public gig at the Screen On The Green in August 76, over The Buzzcocks (making their London debut). The Pistols also played there when looking for a label . . . but record company A&R men were too intimidated to enter!

R&B group Juice On The Loose were all bar fixtures at the Kings Head in Upper Street. The Pied Bull at 1 Liverpool Road was another music pub, often used for rehearsals/auditions.

Pre-Spandau teenagers Martin and Gary Kemp acquired acting skills and social graces at the Anna Scher School in Barnsbury Road.

The 2-Tone label had their offices at 285 Pentonville Road; Bronski Beat made their debut in Autumn 83 at the Bell pub at 259 Pentonville Road.

## N2
## EAST FINCHLEY, FORTIS GREEN

Fairport Convention were so named because they assembled at a house called Fairport in Fortis Green.

## N3
## FINCHLEY

Birthplace of George Michael, 25.6.63. Chas Smash of Madness went to Finchley High School.

In 1967, The New Vaudeville Band scored a hit with their execrable novelty Finchley Central.

Local bands include Eater (early punkers).

## N4
## FINSBURY PARK, STROUD GREEN

During the 50s and 60s, the Finsbury Park Astoria at 232 Seven Sisters Road was a prime package show venue. The Beatles played twice nightly for 17 days over Christmas 63; the Jeff Beck Group made its debut on the same night that Jimi Hendrix set fire to his guitar for the first time (Mar 67). After refurbishment, it re-opened as the Rainbow in Nov 71, when the Who filled it for three nights. The following month, some

# london

pillock pushed Frank Zappa off the stage causing multiple fractures. Its subsequent decline as a venue was slow but sure.

The Hornsey Wood Tavern at 376 Seven Sisters Road was known as Bluesville in the 60s R&B boom, and a sister club operated at the Manor House at 316 Green Lanes.

R&B hero Graham Bond met his death when he leapt in front of an oncoming train at Finsbury Park tube station in May 74.

Free were formed after Paul Kossoff and Simon Kirke saw Paul Rodgers singing at the Fickle Pickle club in early 68.

Johnny Rotten was raised on Six Acres estate.

Mike Barson of Madness married Sandra Wilson at Finsbury Park Register Office in February 81, and soon removed to Holland.

Pathway Studios grand entrance N5

Wessex Studios N5

The Archway Tavern N5

## N5
## HIGHBURY

Birthplace of David White, 2.6.65 (Brother Beyond).

Pathway Studio at 2a Grosvenor Avenue came into its own during the punk era when every major group cut records there. Nick Lowe's Stiff debut So It Goes was made there for £45, Dire Straits made their first demos there in 1977, and Police cut their first single there.

Wessex Sound Studios at 106 Highbury New Park was where the Pistols recorded their earliest works, where The Clash cut London Calling and where Abigail Mead made I want To Be Your Drill Instructor.

In June 77, Johnny Rotten was ambushed and razored when he emerged from the Pegasus pub in Green Lanes.

## N6
## HIGHGATE

Rod Stewart was born here on 10.1.45, and lived in a flat over his parents' newsagent's shop in Archway Road (long since pulled down and redeveloped). Also born here was Dave Ambrose, 11.12.46 (bass player in the Brian Auger Trinity and later the EMI exec who signed up Sigue Sigue Sputnik); Steven Severin (co-instigator of the Banshees).

Fairport Convention's Simon Nicol worked as a projectionist at Highgate Odeon.

The cover of The Kinks' album Muswell Hillbillies was shot inside the Archway Tavern.

# london

Finsbury Park: The Rainbow N22

The Hope & Anchor N1 pub-rock mecca for more than a decade

A local group who benefited from Meek's patronage were the Syndicats, featuring guitarist Steve Howe. They had formed at Barnsbury School for Boys and played their first gig at Eden Grove Youth Club.

Eddy Grant grew up on a council estate in Hornsey Rise and went to Acland Burghley School, where he formed his first group, the Equals. Another Acland Burleigh pupil was Lee Thompson from Madness (when he wasn't doing time in various detention centres).

Ace made their debut at North London Polytechnic on the Holloway Road in Feb 73, and Chilli Willi & the Red Hot Peppers played their final gig there two years later.

The Lord Nelson at 100 Holloway Road was a major venue of the 70s pub rock circuit.

In the pre-fame early 70s, Bob Geldof lived here, in a filthy decaying squat. During this period, he also helped to construct the M 25. (I do urge you to read his autobiography).

Johnny Rotten languished in St William of York School, Brewery Road, for several years ... until his expulsion.

Stranglers frontman Hugh Cornwell languished in Pentonville Prison, Caledonian Road, for six weeks after being found guilty of heroin possession (Mar 80).

304 Holloway Road N7

## N7, 19 HOLLOWAY, TUFNELL PARK

Birthplace of producer George Martin, 1926; guitarist Steve Howe, 8.4.47 (Yes).

Legendary producer Joe Meek had his studio above a leather goods shop at 304 Holloway Road. It was here that he cut such classics as Telstar and Johnny Remember Me, and here also that he blew his brains out with a shotgun in February 1967.

## N8 HORNSEY, CROUCH END

Former students at Hornsey Art School in Crouch Hill (now part of Middlesex Poly) include Ray Davies (Kinks), Danny Kleinman (leader of 70s pub rock group Bazooka Joe), Stuart Goddard (aka Adam Ant), Lester Square (Mono-

# london

chrome Set), Neal Brown (leader of the Vincent Units), Mike Barson (Madness), Viv Albertine (The Slits), Steve Walsh (Manicured Noise), Graham Lewis and Rob Gotobed (Wire), Roger Glover (Deep Purple), Lynsey de Paul, Gina Birch and Ana de Silva (both of The Raincoats, who made their debut here in December 78).

In April 78, Madness played what they considered to be a splendid gig at the Nightingale pub — but were refused further bookings after neighbours complained of the noise.

Local residents include the Kershaws of Radio One (they didn't complain — they weren't there then), Pete Brown, Sheriff Jack and Momus.

The Kinks' recording studio, known as Konk, is at 84 Tottenham Lane.

## N9, 18
## EDMONTON

Birthplace of vocalist/organist Mike Smith, 6.12.43 (Dave Clark Five); Chas Hodges, 28.12.43 (Chas & Dave).

In February 57, Cliff Richard played truant to see his hero Bill Haley at Edmonton Granada — the same place Hank Marvin and Bruce Welch made their London debut in April 58. They were then in The Railroaders Skiffle Group, in the finals of a national contest — which they failed to win. However, they stuck around London and soon became part of Cliff's backing group.

The winner of the above contest was The John Henry Skiffle Group, whose leader later emerged as Chris Farlowe.

Jerry Lee Lewis made his UK debut at Edmonton Regal in May 58.

Local lads Chas & Dave have recorded songs celebrating Edmonton Green and Tottenham Hotspur. Chas went to Eldon Road Junior School and lived in Harton Road. His first day job was apprentice watchmaker at Turners the Jeweller on Edmonton Green, but rocking with Billy Gray & The Stormers at the Kings Head held more appeal.

Cooks Ferry Inn on the River Lea Towpath, Angel Road, was a trad jazz stronghold until the R&B boom when it became the Blue Opera Club, presenting the likes of The Animals, Who, Yardbirds, etc.

## N10
## MUSWELL HILL

Birthplace of Ray, 21.6.44, and Dave Davies, 3.2.47 — founders of The Kinks. Eight years after starting out at North Bank Youth Club they immortalised the area on their 1971 album Muswell Hillbillies. Also born here was Shane Fenton/Alvin Stardust, 27.9.44.

Ray and Dave Davies went to William Grimshaw Grammar (now Creighton Comprehensive) in Creighton Avenue — as did Rod Stewart. During their early hit career, the Davies brothers shared a flat in Connaught Gardens.

## N11
## FRIERN BARNET, BOUNDS GREEN

Fairport Convention's Simon Nicol went to Friern Barnet School.

Professor Bruce Lacey, the hero of Fairport's Mr Lacey, lived in Durnsford Road. He played The Beatles' gardener in Help!

## N12
## NORTH FINCHLEY

The Torrington pub at 4 Lodge Lane has always been a popular rock venue.

## N13
## PALMERS GREEN

Birthplace of Shadows drummer Brian Bennet, 9.2.40, who lived in a council house at 125a Ferndale Avenue and went to Hazelwood Lane School. His first group was local skiffle outfit The Velvets.

## N14
## SOUTHGATE

When Cliff Richard made it, he bought his parents a house here.

## N15, 17
## TOTTENHAM

Birthplace of drummer Dave Clark, 15.11.42.

The Dave Clark Five originally made their reputation as resident group at the Royal Dance Hall at 413 High Road. Their debut had been at South Grove Youth Club in January 62.

Michael Oldfield wrote Tubular Bells when he was living in a Tottenham bedsitter.

98 Beaconsfield Road, N 15 was the first home of independent label Creation.

# london

The (boarded up) roundhouse NW1 – Famous rock landmark

Fishmonger Arms  N22

## N16
## STAMFORD HILL, STOKE NEWINGTON

Birthplace of guitarist Adrian Curtis, 26.6.49 (The Gun); Nathan Moore, 10.1.65 (Brother Beyond).

Marc Bolan attended Northwood Primary and then William Wordsworth Secondary Modern.

Sid Vicious lived in Evering Road.

## N20
## TOTTERIDGE, WHETSTONE

Birthplace of Richard Thompson, 3.4.49 (Fairport Convention).

Paul Young lived here in the late 80s, but the most celebrated local resident is Mickie Most, who lives in a resplendent 30 room Georgian-style mansion.

## N21
## WINCHMORE HILL

Shadows drummer Brian Bennett was educated at Winchmore Hill School

## N22
## WOOD GREEN

Everyone from Led Zeppelin to Fleetwood Mac has played at the Fishmongers Arms at 287 High Road. A heaving R&B/blues club in the 60s, it became known as the Village Of The Damned in the progressive 70s, when Edgar Broughton, Stray, etc played there. The heavy metal band UFO were formed after auditions there in 1969.

In April 67, Alexandra Palace was the venue for the 14 Hour Technicolour Dream — a benefit for the police-beleaguered newspaper International Times. Britain's first Be-In, it featured over 20 acts including Pink Floyd, Arthur Brown, and Soft Machine.

In June 64, Ally Pally was the scene for an All Night Rave headed by The Stones; The Small Faces played their last gig there on New Year's Eve 68, and The Grateful Dead played three nights there in Sept 74.

# london

Magistrates Court, Marylebone NW1

100 Marylebone Road, W1
– Former home of Cliff, Mark & Bruce

## NW1
## CAMDEN,
## MARYLEBONE

In the late 50s, Cliff Richard, Hank Marvin and Bruce Welch shared a flat at 100 Marylebone High St.

Several pupils at the Royal Academy of Music in Marylebone Road opted for rock music rather than classical ... Nicky Hopkins, John Gosling (Kinks), Kerry Minnear (Gentle Giant), producer Chris Thomas, Annie Lennox (Eurythmics), Karl Jenkins (Soft Machine), David Bedford (Kevin Ayers), Steve Nieve (Attractions), Joe Jackson and Elton John.

One of London's most famous rock landmarks is the Roundhouse in Chalk Farm Road. The first gig was an all-night hippie rave to launch underground newspaper the International Times in October 66. Pink Floyd and Soft Machine were headliners, and groovy punters rolled naked in a 56 gallon jelly. Other significant gigs include The Doors/Jefferson Airplane in 68 and Led Zeppelin's London debut in November 68 (they got 150 quid).

Just down the road at Camden Lock is Dingwalls – a favourite rock showcase throughout the 70s and 80s – and in the railway yards between is the warehouse where The Clash got their act together. It was there that they did their first gig, a media only preview, in August 76.

Just up the road is Chalk Farm underground station, where Madness posed for the sleeve of their album Absolutely.

Birthplace of Dickie Valentine, 4.11.29 (50s crooner); Adam Ant, 3.11.54.

Adam Ant and Peter Bardens (Cheynes/Them/Camel) were both educated at Marylebone Grammar.

The coaches taking package shows around Britain would always collect the stars and musicians in Allsop Place, behind the Madame Tussauds.

Former XTC keyboard player Barry Andrews immortalised his residence on a single, Rossmore Road.

Fashionable venues included the Electric Ballroom at 184 Camden High Street, where Sid Vicious played his last UK gig (a benefit concert billed as Sid Sods Off in August 78) and Steve Strange's venture Camden Palace, also in Camden High Street. Once a BBC television theatre, it was known as the Music Machine in the 70s.

The Brecknock at 227 Camden Road was a major pub-rock venue.

The magistrates court at 181 Marylebone Road has dealt with such miscreants as Keith Richards (June 73), John and Yoko (October 68) and Sid and Nancy (May 78) ... all on offences related to drugs. In June 73, Mick Jagger was there answering the charge that he had sired Marsha Hunt's child.

The Register Office just along the road at Council House has witnessed the weddings of Paul and Linda McCartney (March 69), and Ringo and Barbara Starr (April 81), among others.

## NW2
## CRICKLEWOOD,
## DOLLIS HILL

Bow Wow Wow singer Annabella L'Win went to Hampstead Comprehensive in Westbere Road.

Mike Barson of Madness went to Cricklewood Secondary.

## NW3
## HAMPSTEAD

Birthplace of Shadows drummer Tony Meehan; Marianne Faithfull, 29.12.46; guitarist Paul Kossoff, 14.9.50 (Free); Rhoda Dakar, 1960 (Special AKA).

While waiting for stardom (and Dave Stewart) to tap her on the shoulder, Annie Lennox worked at Pippins restaurant.

As a schoolboy, Pink Floyd's Roger Mason lived in Downshire Hill.

The Country Club, approached through an alleyway at 210a Haverstock Hill, was an excellent underground/progressive venue. Mott the Hoople made their debut there in summer 69.

Folk rock stars Chad (Stuart) and Jeremy (Clyde) met at the Central School of Speech And Drama at 64 Eton Avenue. Another pupil was Jon Lord, later of Deep Purple.

Madness singer Suggs was educated at Quinton Kynaston School in Swiss Cottage.

# london

## NW4
## HENDON

Twelve year old John Entwistle made his public debut at Hendon Town Hall, playing french horn with the Middlesex Youth Orchestra.

Dire Straits made the video for Twisting By The Pool at the swimming pool in the Copthall Sports Centre.

Snuff are a currently hot hardcore band.

## NW5
## GOSPEL OAK, KENTISH TOWN

Birthplace of Bam King, 18.9.46, (Ace); Lee Thompson, 5.10.57 (Madness).

Former pupils of William Ellis School in Highgate Road include Richard Thompson, Gerry Conway (Fairport), Hugh Cornwell (Stranglers), Mark Bedford (Madness).

Former pupils of Gospel Oak Primary in Gordonhouse Road include Mike Barson, Lee Thompson and Chris Foreman. All were reunited in Madness, whose first rehearsals were at Mike's mother's house in Chetwynd Road.

Local groups include The Action, Mighty Baby and Ace.

The Tally Ho (later Hudsons) at 9 Fortress Road was the venue which precipitated the mid 70s pub rock circuit. The first groups to establish it as such were Eggs Over Easy, Bees Make Honey, Brinsley Schwarz and Ducks DeLuxe, who made their UK debut there in August 72.

Photos on the sleeve of Muswell Hillbillies show The Kinks cavorting in Retcar Close, not far from Waterlow Park — the title of a song by Mott The Hoople, whose singer Ian Hunter lived nearby.

The Town And Country Club at 9-15 Highgate Road became one of the hottest/coolest late 80s London venues.

## NW6
## KILBURN
## WEST HAMPSTEAD

Birthplace of Tom, 2.7.36, and Dusty Springfield, 16.4.39.

The State Theatre was a prime rock venue in the 50s. Buddy Holly appeared there in March 58 and Jerry Lee Lewis two months later. Ron Wood chose it for his solo debut in July 74.

It was at the Decca studio at 165 Broadhurst Gardens that The Beatles failed to impress the company's A&R team on New Year's Day 1962. They thought Brian Poole & The Tremeloes had more potential and signed them instead!

The Railway Hotel at 100 West End Lane was better known as Klook's Kleek during the 60s R&B boom, and the Moonlight Club during the New Romantics boom.

Shadows drummer Tony Meehan and Bow Wow Wow singer Annabella L'Win were both educated at Beckford Primary in Dornfell Street.

Drummer Keef Hartley gave one of his albums the enigmatic title Battle Of NW6.

Sidelining his pop career, Cat Stevens changed his name to Yusuf Islam and now operates the Islamia Schools Trust at 8 Brondesbury Park.

It was in a Kilburn launderette that the pubescent Annabella L'Win was discovered by Malcolm McLaren, who immediately installed her in Bow Wow Wow.

## NW8
## ST JOHN'S WOOD

Tony Meehan attended Regents Park Central in Lisson Grove.

EMI have long maintained their studios at 3 Abbey Road, but it was the Beatles who put the road and the zebra crossing on the rock map with their 1969 album.

In April 65, Paul McCartney paid out 40 grand for a house at 7 Cavendish Avenue, not far from the studio.

## NW9
## COLINDALE, KINGSBURY

Birthplace of Shadows bass player Jet Harris (in Honeypot Lane), 6.7.39; bassist Chris Squire, 4.3.48 (Yes); singer Mari Wilson, 29.9.57.
Rolling Stone Charlie Watts was educated at Tylers Croft Secondary Modern — now part of Kingsbury High School in Princes Avenue. Another pupil was George Michael.

Local groups include rockabilly hopefuls, The Polecats.

## NW10
## HARLESDEN, KENSAL GREEN

Birthplace of dynamic rocker Johnny Kidd, 23.12.39; Mick Tucker, 17.7.49 (Sweet).

Keith Moon married Kim Kerrigan at Willesden Register Office in March 66.

Reggae group Aswad emerged from Harlesden in 1976.

Punk group The Slits made their debut supporting The Clash on their memorable gig at the Colosseum in March 77.

Local lass Mari Wilson became known as the Queen of Neasden.

# london

Golders Green Chapel, NW11. Farewell Marc & Moon

The Railway Hotel, later The Moonlight Club, NW6

© Global Antar Archive

Old Decca Studios, NW6 – From rock to opera!

The Mean Fiddler at 24 High Street, Harlesden, is one of the best London venues for rootsy, ethnic, interesting, honest, real music.

## NW11
## GOLDERS GREEN

Fairport Convention made their world debut at St Michael's Church Hall (April 67) and the Paul Butterfield Blues Band made their UK debut at briefly popular R&B venue the Refectory at 911 Finchley Road (Dec 66).

At Golders Green Chapel, friends bade farewell to Marc Bolan in Sept 77, and Keith Moon in Sept 78.

Pauly purchases a pad: 7 Cavendish Avenue NW8

# london

## SE 1
## BOROUGH, LAMBETH

Due to the unprecedented clamour of fans at Waterloo Station in February 57, the press described Bill Haley's arrival into London (by train from Southampton) as "the second battle of Waterloo".

Waterloo Station, Bridge and Underground were the setting for The Kinks hit Waterloo Sunset, and Bob Geldof's 1986 follow-up Love Like A Rocket.

The Trocadero Theatre at the Elephant & Castle was renowned for its critical Teddy Boy audience who threw pennies at Cliff Richard, jeered Bobby Darin, but idolised Duane Eddy! Two policemen were injured trying to disperse "juvenile delinquents" who were letting off steam after seeing Rock Around The Clock there. Buddy Holly & The Crickets made their UK debut there in March 58 ... Des O'Connor was the compere!

Fifties rock'n'roller Terry Dene was born in a flat above a sweetshop in the Elephant & Castle 20.12.38, in Lancaster Road, which has since been bulldozed and redeveloped. He was educated at St Johns and All Saints Secondary Mixed in Waterloo Road.

At a house in Waterloo Road known variously as The Cave and The Yellow Door, three unknowns formed a group called The Cavemen ... Tommy Steele, Lionel Bart and Mike Pratt (subsequently the star of Randall & Hopkirk Deceased).

Fifties rocker Dickie Pride was "discovered" singing at the Union Tavern in the Old Kent Road, and Long John Baldry made his debut at The World Turned Upside Down in 1958. The Thomas A Becket at 302 Old Kent Road has been a rock pub since the 60s, and the Ambulance Hut was a hardcore

venue presenting the likes of The Butthole Surfers. On one of their most memorable gigs, in November 84, The Jesus & Mary Chain trashed the place.

The reputation of the Workhouse Studio at 488 Old Kent Road was established by albums like New Boots And Panties (Ian Dury) and No Parlez (Paul Young).

The Royal Festival Hall on the South Bank has presented suitably sedate gigs. Dylan played his first formal UK concert here in May 64, as did Peter Paul & Mary. Three years later, flocks of colourful hippies came to see Emily play at the adjacent Queen Elizabeth Hall when Pink Floyd presented their seminal Games For May.

Late 80s star Roachford was born here on 22.1.65; actress and Eighth Wonder vocalist Patsy Kensit on 4.3.68.

## SE 2
## ABBEY WOOD

Kate Bush was educated at St Joseph's Convent.

## SE 3
## BLACKHEATH

Birthplace of fifties star Marty Wilde, 1939; ace guitarist Albert Lee, 21.12.43; drummer Jon Hiseman, 21.6.44; Virgin boss Richard Branson, 18.7.50 (at Stonefield Maternity Home).

Led Zeppelin's John Paul Jones was educated at Christ College.

## SE 5
## CAMBERWELL

A 1964 flash in the charts, the Joy Strings formed at the Salvation Army training college in Denmark Hill.

Syd Barrett was a student at Camberwell Art School when he and his mates formed Pink Floyd. A bunch of Barrett disciples formed the locally based neo-psych group House Of Love.

Home of Jon Marsh, half of late 80s duo The Beloved.

## SE 6
## BELLINGHAM, CATFORD

Many of the Bonzo Dog Band's early gigs were at the Tigers Head in Catford.

Operational base of the aptly named Crass.

## SE 7
## CHARLTON

Marty Wilde was educated at Charlton Central School, but left at 15 to work in a factory until he became famous!

The Who drew 50,000 fans to Charlton Athletic's ground in May 74, and did an action replay in May 76.

## SE 8
## DEPTFORD

Formed in 1974, Squeeze put the area on the rock map when their first release appeared on the Deptford Fun City label.

During spring 77, Mark Knopfler and his mates sat in their flat at Farrar House and settled on Dire Straits as the name for their new group. Their first gig was that July, on the greensward behind the block.

Other local groups include The Rejects and Electric Bluebirds.

Dee C Lee was raised in Deptford and worked in a boutique there until joining Wham!

# london

Mark Perry published his famous punk fanzine Sniffin' Glue from 24 Rochfort House in Grove Street, and in March 77 formed Alternative TV.

The Albany Empire Theatre became a hip new wave venue in the late 70s.

The Kings Head became a well known venue after groups like The Chords attracted a following in 1979.

Twisted Sister shot the video for Can't Stop Rock'n'Roll at St George's Wharf.

## S E 9
## E L T H A M

As a lad, Boy George lived with his parents at 29 Joan Crescent. He subsequently attended Eltham Green School in Queenscroft Road — until Sept 75, when he was deemed impossible to control.

The Falcon Hotel in Rochester Way was a popular 60s venue presenting chart stars.

## S E 1 0
## G R E E N W I C H

Marty Wilde's first school was Halstow Road Primary.

## S E 1 1
## K E N N I N G T O N

The Who filled the Oval cricket ground in Sept 71. Also on the bill were America, Lindisfarne and The Faces.

## S E 1 3
## H I T H E R  G R E E N ,
## L E W I S H A M

Birthplace of bassplayer Bill Wyman, 24.10.35 (Rolling Stones); drummer Ginger Baker,19.8.40 (Cream); drum-

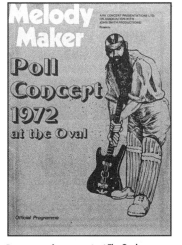

Programmes from concerts at The Oval & Charlton Football Ground SE11

Jon Marsh of The Beloved

mer Pete Gavin, 9.8.46 (Vinegar Joe, Joe Cocker); organist Pete Gage, 31.8.47 (Ram Jam Band); Sid Vicious, 10.5.57 (Sex Pistols); the Goss twins, Matt and Luke, 29.9.68 (Bros).

Cinema smashing and onstreet hooliganism greeted the showing of Rock Around The Clock at Lewisham Odeon in September 56. Teddy boys ran berserk in what the press described as a rock'n'roll riot.

Georgie Fame's audition for Larry Parnes was being shoved onstage at the Gaumont in the middle of a package show (Oct 59).

Deptford Fun City label SE8 Put on the map by Squeeze

# london

13 Chester St (SW1) – Title of Pretty Things brilliant album track

## SE14
## DEPTFORD,
## NEW CROSS

Alumni of Goldsmiths College in Lewisham Way include John Illsley (Dire Straits), John Cale (Velvet Underground), Neil Innes (Bonzos), and Malcolm McLaren.

## SE15
## PECKHAM

Birthplace of Alan Lancaster, 7.2.49 (Status Quo).

Sixties R&B club the Bromel had a Peckham branch at the Co-op Hall in Rye Lane.

## SE16
## BERMONDSEY,
## ROTHERHITHE

Birthplace of Britain's first rock'n'roll star Tommy Steele, 17.12.36 ... not to mention his brother, Colin Hicks. They lived at 52 Frean Street, and Tommy went to Bacon's School for Boys. Coffee bar rocker Wee Willie Harris was also born in Bermondsey, as was Julie Rogers, 6.4.43.

Max Bygraves was born in Rotherhithe, 16.10.22, and went to St Josephs School. He first hit the charts with Cowpuncher's Cantata in 1952!

Setting for the video of The Specials' hit Ghost Town ... which was about Coventry!

## SE18
## PLUMSTEAD,
## WOOLWICH

Birthplace of 50s rocker Terry Wayne, 24.9.41 (loads of publicity but no hits); Kate Bush, 30.7.58 (loads of publicity and loads of hits!)

## SE19
## CRYSTAL PALACE,
## NORWOOD

Crystal Palace Bowl became a rock venue in the 70s, when acts like Santana and Rick Wakeman would headline.

## SE20
## PENGE

Bill Wyman went to Oakfield Junior School.

## SE21, 22
## DULWICH

Birthplace of bassplayer Kim Gardner, 27.1.46 (Ashton Gardner & Dyke); Belouis Some, 12.12.59.

Status Quo (then called The Spectres) used to rehearse in the ATC headquarters in Lordship Lane. Their first professional gig was at the Samuel Jones Sports Club in 1962.

Quiet Sun was an early 70s progressive group formed at Dulwich College. Guitarist Phil Manzanera went on to Roxy Music. Following a night of the excess he advocated as lead singer of AC/DC, Bon Scott died in a car, choking on his vomit while comatose (21.2.80).

## SE23
## FOREST HILL,
## HONOR OAK

Birthplace of Francis Rossi, 29.5.49 (Status Quo).

Operational base of The Only Ones.

# london

## SE24
## HERNE HILL

Brockwell Park was the setting for a Rock Against Racism gig in Sept 78. Elvis Costello, Aswad and Sham 69 entertained.

## SE27
## WEST NORWOOD

Birthplace of John Coghlan, 19.9.46 (Status Quo); keyboard player Barry Andrews, 12.9.56, (XTC/Shriekback: he went to Hitherfield School).

## SW1
## BELGRAVIA, PIMLICO, WESTMINSTER

Birthplace of keyboard player Peter Bardens, 19.6.44 (Camel); Kirk Brandon, 3.8.56 (Theatre of Hate, Spear of Destiny).

It was at Buckingham Palace that The Beatles received their MBEs in October 65 and Bob Geldof his knighthood in July 86. The Sex Pistols relieved A&M Records of a large cheque in a ceremony outside the front gates in March 77.

Roxy Music's Andy Mackay was educated at Westminster City Grammar; Peter & Gordon first met as pupils at Westminster Boys School.

Pop stars of every generation, Larry Page to Adam Faith to Ringo Starr, have got married at Caxton Hall.

On moving down from Liverpool, George Harrison and Ringo Starr shared a flat in Whaddon House, William Mews — but they moved out following a burglary in April 64.

In 1964, Brian Jones shared a flat with The Pretty Things at 13 Chester Street. The address became the title of a Pretty Things album track.

John Lennon first met Yoko Ono in November 66, at Indica Art Gallery in Masons Yard, off Duke Street. A stones-throw away at number 13 was the Scotch of St James, for 60s In-Crowd revellers.

In early 1968, Rolling Stone Brian Jones lived in Chesham Place.

In August 67, Brian Epstein took a drug overdose in his flat at 24 Chapel Street, Belgravia. His butler discovered his lifeless body the next morning.

The ICA (Institute of Contemporary Arts) in Pall Mall has frequently presented rock nights — often of an avant garde nature. Adam & The Ants made their debut there in May 77.

Haircut 100 played their first gig at the Ski Club in Eaton Square — operated by Nick Heyward's parents.

In 1967, The Troggs recorded a song Number 10 Downing Street. 22 years later Elvis Costello expressed his contempt for the current incumbent in Tramp It Down.

The sleeve of his album New Boots And Panties shows Ian Dury and his son Baxter standing outside Axton's at 306 Vauxhall Bridge Road. He used to wait for the bus there and often popped in "to buy his two tone crotchless panties".

## SW2
## BRIXTON

Following a drug conviction in June 67, Mick Jagger spent a night in Brixton prison.

Brixton prison was also the setting for Simon & Garfunkel's first British concert ... in 1965, some months before they became famous.

Before joining Fleetwood Mac, guitarist Danny Kirwan led local blues group Boilerhouse.

Joe Strummer's group The 101-ers played their first gig at the Telegraph pub at 228 Brixton Hill in September 74.

## SW3
## CHELSEA

In 1968, Mick Jagger purchased 48 Cheyne Walk, overlooking the Thames, while Brian Jones moved into Royal Avenue House on the Kings Road. Police tracked him down and found cannabis concealed in a ball of wool. "I don't knit" said Brian.

Pre-fame Sandy Denny was a nurse at Brompton Hospital.

It was at Sound Techniques Studio in Old Church Street that Pink Floyd recorded their first single, Arnold Layne; that Richard Thompson met his future wife Linda Peters (she was recording a cornflakes commercial!).

The cover of Richard Thompson's album Hand Of Kindness was shot on a deserted Chelsea Embankment.

It was at Chelsea Art School that John Martyn first encountered his future wife Beverly.

The Pet Shop Boys are said to have first met each other in a Kings Road music shop.

Fifteen year old Boy George worked at Shades, a clothes stall in Chelsea Antique Market.

# london

102 Edith Grove SW10 – the Stones' gruesome flat

Under Neath What's Andy Berenyi
outside their Brixton Squat in Barrington rd. SW9

Bands have lived in this squat
for several years. Under Neath
What's material is often about
Brixton life

430 Kings Road (SW10 – formerly 'Sex':- birthplace of the
Pistols

Never Stop "Discotheque" / Echo & The Bunnymen

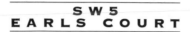

Liverpools finest wear Alberts Hall on their sleeve

## SW5
## EARLS COURT

The Troubadour at 265 Old Brompton Road has been a coffee house/folk venue since the 50s. Bob Dylan gave an impromptu performance on his first UK visit.

Earls Court Exhibition Centre has presented various rock music extravaganzas: Pink Floyd played and built The Wall there for six nights in August 80; Bob Dylan filled it for six nights in June 81.

## SW4
## CLAPHAM

Among Clapham's residents have been Bob Geldof and Paula Yates, Kevin Coyne and Thunderclap Newman (his dog does tricks in the local pubs!).

Sting, Sade and Boy George were among those singing at an Anti Apartheid concert on Clapham Common in July 86.

Local groups include Rock Goddess (early 80s HM).

Birthplace of Dennis Waterman, 24.2.48 (top three in 1980). He starred in Up The Junction, set locally; Squeeze sang about it.

# london

## SW6 FULHAM, PARSONS GREEN

Birthplace of 50s rocker Duffy Power, 9.9.41; singer Simon Climie, 7.4.60 (Climie Fisher).

Fleetwood Mac held their first rehearsals at the Black Bull in Fulham Road.

After taking acid in 1967, Yes bassplayer Chris Squire spent two days in St Stephens Hospital.

## SW7 SOUTH KENSINGTON

The Royal Albert Hall has presented prestigious rock gigs since the 50s. Janis Joplin made her UK debut there, The Nice burnt an American flag, and Cream said goodbye, but boisterous fans and bizarre groups saw policy changes in 1971 when Frank Zappa and Mott The Hoople were both banned. Rock was again deemed permissible in the 80s, when groups like Siouxsie & the Banshees (originally the wildest, most untutored punks of all) drew well behaved audiences.

The Royal College of Music in Prince Consort Road has educated such rock luminaries as Darryl Way (Curved Air), Tony Kaye and Rick Wakeman (Yes), Davy O'List (Nice), Steve Nieve (The Attractions), Richard Harvey and Brian Gulland (Gryphon), and Mike Moran (writer/arranger).

Ian Dury, John Foxx (Ultravox) and Sarah Jane Owen (Belle Stars) all made it to the Royal College of Art in Kensington Gore.

When John and Cynthia Lennon moved down to London in early 64, they took a flat at 13 Emperors Gate.

In summer 66, Brian Jones and Anita Pallenberg shared a flat in Courtfield Road. That same year, Donovan had an album track called Sunny South Ken.

A popular 60s night spot was Blaises, a basement club in Queensgate. Jimi Hendrix made his UK debut there in Oct 66, guesting with the Brian Auger Trinity.

Equally thronging was the Cromwellian at 3 Cromwell Road ... described as "three floors of fun"! It was here that Long John Baldry asked Elton John if Bluesology would be his backing group.

The Elizabethan Room of the Gore Hotel in Queensgate was the setting for the press launch of the Stones album Beggars Banquet in December 68. Everyone threw food around. How jolly.

## SW9 BRIXTON, STOCKWELL

David Bowie was born at 40 Stansfield Road on 6.8.47.

One of the most famous of all 60s R&B/soul clubs was the Ram Jam at 390 Brixton Road, owned by Geno Washington's manager and named after his band. From here, the cry of "Geno! Geno!" spread throughout the land.

Residents have included Nico, and local groups include Local Heroes SW9 (!) and Under Neath What.

## SW10 CHELSEA

During the gestation of The Rolling Stones, Mick Jagger, Brian Jones and Keith Richards shared a gruesome flat at 102 Edith Grove, bereft of food, furniture or heat.

They used to rehearse in a room above the Weatherby Arms at 500 Kings Road.

In 1971, Malcolm McLaren and Vivienne Westwood opened Let It Rock at 430 Kings Road. After a brief spell as Too Fast To Live Too Young To Die, it became Sex in 1975. It was here that Chrissie Hynde and Glen Matlock worked, Johnny Rotten was discovered, and the Sex Pistols were created.

The grooviest shop of the psychedelic era was Granny Takes A Trip at 488 Kings Road.

## SW11 BATTERSEA

Birthplace of one of Britain's earliest rock'n'rollers, Rory Blackwell. Terry Dene and Georgie Fame both made their professional debuts in his band.

One of London's earliest blues clubs was the Blue Horizon, which ran at the Nag's Head at 205 York Road. Producer Mike Vernon was the promoter. Free played their first gig here in May 68; Alexis Korner, who named them, was in the audience.

Whilst The Who were inside Battersea Dogs Home buying a guard dog in Sept 65, a thief stole their van and scarpered with 5000 quids worth of equipment. (Sounds apocryphal to me, but it's a good story!)

Reggae pioneers Matumbi emerged from Battersea in 1972, and the Pasadenas appeared in 1988.

In December 76, during a photo shoot for Pink Floyd's album Animals, a 40 ft inflated pig, moored to Battersea Power Station, broke loose, floated heavenwards, bewildered pilots, and was never seen again. The Power Station was also used as the backdrop to Toyah's video of Brave New World.

# london

The Half Moon Putney (SW15) enduring jazz/folk/rock/blues stronghold

Olympic Studios (SW13) — First recordings of the Stones and Led Zeppelin happened here

Marc Bolan's last encounter with a tree, on Barnes Common SW13

Everything But The Girl's Ben Watt

© WEA Records (U.K.)

Bongoes Over Balham — by Chilli Willi (ulp!)

© Zippo Music Group

## SW12
## BALHAM

Birthplace of Dee C Lee, 6.6.61.
Chilli Willi & The Red Hot Peppers called their album Bongos Over Balham, and a bunch of pub rock cajuns call their group The Balham Alligators.

## SW13
## BARNES

The Rolling Stones first official recording session took place at Olympic Studios in Church Street in May 63, yielding top 30 hit Come On. In Oct 68, Led Zeppelin recorded their first album there — in 30 hours!

# london

In Sept 77, a purple mini GT driven by Gloria Jones went out of control crossing Barnes Common. It veered off the road and smashed into a tree, killing the passenger, Marc Bolan. Fans still visit the spot to lay flowers beside the tree.

Home of Ben Watt, half of Everything But The Girl.

## SW14
## EAST SHEEN, MORTLAKE

Birthplace of singer/songwriter Bridget St John.

## SW15
## PUTNEY, ROEHAMPTON

In July 67, Rolling Stone Brian Jones booked himself into the Priory, a psychiatric hospital in Priory Lane, for 20 days. "I need treatment" he told doctors.

Hedonistic behaviour at the mid-60s home of The Moody Blues in Roehampton made sex-and-drugs style headlines in the Sunday papers.

Peter Green lived in Putney; he went to Ronald Ross Primary and Elliot Secondary School.

In the early 70s, Elvis Costello and his band Flip City shared a house at 3 Stag Lane.

The Pontiac Club in Zeeta House, 200 Upper Richmond Road was a R&B/mod venue decorated in classic 60s op-art style. It was here that Peter Green blagged his way into John Mayall's Bluesbreakers.

Rather more enduring is the Half Moon at 93 Lower Richmond Road — a jazz/folk/blues/rock stronghold forever.

Police played their first headlining gig at the Railway Hotel in Putney in May 77.

## SW16
## STREATHAM

In the 50s, the Dolphin was the place to be, but the action had crossed the road by the 60s when punters could carry on skating at the Silver Blades Ice Rink (386 Streatham High Street) while bands like The Pretty Things entertained them!

When Eden Kane hit number one with Well I Ask You in 1981, he was living in Norbury Crescent. His brother, Peter Sarstedt was still living there eight years later when he reached number one with Where Do You Go To My Lovely.

## SW17
## TOOTING

Birthplace of Phil Lithman, 17.6.49 (Chilli Willi, The Residents).

In May 58, after his appearance at Tooting Granada (50 Mitcham Road), Jerry Lee Lewis' UK tour was aborted by theatre chain moguls who were incensed that his wife (his third one!) was only 13.

Gene Vincent made his UK debut at the same venue in December 59. During his act, he suddenly swung his steel-braced leg over the microphone, pole-axing guitarist Joe Brown as he leapt forward to take a solo.

Three years later, Vincent was treated at St Georges Hospital when he aggravated his dodgy leg. Brian Jones was also treated at St Georges — for nervous exhaustion in 1967, and Cilla Black had her babies here.

When he left school, Marc Bolan worked in Edgar's, a clothes shop on Tooting Broadway.

In December 80, Sting played two gigs in a sardine-packed 5000 capacity tent on Tooting Bec Common.

## SW18
## WANDSWORTH

Birthplace of Jon Moss, 11.9.57 (Culture Club).

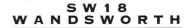

## SW19
## WIMBLEDON

Birthplace of guitarist Tom McGuinness, 2.12.41 (Manfred Mann); guitarist Peter Thorp, 25.5.44 (Roulettes); Sandy Denny, 6.1.47; keyboard player Mick Talbot, 11.9.58 (Style Council).

Jeff Beck went to Wimbledon Art College, and punk group The Art Attacks made their debut there in summer 76.

In December 63, The Beatles played a special Fan Club concert at Wimbledon Palais.

The Yardbirds cut their early singles at R G Jones Studios in Beaulah Road. Twenty five years later, Cliff Richard cut Mistletoe And Wine here.

Wimbledon Common is the ancestral home of The Wombles — television puppets who scored top tenners under Mike Batt's direction. Notorious rock manager Don Arden also lived there before moving to Nevada.

Local groups include The Outsiders (new wave) and The Merton Parkas (neo-mods).

Before he started Sham 69, Jimmy Pursey worked at Wimbledon Greyhound Stadium.

# london

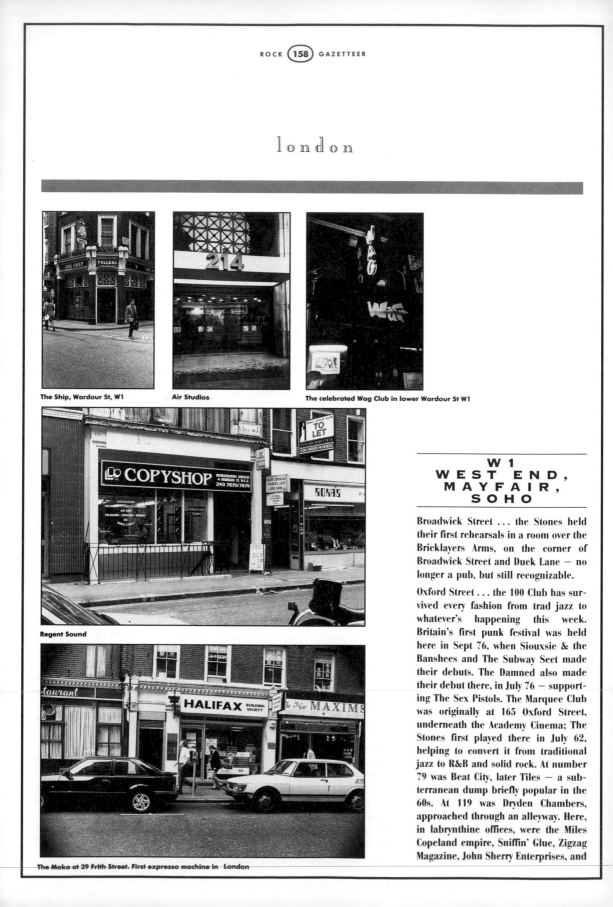

The Ship, Wardour St, W1

Air Studios

The celebrated Wag Club in lower Wardour St W1

Regent Sound

The Moka at 29 Frith Street. First expresso machine in London

## W 1
## W E S T   E N D ,
## M A Y F A I R ,
## S O H O

Broadwick Street ... the Stones held their first rehearsals in a room over the Bricklayers Arms, on the corner of Broadwick Street and Duck Lane — no longer a pub, but still recognizable.

Oxford Street ... the 100 Club has survived every fashion from trad jazz to whatever's happening this week. Britain's first punk festival was held here in Sept 76, when Siouxsie & the Banshees and The Subway Sect made their debuts. The Damned also made their debut there, in July 76 — supporting The Sex Pistols. The Marquee Club was originally at 165 Oxford Street, underneath the Academy Cinema; The Stones first played there in July 62, helping to convert it from traditional jazz to R&B and solid rock. At number 79 was Beat City, later Tiles — a subterranean dump briefly popular in the 60s. At 119 was Dryden Chambers, approached through an alleyway. Here, in labyrinthine offices, were the Miles Copeland empire, Sniffin' Glue, Zigzag Magazine, John Sherry Enterprises, and

# london

various other rockbiz enterprises. At 214 are Air Studios, tucked away on the fifth floor near Oxford Circus. George Martin is the most visible co-owner.

Old Compton Street ... the 2Is coffee bar at number 59 was mecca to fifties teenagers. Among those who played or got their big break there were Tommy Steele, Terry Dene, The Vipers, Cliff Richard, Hank and Bruce, Mickie Most, Tony Sheridan, Adam Faith and Emile Ford. BBC-TV broadcast a live 6.5 Special there and Wee Willie Harris celebrated the place on Rockin' At The 2Is.

Other 50s rock'n'roll venues were Vince Taylor's Top Ten Club in Berwick Street, and the Condor Club, where Marty Wilde was discovered.

Other coffee bar/skiffle clubs in the locality were the Heaven And Hell (next door to the 2Is) at 57 Old Compton Street, the Freight Train at 44 Berwick Street, the House of Sam Widges at 9 D'Arblay Street, the Partisan at 7 Carlisle Street, Russell Quaye's Skiffle Cellar at 49 Greek Street, Le Macabre at 23 Meard Street (the tables were shaped like coffins!), and the Breadbasket at 65 Cleveland Street (where The Vipers first started in early 56).

By the mid 60s, the Skiffle Cellar had become Les Cousins — the best folk club in Soho. The likes of Bert Jansch and Al Stewart made it famous.

Good too was the Ballads & Blues Club at the Black Horse, 6 Rathbone Place. That was started in 1953 by Ewan McColl — author of First Time Ever I Saw Your Face and father of Kirsty.

Folkies and beatniks drank in Finch's in Goodge Street — the setting for a Donovan song.

Heddon Street ... Bowie was photographed here in January 72 for the sleeve of Ziggy Stardust.

Wardour Street ... the second and most famous home of the Marquee Club was at number 90 — opened by the Yardbirds in March 64. Every one from the Stones to Pink Floyd, Bowie to Marillion played here in their hungry years.

Just up from the Marquee was La Chasse (number 100), a private drinking club in a mangy, smoke filled first floor room containing a bar and sundry bullshitters. Yes were formed here in May 68. A more traditional meeting place/watering hole was nearby pub the Ship. It's difficult to find a muso who hasn't stuck his head in here at some time or another.

Crackers was a mid 70s funk disco at the top end of Wardour Street (number 201). In 1976, it became the Vortex to catch the punk boom. Sham 69 played at the opening ceremony; Jimmy Pursey was arrested and fined 30 quid for breaching the peace. The nearby St Moritz (number 159) became a primo New Romantics haunt a few years later.

The Roundhouse (not to be confused with the Chalk Farm venue) was a pub at 83 Wardour Street — the mid 50s home of the London Skiffle Centre, run by Alexis Korner and Cyril Davies, who modified it to the Blues and Barrelhouse Club in 1958. These days you can pay three quid to see "Live Show: Male And Female In Bed"!

The Flamingo, a cellar at 33 Wardour Street, was a 60s jazz/R&B stronghold originally populated by hookers, black GIs, gangsters and cool fans. The Stones failed there, but Georgie Fame was welcomed with open arms. During the hippie/underground era, it became The Temple — a grisly unwelcome hole if ever I saw one. In the early 60s, the ground floor housed one of London's first discos, the Whiskey A Go Go, and became the premises of the trendy Wag Club in the early 80s.

Other 60s rock/R&B venues included Giorgio Gomelsky's short lived Piccadilly Club in Ham Yard, at 41 Great Windmill Street. This was later acquired by Lionel Blake and Ronan O'Rahilly (soon to float Radio Caroline) and made famous as The Scene Club — patronised by the Who/Stones/R&B/mod elite. Monday was R&B night with manic disc jockey Guy "too fast to live" Stevens. Punters divested themselves of dubious possessions when the police waded in one night and the place was knee-deep in pills!

The Ad Lib Club was a mid 60s In-Crowd haunt on an upper floor of 7 Leicester Place. In the basement was the short-lived London Cavern, where The Small Faces got their act together. It subsequently became known as the Notre Dame Hall and is still used for gigs. The Revillos made their London debut there in September 79.

Regent Street ... upper crust revellers at the Cafe Royal were amused by Tommy Steele's novel rock'n'roll act in 1956; David Bowie held his star-studded "retirement party" there in July 73. Pink Floyd instigators Nick Mason, Roger Waters and Rick Wright were all students at Regent Street Polytechnic's School of Architecture.

Tottenham Court Road ... Bill Haley & his Comets made their UK debut at the Dominion Theatre in February 57, and The Pentangle's first gig was at the Horseshoe pub next door (number 264) in Oct 67.

London's first and best flower power/underground club was UFO, in the basement of 31 Tottenham Court Road. Opened in December 66 and presented the likes of Pink Floyd, Soft Machine and Procol Harum. It was here that Pete Townshend saw Arthur Brown and signed him to Track.

# london

Carnaby Street ... Pet Shop Boy Neil Tennant (editor at Smash Hits), Ian Matthews (shoe seller at Ravels) and Boy George all worked here. Centre of Swinging London in the 60s, it was celebrated on Dedicated Follower Of Fashion by the Kinks and Carnaby Street by The Jam.

One of central London's first black clubs was the Roaring 20s in the basement of 50 Carnaby Street. Opened in 1961, it featured Count Suckle playing bluebeat on his (pre-discotheque era) sound system. Georgie Fame was one of the few white acts to gig there regularly.

Argyle Street ... home of the Palladium, which has been presenting rock shows since the days of Johnnie Ray and Frankie Lymon & the Teenagers. The TV show Sunday Night At The London Palladium featured many rock acts, including the Stones who caused national indignation when they refused to wave from the revolving stage in the traditional finale (January 67).

Shaftesbury Avenue ... home of the Saville Theatre, which Brian Epstein used to promote a series of seminal concerts in 1967. The Who, Cream, Hendrix, Bee Gees (their London debut) all played there. It was converted into a cinema complex in 1970. Opening in July 81, the Limelight Club, in a converted church, became a honey pot for famous neo-popsters. The first line-up of Yes rehearsed in a basement under the Lucky Horseshoe Cafe. Dire Straits mention Shaftesbury Avenue in Walking In The Wild West End (not to mention the number 19 bus!).

Berkeley Street ... Kajagoogoo heartthrob Limahl once worked as a drinks waiter at the Embassy Club.

Baker Street ... The Beatles' boutique Apple was at number 94. Opened December 67; closed July 68. Gerry Rafferty wrote his most enduring hit while staying with friends in Baker Street.

Margaret Street ... the Speakeasy (basement of number 48) was a primo groover/starwatchers hangout in the 60s/70s — even though some observers likened it to an upholstered sewer. It was here that Yes successfully auditioned for Atlantic Records, that Thin Lizzy made their English debut (Dec 70), and that a drunken roadie urinated into Tony Stratton Smith's supper. Hendrix would jam, people would be gay.

Kingly Street ... the Bag O'Nails club at number 8 found favour with the 60s rock elite. It was here that John McVie proposed to Christine Perfect, and that Paul McCartney first encountered Linda Eastman.

The Revolution Club at 14-16 Bruton Place was another late 60s/early 70s rock biz watering hole.

Louise's in Poland Street was the home of the early punk set and Rusty Egan's Bowie Nights (March 79) drew peacock punters to Billy's at 69 Dean Street. Later, both Le Beat Route (number 16) and Le Kilt (number 60) in Greek Street fostered the class of 81 new romantics. The Gargoyle Club in Meard Street was the first home of the ghoul'n'gothic Batcave in October 82. Spandau Ballet made their Chant No 1 video at Le Beat Route; Culture Club filmed Do You Really want To Hurt Me at the Gargoyle.

After operating from 95 Wigmore Street, The Beatles moved their Apple/business offices to 3 Savile Row, which they purchased in June 68.

In July 74, Mama Cass died in a service flat in Curzon Place. In Sept 78, Keith Moon died in the very same room.

John and Yoko were living in Ringo Starr's flat at 34 Montagu Square in late 68, when they were busted for drug possession.

Great Marlborough Street Magistrates Court (opposite the end of Carnaby Street) has seen many rock stars pass through its portal — including Brian Jones, Mick Jagger, Marianne Faithfull, Keith Richards and Johnny Rotten.

It was from a stall on the corner of Dean Street, in the early 70s, that Bob Geldof embarked on an abortive career as a hot dog salesman. Further down Dean Street, within the Nellie Dean pub, ex-pop stars with beer guts would lie about their lives. The Good Earth Studio at number 59 was designed by Tony Visconti.

Gerrard Street once housed Happening 44 (psychedelic club at number 44 — now a Chinese super market), the first location of Ronnie Scott's Jazz Club (number 39), and the Rik Gunnell Agency — England's biggest R&B booker with the likes of Mayall, Price, Fame, Farlowe, Geno, Zoot (at number 47).

Ronnie Scott moved his jazz club to 47 Frith Street, where it has since remained. The Who gave their first public performance of Tommy there in May 69. Just across the street at number 23b is Angelucci's coffee shop — where Mark Knopfler stepped out in the first line of Wild West End.

The Moka at 29 Frith Street was (in 1953) the first coffee bar in London with an Espresso machine.

Madness dancer/singer Carl Smyth was born in the Middlesex Hospital, Mortimer Street on 14.1.58.

Before he bought his St John's Wood gaff, Paul McCartney lived with Jane Asher's parents at 57 Wimpole Street.

The offices of the Music Of Life label are at 22 Hanway Street. In 1989, four of its five stars had been imprisoned within the past twelve months!

# london

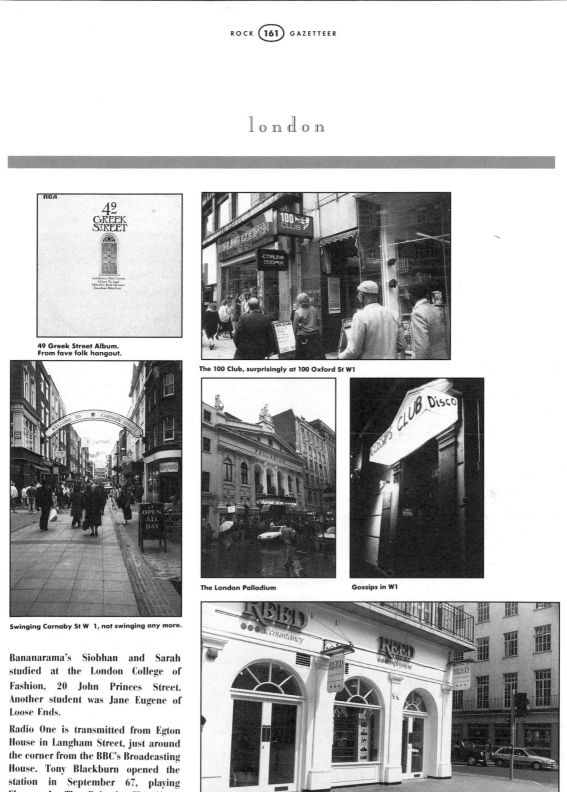

49 Greek Street Album.
From fave folk hangout.

The 100 Club, surprisingly at 100 Oxford St W1

The London Palladium

Gossips in W1

Swinging Carnaby St W 1, not swinging any more.

Bananarama's Siobhan and Sarah studied at the London College of Fashion, 20 John Princes Street. Another student was Jane Eugene of Loose Ends.

Radio One is transmitted from Egton House in Langham Street, just around the corner from the BBC's Broadcasting House. Tony Blackburn opened the station in September 67, playing Flowers In The Rain by The Move. Former studio managers include Alexis Korner (Blues Inc) and Bill Sharpe (Shakatak).

94 Baker St – once the short lived APPLE BOUTIQUE

# london

Ex-Equinox book shop (W8)

The Old Byam Shaw School of Art (W8)

8-10 Basing St, was Island Studios, now part of Trevor Hornes Sarm empire W11

22 Landsdown Crescent, W11

Also in Praed Street was the Paddington Kitchen (opposite the hospital) where Mick Jones and Tony James planned their prototype punk group London SS. They used to rehearse in the basement of the pub on the corner, the Fountains Abbey.

32 Alexander Street was the home of both Blackhill Enterprises (managers of Floyd, T Rex, Dury, etc) and Stiff Records. It was here that the likes of Wreckless Eric and Elvis Costello brought their demo tapes and daydreams, and here that Marc Bolan charmed his future wife June, who worked as a secretary for Blackhill.

## W 3
## A C T O N

Birthplace of Adam Faith, 23.6.40, at 4 Churchfield Road East. He went to Derwent Water School, John Perring Junior in Long Drive, and Acton Wells Secondary.

Former pupils of Acton County Grammar include Pete Townshend, Roger Daltrey and John Entwistle (all of The Who), Ian Gillan (Deep Purple).

In 1968, the newly formed Deep Purple shared a house at 13 Second Avenue, Acton Vale.

The White Hart at 264 High Street was a popular 60s/70s venue. It was here that John McVie played his first gig with John Mayall's Bluesbreakers (Feb 63).

## W 4
## C H I S W I C K

Birthplace of John Entwistle, 9.10.44; Pete Townshend, 19.5.45; Davy O'List, 13.12.48 (the Nice); Phil Collins, 30.1.51; Kim Wilde, 18.11.60; Ian Spice, 18.9.66 (Breathe).

## W 2
## B A Y S W A T E R ,
## P A D D I N G T O N

Birthplace of Jerry Lordan, 1933 (he wrote The Shadows hit Apache); Mike Sarne, 6.8.39 (he and Wendy Richard had number one hit with Come Outside); drummer Ian Mosley, 16.6.53 (Marillion); Elvis Costello, 25.8.54; Pepsi, 10.12.58 (Shirlie And . . .).

Rolling Stone Brian Jones was briefly employed as a salesman at Whiteley's

department store in Queensway, and Madness drummer Dan Woodgate worked in their design department for a spell.

Hyde Park free concerts drew fans from all over Britain. First show, in June 68, featured Pink Floyd and Jethro Tull; Blind Faith made their debut there in June 69; the Stones bade adieu to Brian Jones and welcomed Mick Taylor in July 69.

The Cue Club in Praed Street was a great 60s reggae/black music venue.

# london

Residents have included Midge Ure, Bruce and Pete Thomas (Elvis' Attractions), Rat Scabies, Nick Lowe, Jack Good, John Spencer (Home Service) and Peter Blake — noted painter, but also Sgt Pepper and Band Aid sleeve designer.

Steve Marriott wrote Lazy Sunday after protracted disagreements with his middle class neighbours in Chiswick Walk.

Mott The Hoople's bassplayer, Overend Watts, has an antique shop (The Duke of Bedford Park) in Southfield Road.

The most memorable gig in the area seems to have been at the Town Hall (on the Green) in 1966, when sundry mod/skinhead thugs from Devonshire Road (now trendy middle class) invaded the stage and attacked the Graham Bond Organisation. Observers recall Ginger Baker and Jack Bruce defending themselves with their instruments while the yobbo horde took the place apart.

Elvis Costello's biggest hit, Oliver's Army, was recorded at Eden Studios, 20 Beaumont Road. So were Shakin Stevens' chart toppers This Ole House and Green Door.

## W 5, 7, 13
## E A L I N G

Birthplace of pianist Nicky Hopkins, 24.2.44; singer/writer Speedy Keen, 29.3.45 (Thunderclap Newman); guitarist Ian Gomm, 17.3.47 (Brinsley Schwarz); drummer Mitch Mitchell, 9.7.47 (Jimi Hendrix Experience); bass player Tony Butler, 13.2.57 (Big Country).

London's first rhythm & blues club was in a cellar below the ABC teashop in Helena Chambers, Ealing Broadway. Started by Alexis Korner and Cyril Davies in March 62, it was a source of inspiration to a generation of R&B

groups. It was here that Mick Jagger and Keith Richards first met Brian Jones and Paul Jones.

Star pupils from the Ealing Art School in St Marys Road include Ron Wood, Roger Ruskin Spear, Thunderclap Newman, Freddie Mercury, and Pete Townshend, who met his wife Karen Astley there.

## W 6
## H A M M E R S M I T H

Birthplace of Roger Daltrey, 1.3.45; Cat Stevens, 21.7.47; Gary Numan, 8.3.58; Mikey Craig, 15.2.60 (Culture Club).

Whilst looking to get Roxy Music off the ground, Bryan Ferry taught ceramics at St Pauls School for Girls in Hammersmith. Among the pupils there was subsequent singer/songwriter Bridget St John.

Even as Release Me was zooming to number one in 1967, Englebert Humperdinck was living in a flat above Times Furnishing in King Street.

Island Records HQ is a stately town house at 22 St Peters Square. Bob Marley's UK residence was tucked away behind it in British Grove.

Hammersmith Odeon in Queen Caroline Street has always been a top rock showplace. Bruce Springsteen made his UK debut here in Nov 75.

The Greyhound at 175 Fulham Palace Road has always presented rock groups. On their London debut in 1974, The Jam supported Stackridge, whose idiosyncratic yokel fans threw turnips at them. The Only Ones made their debut there in January 77.

The Red Cow at 157 Hammersmith Road is a similar establishment.

The Clarendon was a popular 80s venue for up and coming bands. Stiff boss

Dave Robinson had his wedding reception here in August 79 ... Madness provided the music.

Hammersmith Art School pupils included Cat Stevens and Mick Jones (The Clash).

## W 8
## K E N S I N G T O N

Jimi Hendrix was pronounced dead on arrival at St Mary Abbots Hospital in September 70.

Pink Floyd's debut was in 1965, at the Countdown Club in Palace Gate. They got 15 quid.

Queen made their debut at the College of Estate Management in St Albans Grove, 1971.

The New York Dolls made their only UK appearance at Bibas's in Kensington High Street in Nov 73.

Jimmy Page was owner of the Equinox, an occult bookshop at 4 Holland Street. It closed in 79.

Cat Stevens, now Yusuf Islam, married Fouzia Ali at Kensington Mosque in Sept 79.

In Kensington High Street, Kensington Market was where Sigue Sigue Sputnik first got together, where The Cult's Billy Duffy worked between gigs, and where promoter Harvey Goldsmith used to flog posters in the 60s.

Kensington High Street was immortalised by 60s band Dead Sea Fruit, and a late 60s American group had the temerity to call themselves Kensington Market.

Clash bassplayer Paul Simonon attended the Byam Shaw School Of Art at 70 Campden Street.

Paul Hardcastle of 19 fame was born in Kensington on 10.12.57.

# london

© Global Antar Archive

**The Mountain Grill frequented by Hawkwind and assorted Ladbroke Groovers W11**

**Vernon Yard W11 – First home of Virgin record label – now used by other branches of the Branson Empire**

**W8 Island Records headquarters in a former laundry**

## W9
## MAIDA VALE, WESTBOURNE GROVE

Birthplace of drummer Dan Woodgate, 19.10.60 (Madness).

The Zigzag Club flourished very briefly at 22 Great Western Road. It opened in Nov 81 with Bow Wow Wow — who also flourished very briefly.

The Windsor Castle at 309 Harrow Road was a highly popular pub-rock gig. The Bodysnatchers made their debut there in Nov 79.

Equally popular was the Chippenham in Chippenham Road. The Modettes made their debut here and The Derelicts were resident band.

## W10
## KENSAL RISE

The Acklam Hall in Westbourne Park became a popular post punk venue favoured by the likes of The Vincent Units, The Derelicts, Prag Vec and The Raincoats. It was here in November 78 that Madness, supporting The Tribesmen, were attacked by iron bar and razor wielding skinheads — as re-enacted in their film Take It Or Leave It.

Hit group The Passions lived in a squat in Latimer Road — as did activist group the Derelicts.

Dexy's Midnight Runners shot the video for Celtic Soul Brothers around the Kensal Rise Canal.

# london

## W11
## NOTTING HILL

Portobello Road ... 60s flower power stars bought flamboyant clothes there — Dr & The Medics still do; Cat Stevens sang about it on the b-side of his first single; Virgin Records had their offices in adjacent Vernon Yard during their 70s/80s heyday; the Mountain Grill cafe was favoured by blacks, hippies, navvies, arty types and even Bolan and Bowie. Regular noshers Hawkwind named their fifth album after the place — Hall Of The Mountain Grill.

Basing Street ... the title of a dramatic Nick Lowe song about the 1977 racial disturbances. Island Records had their HQ here (8-10) in the 70s, when classic Traffic/Mott/etc albums were recorded in their studios. When Island moved to Hammersmith Trevor Horn took the place over for his ZTT/Sarm set up. Multi-million sellers by Frankie Goes To Hollywood and Band Aid were recorded here — not to mention the first Dire Straits album, which cost all of twelve grand.

All Saints Hall in Powis Gardens housed the London Free School in 1966, when Pink Floyd were regular performers. Having made their debut here in 1969, Quintessence recorded Getting It Straight In Notting Hill Gate on their first album. Hawkwind also debuted here.

Joe Strummer's group The 101-ers had a residency at the Elgin pub.

Van Morrison lived in Ladbroke Grove during the heydays of Them (as recalled in Slim Slow Slider). Other residents have included Hawkwind, Skin Alley, and the Third Ear Band (though most of them lived the other side of the Westway in W10).

It was at Lansdowne Studio at 2 Lansdowne House, Lansdowne Road, that Joe Meek was apprenticed as a recording engineer in the mid 50s.

Jimi Hendrix spent his last night on earth in Monika Danneman's basement flat at 22 Lansdowne Crescent.

## W12
## SHEPHERDS BUSH

Birthplace of Chip Hawkes, 11.11.46 (Tremeloes); Yasmin Evans, 19.5.60 (better known as Yazz).

Cliff Richard was discovered, by agent George Ganjou, playing a Saturday morning show at Shepherds Bush Gaumont in June 58. He paid for the demo which won Cliff his EMI contract.

The Social Club at 205 Goldhawk Road was an early Who stronghold. Roger Daltrey's childhood home was around the corner at 15 Percy Road.

Wormwood Scrubs prison was the temporary residence of two Rolling Stones, Keith Richards (June 67) and Brian Jones (Oct 67) — both found guilty of dope possession.

## W14
## WEST KENSINGTON

A prime venue on the 70s pub rock circuit was the Kensington in Russell Gardens.

More prestigious was the Nashville Rooms at 171 North End Road. Every pub rock group played here, every punk group worth its salt. Rockpile made their debut here in February 77.

When they first moved to London, The Animals lived in Fitz James Avenue — in a mansion block flat owned by one of the partners in the Scene Club. Peter Grant was their roadie!

## WC1
## BLOOMSBURY

The Central School of Art in Southampton Row has fostered many a musician — including Legs Larry Smith and Vivian Stanshall (Bonzo Dog Band), Dick Taylor (Pretty Things), Joe Strummer (The Clash), and Lene Lovich. The Pistols played their second ever gig here in November 75, and Generation X debuted here in December 76.

On their first London trip, to audition for Decca on New Year's Day 62, The Beatles stayed at the Royal Hotel in Woburn Place.

Bob Dylan made a pre-fame (December 62) appearance at the Pindar Of Wakefield pub in Grays Inn Road — the same place the Pogues made their debut in October 82.

Around the corner in Sidmouth Street, Johnny Rotten met Jah Wobble when both were students at Kingsway College.

Both Ringo Starr (November 64) and George Harrison (February 69) had tonsillectomies at University College Hospital in Gower Street — the birthplace of Madness guitar player Chris Foreman, 8.8.55, and S'Express frontman Mark Moore, 12.1.65.

Along the road at the Royal Academy of Dramatic Art (number 62), Brian Epstein was quickly disillusioned about any future on the stage.

A short-lived 70s venue was Kings Cross Cinema, where Iggy & the Stooges played their only UK gig in July 72.

It was at the Scala Cinema in Pentonville Road that Janet Street Porter and London Weekend made the documentary which rocketed Spandau Ballet into public consciousness in April 80.

# london

43 King St WC2 Former home of Middle Earth, London's premier underground freak beat club

Bunjies folk cellar WC2 site of Paul Simon and Al Stewarts London debut

The new Marquee (W1)

41-43 Neal St WC2 home of The Roxy

## WC2
## COVENT GARDEN

It was at The Gyre And Gimbal, a coffee shop behind the Strand, that Larry Parnes laid eyes on Tommy Steele — his first protege and the cornerstone of British rock'n'roll.

Many musicians have dragged their sack of woe to the High Court in the Strand . . . among them The Kinks, The Troggs (67), The Beatles (71), Fleetwood Mac (74), Gilbert O'Sullivan, Sting, Hazel O'Connor (82), Ray Jackson, Elton John (85), The Sex Pistols (86) and Holly Johnson (88).

Originally an upper crust stronghold, the Savoy Hotel in the Strand learned to accept nouveau riche rock stars as soon as Bill Haley set foot in the country. Bob Dylan's ructions with the management were captured in Don't Look Back and his video for Subterranean Homesick Blues was shot in the street behind the hotel . . . he and Donovan had sat up all night writing out the caption boards. Elton John also had trouble with the management; he left a bath tap running when he phoned his wife and caused £5000 worth of damage!

Around the corner at 9 Villiers Street is the Griffin, where head Pogue Shane MacGowan was a barman during the mid-70s. Just down the street, within the arches, is gay disco Heaven, where Spandau Ballet played a seminal gig, and numerous provincial bands made

# london

their London debut ... like Southern Death Cult in 1981. It was previously known as the Global Village, an early 70s progressive club.

Around another corner is the Lyceum ballroom, where every band worth its salt played during the 60s and 70s. Derek & The Dominos made their world debut there in June 70.

Both Mick Jagger and Robert Elms completed their formal education at the London School of Economics in Houghton Street. One of the lecturers there was Peter Jenner, who later discovered and managed Pink Floyd and now manages Billy Bragg.

Studio 51, a cellar club at 10/11 Great Newport Street, was a prime trad jazz/R&B hangout during the early 60s. The first rock group to play there was The Rockets (led by jazz drummer Tony Crombie) in September 56. Until they got too popular, The Stones had a Sunday residency and The Downliners Sect made their first recordings there.

Al Stewart and Paul Simon made their London debuts in Bunjies, a perennial folk venue at 27 Litchfield Street.

In 1963, Bob Dylan assisted on a Richard Farina album recorded in the basement of Dobell's Record Shop at 77 Charing Cross Road. He used his alias Blind Boy Grunt for the first time.

While putting the Stones together, Brian Jones worked fleetingly at the Civil Service store in the Strand.

A popular 50s rock'n'roll club was the Nucleus in Endell Street — conveniently situated up the road from the VD clinic. To be "on the slab at Endell Street" was a fear expressed by many a musician.

The Rolling Stones recorded I Wanna Be Your Man in Kingsway Studios, beneath the church opposite Holborn tube station. It was there also that The Animals cut House Of The Rising Sun. Ian Gillan was a subsequent co-owner of the place.

Denmark Street is London's traditional Tin Pan Alley, thronging with publishers, managers, agents and peripheral hustlers. The Giaconda snack bar invariably contained daydreaming musicians, waiting for their big break. Any number of people claim to have loaned Tom Jones half a crown so he could buy egg and chips.

It was at Regent Sound Studios, 4 Denmark Street, that the Stones recorded Not Fade Away in January 64 (Phil Spector and Gene Pitney were also in the studio) and that Elton John recorded any number of cover versions for the Woolworth's label Embassy.

St Martins Art School at 109 Charing Cross Road has nurtured many aspiring musicians ... like Lionel Bart, Rodney Slater (Bonzo Dog Band), Patrick Campbell Lyons and Alex Spyropoulos (Nirvana), Sade, Lora Logic (X-Ray Spex), Glen Matlock (Sex Pistols), Jarvis Cocker (Pulp), and Pennie Leyton (Belle Stars). Sarah Jane Owen (another Belle Star) was a lecturer there.

The Sex Pistols made their world debut at St Martins in November 75. A horrified social secretary cut the power after five numbers.

Cat Stevens (who used to live in the flat above his dad's restaurant, the Moulin Rouge at 49 New Oxford Street, WC1), went to Drury Lane Roman Catholic School.

The Arts Lab at 182 Drury Lane (the first of several in Britain) was a late 60s hippie hangout. The Third Ear Band started there.

Middle Earth was a flower power club in the basement of 43 King Street. It transferred to the Roundhouse after police and media hassle. 150 cops swooped in for a drug raid in March 68.

At the Africa Centre next door, The The made their debut in May 79. Waggish manager Stevo got CBS boss Maurice Oberstein to negotiate The The's contract while sitting on one of the lions in Trafalgar Square!

A hop, skip and a jump away from the Africa Centre is the Rock Garden, a popular 70s/80s venue in the Piazza.

Chaguerama's at 41-43 Neal Street was popular with the clothes-horse clique in 1975 and became the best punk club in London when it re-opened as the Roxy in Dec 76 ... with Generation X headlining. Every significant group played there, even though it closed after four months.

The Blitz at 4 Gt Queen Street was the favourite haunt of the new romantic poodle people. Both the club and the movement were launched by Steve Strange and Rusty Egan. It opened in June 79 and reached a peak of chic that September when Bowie swooped in with Bob Geldof.

The Sex Pistols celebrated Jubilee Day, June 77, by meeting numerous friends at Charing Cross Pier and taking a boat trip up the Thames. Police interrupted the cruise, arresting Malcolm McLaren and Vivienne Westwood among others.

In 1988, the Marquee Club moved to its third location at 105 Charing Cross Road; Kiss played on opening night.

Boy Georges modest abode in NW3

The home of Mr Personality: Mickie Most (N20)

Fairly well known Abbey Road studio & crossroads NW8

The ABC tea room – The Basement was London's first Rhythm 'n' Blues Club

© Global Antar Archive